THE CONTENTED POACHER

THE CONTENTED POACHER

Tales and Recipes
from an Epicure
in the Wilderness

Text and Illustrations
by Elantu B. Veovode

TEN SPEED PRESS
Berkeley | Toronto

Ten Speed Press
P.O. Box 7123
Berkeley, California 94707
www.tenspeed.com

Distributed in Australia by Simon & Schuster Australia, in Canada
by Ten Speed Press Canada, in New Zealand by Southern Publishers
Group, in South Africa by Real Books, and in the United Kingdom
and Europe by Airlift Book Company.

Cover design by Betsy Stromberg
Interior design by Karen Schober

Library of Congress Cataloging-in-Publication Data

Veovode, Elantu B.
The contented poacher: tales and recipes from an epicure
in the wilderness / Elantu B. Veovode.
    p. cm.
ISBN 1-58008-554-7
TX751 .V476 2003
641.6'91—dc21
                2003009066

1 2 3 4 5 6 7 8 9 10 — 07 06 05 04 03

DEDICATION

I'd like to dedicate this odyssey to my son, Chris, who has
put up with me now for more than thirty-five years and who turned out to
be a fine man, despite all my contrary teachings. And to my husband, Harry,
who has always allowed me to be me.

ACKNOWLEDGMENTS

In sincere acknowledgment, I'd like to mention
three good men and a special woman: Lt. Col. David Grossman and
his wife, Jeanne; Bob Mecoy; and Buck Peterson. These folks made up their
minds that my activities ought to be part and parcel of the public record,
and not a one of them slacked off until the dirty
deed was done. Thanks, guys.

A respectful bow to my editor, Fabrienne Mazurek, who learned
to speak my language in record time.

And last but not least, I'd like to thank all my friends
whose endeavors have supplied me with so much comic material to work
with. Such dedication, at the risk of life and limb, cannot be overlooked.
Guys, I hope you can forgive me for telling the truth like that,
but it had to happen eventually.

CONTENTS

Smaller Game

Fish and Seafood

INTRODUCTION

Don't get out your high hat.
If you ever borrowed an apple from a neighbor's
tree, then you're a poacher, too.

The original meaning of "poacher" was a person presumptuous
enough to harvest something that rightly belonged to the king. This
definition began to apply to the average overworked and underfed
peasant about the time that kings scraped up enough power to award
themselves "the divine right of." Thereafter, the land, the animals,
and generally anything and everything of value, including the miserable poacher, belonged to the king. Hunting deer, picking apples, or
gathering a pumpkin here and there all constituted poaching. Hanging or quartering usually ensued.

Nowadays, poaching is generally defined as either hunting a
protected animal using some form of nefarious stealth and thereby
endangering that animal's future for personal gain, or hunting an
otherwise legally hunted animal without the required licenses.

Believe it or not, a third definition of poaching exists in the reams
of official paperwork that currently pass for the words of the king.
Namely, that any person who presumes to hunt without a gun, even
if he or she is possessed of the regulation license and does not presume to exceed the number of animals listed on that license, is
deemed a poacher and equal to the above-mentioned villains in the
eyes of the law.

I guess that third one means me.

The way I figure it, we're having quite enough hoorah in this
country over guns without my being forced by some law to go out
and acquire one.

There is a special provision made for bow hunters, but I'm not good enough with one and never will be, and besides, you can't hunt without a bow in bow-hunting season either.

I joined the ranks of the poachers in this country after the third time I was shot at by another hunter, who deemed it perfectly legal to shoot at movement. Lots of hunters shoot at movement whether or not they know who or what was moving. Funny thing is, if you shoot someone while out hunting, then no matter what stupid excuse you have for it, the law deems it an accident . . . so long as you have the required license. A woman in Maine was shot in her own kitchen while taking cookies out of the oven, and the shooting was ruled an accident. I don't know about you, but I've never seen a deer in an apron before, much less baking. Funny how that works: I can kill all the humans I want, so long as I have a deer license in my pocket, but I can't kill the deer unless I follow the proper procedure.

The gun folks have way too much power for me to take this situation lightly.

I'm not against guns. It wouldn't bother me a bit if every American had two or three. What bothers me is how many people own them and have no idea how to use them correctly, but in the words of the king, you don't have to demonstrate knowledge of guns or safety rules in order to have one . . . or two . . . or a dozen, if it suits you.

That's what makes me a poacher. Well, that and the law that says my license isn't worth the paper it's printed on if I can't show the game warden my shiny new gun.

Hunting Ethics

I learned to hunt mostly from my grandfather, who was also a poacher from time to time. He taught me how to fish by playing with the animal, feeding it for a while, and then teasing it out of the water. Sometimes, we'd make a shadow for enterprising surface feeders to hide in, and then slap them out onto the bank with our hands. Listening to him at night by the fire, or walking with him in the woods, I learned to respect animals and to study their habits. Grandpa died when I was still fairly young, but his example inspired me to study the pre-gun era of hunting. Lacking a handy .30–30, native populations in the Americas were forced to depend upon stealth and knowledge of the animal's habits to get them close enough to their quarry to make a kill. Nobody has ever hunted an animal successfully who didn't spend some time learning how that animal thinks.

I'm not talking about the sort of guys who go out and buy themselves a pack of dogs and then equip the dogs with GPS collars. I figure those guys think they're in some sort of video game, and that's scary enough without the law demanding that they carry a gun. Your greatest weapon is your brain—not your gun, or your knife, or any other piece of technology. Hunters are people who gather information and use that information to their advantage. My grandfather taught me how to use guns. I'm a good shot, both with a pistol and a rifle. More important than the manual dexterity involved, he taught me to respect the power of these tools. Careful observation, intellectual deduction, and patience are also powerful tools. These are the ones I prefer. You don't need a gun if you've watched the moose population year after year and gleaned the information you need that will make the bull's instincts play in your court. You don't need a gun if you've watched pheasant hiding in the grass waiting for the next sound to tell them which way to fly. That information is all you need. Sometimes I win and take home dinner. More often, they win and I make do some other way. That's fair.

For those of you who tear your hair and cry out over the fate of a deer shot through the heart by a hunter, I have one question to ask: have you ever seen what a fawn looks like who's starved to death because the local deer population exceeds twice what the land can support?

So long as we award ourselves the privilege of clearing the land to make room for our grain, our cornfields, our orchards, our truck farms, and our domestic grazing cattle, then we inherit the responsibility of either feeding the animals we displace or at least providing the young with a fighting chance to grow up. States collect revenues in the form of license fees that allow them to monitor animal populations, and they issue licenses that account for the judicious weeding of males to allow females and children to exploit their environment to best advantage. As long as our own population continues to grow, this system is an unfortunate reality.

Strict vegetarianism is not the answer either. Unless you can figure a way to grow what you need in thin air without the use of any land space whatsoever, then every apple, orange, and soybean patty that you consume is grown where some animal used to live before the area was cleared for human use. It's not our eating habits that threaten animal populations, it's our increasing numbers.

The fact that cities like Pittsburgh have a deer problem inside the city limits is testament to the success of the licensing system. I once had to stop in the middle of the day on Forbes Avenue for a doe and her fawn to cross the road.

The Creative Power of Intermittent Poverty
(Or, the Shocking Truth on How and Why This Book Got Written)

Starting around five years of age, I began practicing for my career as an artist. That may or may not have been entirely of my own choosing, but the point is, I agreed to it and here we are. From what I hear, I was the kind of child who inspired every adult within range to find me something to do that did not involve any undue noise. To this end, on my fifth birthday, I received enough art supplies to keep me busy for about fifty years . . . and then I was asked to sit down somewhere and commence to using them.

It seemed to work, and I've been supporting myself, more or less, with my art since I was about eighteen. I say more or less because the truth is, an artist's income is always dependent on the health and welfare of everybody else's pocket first and foremost.

The recipes and stories in the book are the result of my intermittent poverty and my personal taste for good cooking. If beans and cornbread won't satisfy you for two nights running, and your income has been stretched so far that it got itself a case of permanent neck strain, then, friends, you have two choices in front of you: you can rob a bank, or you can get creative.

I began applying my artistic bent to foods when my son was a small child and money was flowing through my hands like water—but not in a good way. We were living in Colorado, and even though my grandfather had long since passed away, I took him with me every time

I ventured into the woods hunting for decent vittles. My son and I started to eat pretty well, and most of the time we were doing well enough to host friends. The stories came about as a means of recording audacious events in history that are best not forgotten, lest we find ourselves entertaining such things more than once.

A Few Warnings Fairly Given

If you're going to go out hunting, remember that you aren't the only hunter in the woods. The biggest danger to hunting any animal comes from the parasites they carry with them—namely fleas and ticks. Few people hunt rattlesnakes who don't know they bite or hunt porcupine without being aware of the animal's unique defense system, but scores of people every year fall victim to everything from black plague to Lyme disease because some little detail with legs snuck past their guard.

When you shoot an animal, the parasites who have called his hide home are naturally going to look to you first as the source of their next meal. They've been deprived of hearth, home, and personal security and are quite like to feel a bit cranky about the way things have turned out for them.

The insects that stay with the skin after you have taken the meat and left the area generally fall victim to birds and other clever predators, unless they are lucky enough to hitch a ride on another host as soon as possible. To this end, your carcass probably looks pretty inviting. There's a lot you can do to change that perception.

Most bites occur on the hands, face, and neck, so wear gloves and a turtleneck that fits snugly. Tie your hair up and conceal it with a knit hat or some other cover that is difficult for an insect to penetrate. Experiment with odoriferous substances that deter interest in your person. Eating three or four cloves of raw garlic goes a long way towards repelling insects from the area around your face. Garlic oil on the wrists of your gloves and around your cuffs and socks works great as well. Investigate the commercial products available and make use of them. So it smells bad. Good! That's the whole point. You can wash it off when you get home—you have to do that anyway.

I've heard guys complain that they smell so bad that the deer know they're there and sitting all day in the woods turned into a grim and entirely unrewarding experience. Frankly, I'm amazed that these boys would go so far to demonstrate how stupid they are. Duh, cowboy, ever hear of sitting downwind of the prey? I'm here to tell you, friend, to a deer, you smell like holy hell two minutes after you've had a bath. A few herbs and oils here and there aren't going to change that one iota. Bug repellents or not, you still have to make sure that whatever it is that you are hunting can't get a good whiff of you. If you haven't figured that out, which by the way is rule one in the book of hunting knowledge, then I have one question to ask: who the hell let you out of the house with that gun in your hand?

Okay, so maybe you aren't the most brilliant specimen who ever plunked down a few bucks for a hunting license. You are, after all, my own species, and I feel a certain attachment to you. So before you take off half-cocked, check out one or two official sources that list the hazards inherent in whatever area you plan to run amuck in, and arm yourself against them. Before you do any hunting, read up on what's out there, take a camera, and learn to appreciate the place, and the first few times you venture out, take a native with you.

It can't hurt, can it?

Take seriously anything that you are hunting, be it a moose or a mouse. Remember that nobody that's fighting for his life has to obey any Tomfool Rules of Engagement that you might consider fair play. Life and death isn't fair, and if you get hurt in pursuit of dinner, then think about what you were doing when the prey won a round and don't try that approach again. You've got the best trained predator's brain on the planet—use it.

Finally, if you're the sort of person who normally buys fruits and vegetables already cut up in those little plastic containers that stores provide (because you've sliced your own fingers so many times that no one trusts you with a knife anymore), then do the world a favor and stay out of the woods. Buy your meat in a store and save law enforcement the expense of hunting for your carcass after you've gone missing for a week or more. Try imagining the grief of the forensics experts as they try to figure out just what it is that you did to yourself in those

last confusing hours of your life, and have pity. Some folks are born and
bred to the city. There's no shame in that. If you are one of those, then I
urge you to be true to yourself. If you just have to stomp around in the
hinterlands, go with somebody who feels just as out of place with a
microwave as you do cooking over a campfire.

Included in the recipes are some general warnings and a few helpful
hints that you might find useful. *Bon appétit,* and make sure you are the
one doing the biting, because it makes for a much happier camper if
nobody gets a complimentary trip to the hospital out of the deal.

On Using the Recipes

Pretty much everyone in my family knew how to cook somewhat. We
all started learning about the time that we had mastered utensils.

Most of the recipes my family shared with me went a little like this:
"Take a handful of flour and stir in a bit of salt and a pinch or two of
baking powder. Cut it with butter until it beads. Add milk until you get
a smooth dough. Roll it out, cut it with a can, and bake in a medium
oven." That's an authentic biscuit recipe. There are no amounts given
because the number of people present to dinner might not be the same
as the night before.

The truth is, my editor has earned herself a sizable vacation teaching
me how to measure stuff out for you folks. It's just not something that I
ever learned to do. Mostly, over the years, I've written down amounts
and pretty fair directions because friends liked what I cooked for them
and wanted to try it for theirselves. In some cases though, I can't make
myself be too exact when a little variation is the norm.

Also, by now, if you've been doing any cooking at all, then you
should have stuff in your kitchen like flour and oil and salt and a few
basic spices. So when I say, "brown something in a little peanut oil," I
don't expect to have to tell you to use ¼ cup oil, especially since I don't
know what kind or what size frying pan you might be using. Adding a
little flour to thicken a sauce depends entirely on where you live. I live at
over 7,000 feet, so what might work wonders for me will not do you at
all if you live in Boston. I'm not going to mislead you by putting down a
measurement and pretending it's an absolute.

For you city folks, I've tried to do my duty by you and yours and provide you with a means to enjoy the recipes in this book that call for ingredients that are a tad hard for you to come by without you risking life and limb in ways that I have already cautioned you against. I'd rather you live a long and happy life rather than try something that's not truly in your nature and perhaps get yourself in a situation over it. To that end, I have suggested substitutions for everything for which any manner of substitutions exist. Handy substitutions are also there for you folks that suffer from squeamish nerves. I know that some of you folks can't bring yourself to scoop the guts out of an animal nor maybe even skin it. Don't you feel bad about that. If you wasn't brought up with it, then these things can take some getting used to.

Tools and Techniques You Should Learn to Love

Always use a good, sharp knife when boning a bird or cutting meat of any kind. Some people like to struggle with dull implements. If you enjoy a challenge, feel free; but for myself, my life has enough hurdles, and I don't need to fight with a dead creature in my kitchen to liven things up. Oddly enough, you are less likely to cut yourself with a sharp knife than a dull one. The theory is that with a dull knife, you tend to put your weight into the handle instead of your attention and thus suffer the possibility of running yourself through if your knife encounters a pocket of lesser resistance than your back muscles have prepared for. Also sharp knives have a way of demanding the kind of respect that keeps your mind focused on the work at hand instead of on the last beer in the fridge or the fishing trip you're planning this weekend.

Do yourself a favor and throw away that electric knife somebody gave you for a present. They abuse the meat and deliver ugly slices to the table that look like they were chewed from the carcass and spat out onto the plate. If you haven't the heart to throw away a present, then save it for cutting Styrofoam, which is about all it's good for.

Test meat for doneness with a cheap wooden chopstick inserted in the center. I like to hone the stick down with a whittling knife until it comes to a true point. Chopsticks are cheap, readily available, and cut from durable stuff—one of the few kitchen tools you will ever own that can claim all three. Testing with wood works much better than simply poking the meat with a fork. With a fork, you only get the ooze, but a sharpened stick inserted into the meat tests the depths, giving you a more accurate picture of the interior.

Using the Bad Stuff to Do Good Work

A number of recipes in this book call for brandy, either in the recipe or in the cook. I like to cook with Christian Brothers brandy myself. It has a warm, mellow flavor, and it costs a spare dollar or two more than the stuff my cousin uses for stripping paint. Christian Brothers is good for drinking when you're not cooking with it, but that other stuff has its uses as well.

A really cheap brandy comes in handy when your in-laws come to visit and you want to offer them a drink so you can get rid of them and get back to the business of happy domesticity with your family. Sure, they'll talk about you for it, but they're going to do that anyway, so what the hell.

═══

The purpose of this book is to bring a smile to your lips. Lord knows there's plenty of work to do and long hours doing it that surely help you forget how good it feels to laugh. Laugh at me or laugh with me, it doesn't matter one bit so long as your heart feels lighter when you're done. Friends, I hope you're never done with laughter in your life.

While you're about having a good time, don't let yourself get caught up in exactitudes when you're fooling with the recipes. Feel free to add stuff I never mentioned or substitute something you like. Play with it. It's only cooking, not rocket science, besides which, the key to creating your own recipes is to learn to be comfortable messing around with stuff. Have yourself a little glass of brandy, and don't let it worry you.

POULTRY

Pheasant

Pheasant look big, but it's an illusion. Most of that impressive size is feathers. A mature cock can measure up to 3 feet in length, but half of that is tail feathers. Dressed out, a large mature bird will weigh in at about 3 pounds. A female, on average, measures about 12 or 18 inches shorter than the male and weighs about 2 pounds.

Pheasants like to hang out in rows of brush conveniently near a field planted in corn or grain. Hunt them in the late fall or early winter. I prefer early winter myself, especially on a slightly windy day. A cool wind makes the birds less likely to fly. Situate yourself along the edge of a clump of willow or a bit of brushy bottomland. Pheasants prefer to winter over someplace that's protected from the wind. Unfortunately for them, these areas are not rife with food for one and all. This makes them all the more likely to take a chance on your offering of corn.

Even if there were no hunters at all seeking a bit of pheasant meat, a sizable portion of the population would die over the winter anyway. Those beautiful feathers are not exactly designed to keep the bird warm. Wind, even relatively light wind, blows the feathers up and allows snow and freezing rain to pack beneath them. Twice as many males freeze to death in winter as females because more of their plumage is dedicated to display. Don't you go feeling bad about tricking that bird and taking his life. It may not be a natural death, but getting your neck broke after a good meal is way yonder faster than freezing to death under a ratty willow hedge.

You'd think the birds would pack up and move south, but the southern U.S. is one place where you won't find pheasants. Draw a line just south of Kansas and that's about as far south as you'll ever find a pheasant. Current theory offers up the notion that the eggs are sensitive to ground heat. Maybe. There's got to be some reason why they choose to live in places where the struggle to survive is iffy at best.

Field Dressing and Preparation

It is always easier to gut and pluck a bird that has been chilled for an hour or so. Always cut game birds—pheasant, quail, sage hen, etc.—down the back to clean and dress. There's no meat to speak of on the back, and you want to avoid compromising the breast meat. Slit from neck to tail and wash thoroughly, bleeding free as soon as is possible. Don't tie up the neck until the bleeding subsides. Make sure to cut away the oil sac at the base of the tail by cutting a generous circle high up on the back, scooping the meat to the bone and taking away the tail area.

Draw out the internal organs with your hands, using caution so as not to rupture the intestines. If that happens, then mix one teaspoon of baking soda with a quart of cool water and rinse out the abdominal cavity with it, finishing your rinse with a plain water wash; if possible, carry water into the field for this purpose. Don't forget to remove the crop.

After you've gutted and plucked the pheasant, dip the bird into scalding water in order to release the down that still clings to the body. That done, remove the head and feet and set aside. Tie a bit of neck skin into a knot so that when you bake the bird, those precious juices don't flow out into the pan. Tying off the neck forces the juice to do its job of keeping the breast meat moist.

If you intend to freeze the bird before you cook it, keep a portion of the scaly part of the leg attached. Later, when you remove the bird from the freezer, wait for about an hour until the meat begins to soften only slightly. Then remove those annoying tendons from the drumstick. Just cut sparely through the skin above the knee joint, then lean the joint over the edge of the kitchen counter and break it until you are sure that the bones have been separated. Pull on the lower portion of the leg slowly, and the tendons in the upper portion will come with it.

Most folks think that pheasant needs time to adjust to the concept of dinner. To my way of thinking, the flavor is just fine if eaten after aging for about eight hours, but if you prefer your meat to be a tad less aggressive on the palate, then let the bird rest for a full day in a ceramic, glass, or plastic bowl in your refrigerator. Don't store the pheasant in anything metal, since the part of the bird that lays against a metal surface will have a vaguely electric taste to it—elusive but disturbing to the taste buds nonetheless. If you use plastic, sniff it first for any odors the pheasant might want to borrow. Be prepared to throw the bowl away after one use, if you're not willing to mark it with a marking pen "for use with pheasant only" and stick by that. Be sure to cover the bowl to prevent a bit of pungent pheasant flavor from creeping into the cheese or other impressionable foods in your refrigerator.

To Swing or Not to Swing Your Partner

Every year, hunters fan over the Great Plains, guns in hand, intent on bringing down a few pheasant. I gather that the Marquis of Queensbury rules on hunting pheasant state that you have to tromp around in the weeds—with or without a dog—and make noise so as to alert the quarry and then see who is the fastest on the draw. To my way of thinking, this approach sounds like folk dancing with shotguns. Did I also mention the fact that pheasants aren't really big enough to effectively kill with a gun unless you are willing to sacrifice a bit of the meat? I'm not. Plus, I really hate picking shot out of a bit of succulent breast. All you have to do is miss one, and you're on your way to the dentist. I may be a scoundrel, but I don't see anything wrong with tricking the bird into my game bag. Besides, I can surely do without all that stomping around and shooting. Dancing and playing with guns is a good way to get somebody hurt.

My way is easier . . . and safer. Trust me.

As pretty as pheasant are, they aren't exactly overwhelmed with brain-power, and most of their behavior is based on instinctual escape mechanisms. Most humans aren't that pretty, so we have to get out there and use our heads to our best advantage. If you can't outsmart a pheasant, then maybe you ought to stick to TV dinners.

You will need: a poncho big enough to cover you completely or an old blanket with a slit cut in it from the middle to one edge; a small bag of dried corn; a couple of cardboard toilet-paper rolls; a thoroughly dry stick about ½ inch in diameter (I like to use oak because it makes such a satisfying snapping sound) best to carry one for every pheasant you hope to bring home; and a canvas bag to carry your birds in.

Once you've picked your hunting ground—generally a small open spot surrounded by grass that's one and a half to three feet tall is ideal—all you need do is set your trap and wait for volunteers. You might very well get a mess of quail and never even see a pheasant, but hey, if that's what you get, take it and be happy. When you set up your trap and your corn, it's best to work under cover of the blanket lest you have spectators that become suspicious. There isn't a game bird old enough to fend for hisself that isn't naturally suspicious of a man and his goings on, but with a blanket over you, you aren't a man anymore, at least in the perception of birds. You aren't gonna fool crows or even simple-minded magpies, but their opinion hardly matters, since we're not after them. To a pheasant, a man under a blanket is a fuzzy haystack, a feature of the landscape that presents no threat to their continued happiness.

To lay your trap, place a cardboard tube in plain sight on the ground and scatter a few grains of corn around it, being especially careful to place one or two inside the tube itself, somewhere near dead center. Squat on the ground under your blanket within a ten-foot circle of the trap. Keep the blanket humped around you in a nondescript mass, but be sure to leave a small gap in the slit so you can watch for visitors. Now wait. Usually it doesn't take too long—a couple of hours at most—before a bird will spot the corn and come in for it. Hold your peace while he takes the offering you laid out on the ground. It's his last meal, and you can afford to wait for the perfect moment. When all the corn that's easy to reach has been consumed, your volunteer will naturally spot the last bit that's only a short reach down that tube. He'll go for it. By now he knows just how tasty that corn is, and he's not willing to leave until he has it all, especially since there are no predators around to stop him.

Wait for it. . . . Wait for it. . . . Good things come to those with patience.

When he's sure that it's safe, he'll stick his head in the tube to get that last, irresistible piece of corn. That's when you make your move. In the privacy of your blanket hideout, snap that oak stick in half.

A pheasant, or a quail for that matter, has learned by tried-and-true instinct that when he hears a threatening noise close by, the only way to save himself is to freeze until he hears it again. One noise is practically impossible to locate—two tells you which direction the threat is coming from. With his head in the tube, he can't look for what is threatening him, and he won't move his head to look until he hears that sound again. Instinct will freeze him in place with that tube over his eyes. Quick, before he makes up his mind to chance it, reach forward and grab him by the neck. One snap and the dilemma is over. Put your first bird in the bag and reset the bait.

Lately, I've heard an ugly rumor that most states consider this method to be poaching and intend to visit a healthy fine on the perpetrators. I suggest you find out the rules in your state before you head out to the fields. Game wardens rarely have a sense of humor, and they invariably enforce the rules that are on the books, whether those rules make much sense or not. Seems to me that if you have a license to take a couple of pheasants, it shouldn't matter how you do it, so long as you stay within your limit. Bureaucracy being what it is, I would definitely check it out.

Pheasant Stuffed with Rice and Pistachio Nuts

Serves 3

I find that dinner guests like to see the birds nestled beautifully on a lovely serving platter with just a bit of dressing arranged for presentation. It piques a hungry guest's appetite to observe the slices of breast meat being cut from the bird. Use a sharp knife and work quickly so the slices don't dry out. Serve with your choice of greens. Steamed string beans go well.

If you can't get your hands on a pheasant, then use poultry—any variety. If you should choose to use domestic duck or domestic goose, you have to bake the stuffing separately. Bake the duck or goose with a big white potato inside to absorb the grease, then throw the potato away and serve with the dressing, which you have baked in a covered dish separate from the bird.

Orange, lemon, and lime peel can be dried simply by arranging them on a stretched screen and placing them in a sunny location. If you live in an area with a lot of insects, you might want to put one screen over the other, thus trapping the peels between them and keeping out the bugs. How long it takes to dry depends on the humidity in the air. It could take one day or it could take three. If the fourth day dawns and your peels haven't dried, then you're probably on the way to mold and you should start over. Try starting the next batch in the oven on warm for about an hour before you place them on the screen. Once dried, you can grind them into powder using a coffee bean grinder that has never been used to grind coffee beans. (Those beans have a lot of oil in them, and once the grinder has been used for that purpose, the oil will always lend its flavor to anything else you grind in that particular grinder.)

> *2 cups water plus ¼ cup hot water*
> *1 cup rice*
> *½ cup pistachio nuts, quartered*
> *3 tablespoons peanut oil*
> *¼ cup finely slivered dried orange peel*
> *1 tablespoon sugar*
> *½ teaspoon saffron threads*
> *1 cup garlic-flavored croutons*
> *1 pheasant*

Bring the 2 cups water to a boil. Throw in the rice. Cover, decrease the heat to a simmer, and cook for 25 minutes.

While the rice is cooking, sauté the pistachio nuts in the peanut oil over low heat for about 3 minutes, stirring constantly to prevent scorching. Add the orange peel approximately 1 minute before the pistachios are done and continue to sauté, stirring constantly, for 1 to 2 minutes more, until the nuts appear toasted. Stir in the ¼ cup hot water, sugar, and saffron.

In a large mixing bowl, stir together the cooked rice, croutons, and pistachio mixture.

Preheat the oven to 325°F.

Arrange the pheasant breast side down in a large roasting pan and stuff the cavity with the rice mixture. Arrange the leftover rice in the bottom of the pan. It'll be crispier on top and juicier on the bottom than the stuffing is, which will be pretty uniform in texture but really tasty in its own right.

Bake, covered, for approximately 20 minutes per pound. Check for doneness by inserting a stick between the thigh and the body; the juices should run clear. If the juices come out pink, let it cook a little longer.

Serve hot.

A Greengrocer All Unaware

It's possible to get so good at what you are doing that you forget how to do it right. I've been doing the pheasant thing for so long that I'm as relaxed sitting under a poncho as I am kicking back in a La-Z-Boy with a baseball game commencin' between my feet.

Keeping metaphorically on your toes is a good thing to bear in mind if you want to continue to be a successful hunter and not a greengrocer to the wildlife.

One day whilst I was about the business of fooling my dinner into joining me, I was balanced on the edge between sitting patiently under cover and catching a few Z's. (I gather that the birds were sitting off somewheres close by, playing the waiting game with me, 'cause I hadn't seen head nor feather in upwards of two hours.) Anyway, I was made aware of the fact that sleep had won the argument when I felt a distinct tug at the backside of my poncho. The ground out in front of me was innocent of the corn I had sprinkled on it, and my cardboard tube had received assistance in walking the distance to the grass directly opposite my hiding place.

That gentle tug came again, reminding me that I had a visitor here-abouts, and I turned my head ever so slightly to get some idea of who I was hosting. Friends, I peeked through that holey fabric right into the eyes of a year-old buck. It had been a dry winter and a thin spring, and I suspect that he had smelled the corn I'd brought with me and fancied some of it. He was so close I could have reached up and cut his throat if I'd a mind, but my heart wasn't in it. He was a pretty boy and would grow into a fine addition to his species. I dumped some of the corn on the ground and pushed it out from under the poncho where he could see it.

I guess when I rebooted my brain after my little nap I left out a couple of major files 'cause I figured that he'd be satisfied with finding some corn and leave me in peace after that. Wrong! When the last kernel had disap-peared, he followed it back to the source and plucked at my bag for the rest. Friends, I either had to disappoint those big, brown soulful eyes of his or give up the rest of the corn and smile about it.

I went out hunting and ended up spending the day feeding the wildlife. First, the pheasant robbed me of my setup, and then the deer cleaned me out.

There's only one thing you can do when you've been bested: review the situation and glean what knowledge you may. That day I learned that the price of a good nap and a pretty face was a bag of corn. A cheap price to pay it was, though I do think I coulda been just as happy not hearing the birds laying on their backsides laughing at me. It's kinda hard when a guy with a brain the size of half a pecan gets a laugh at your expense.

I went home empty handed and fixed myself a mess of cornbread and beans for dinner, and I'm here to say that it was right good.

Pheasant and New Potatoes Marinated in Bordeaux

Serves 3

You can use this recipe with any bird except domestic duck or goose. Both are way yonder too fatty to bake in such close confines with a batch of innocent vegetables, and if you wish to remain good friends with your heart, don't disregard this warning. The potatoes will soak up the fat and taste grainy, and the broth will congeal before you can get the dish to the table. Don't get discouraged if the stores in your areas are less than helpful in assisting you to acquire a pheasant through the fair-market exchange method. This recipe is easily accomplished (as well as delicious) when prepared with Cornish game hens. Get yourself a large oval roasting pan and six game hens, and arrange them in two rows of three with the potatoes and carrots between and the leeks laid out in a herringbone pattern on the top. Not only is this a lovely presentation, it's quite a toothsome delight.

Patience is required for this recipe. You must wait for your reward for 18 hours while the bird bathes in Bordeaux in the fridge. It also requires a large piece of cheesecloth and a bottle of Bordeaux, and whatever you don't pour over the pheasant will go down nice with dinner. Serve with any good, crusty bread. Sourdough is a good choice, but you be your own cook and pick what you like. If you choose something too soft, it will soak up the Bordeaux sauce and turn into a sticky reddish paste. Use a bread with body and resistance to suggestion.

1 pheasant
1 bottle Bordeaux wine
¼ cup all-purpose flour
¼ cup peanut oil
1 cup chicken stock, fat skimmed off
10 to 12 carrots, cut into 3-inch sections
4 whole leeks, rough outer leaves cut away
3 stalks celery, chopped
6 to 7 new potatoes, scrubbed
2 teaspoons ground nutmeg
1 teaspoon ground cinnamon
Freshly cracked black and white peppercorns, mixed half and half

Cut the pheasant into 3 large pieces by separating the legs from the body. Free the breast meat from the back and throw that bony back away. (If you're the sentimental kind, then simmer it for about half an hour in as little water as you need to cover it, placing it in the pan meat side down for efficiency's sake, and then use the broth in place of the chicken stock recommended above.)

Wrap the pheasant in cheesecloth and pour enough of the Bordeaux over the bird to cover it entirely. If you were cheap and bought a small bottle then you won't have any to drink and that's truly sad, as a glass of Bordeaux goes a long way towards elevating the quality of dinner. Allow the pheasant to bathe in the wine for 12 to 18 hours in the refrigerator to give it time to drink in as much as the meat will hold. The time is a variable that you can use to arrange your schedule so that it's not a slave to cooking, but if 24 hours goes by and you haven't rescued that bird from the wine yet, time's a-wasting. Drop what you're doing and get on with the task to hand, namely, cooking and eating the bird before it starts to go downhill into the leftover range before it's ever made it through a first run.

When you're ready to cook, pour off the wine, but don't throw it away—it'll be put to good use presently.

Roll the pheasant in flour and brown it in peanut oil over medium heat.

In a separate pan, heat the Bordeaux you poured off the bird and slowly boil away a fair amount of the alcohol until you have a thick syrup remaining. You have to watch the heat and stir this now and then to keep it from scorching. When you have reduced the Bordeaux, add $^1/_2$ cup of the chicken stock and stir it in thoroughly.

Remove the pheasant from the pan you browned it in and throw in the carrots, leeks, and celery. Sear them until they begin to get tender. Add the remaining $^1/_2$ cup chicken stock a few drops at a time to aid this process. When you can spear the carrots without them skittering away from your fork, add the reduced marinade and simmer for about 10 minutes.

While you are searing the vegetables, boil the potatoes until just barely tender, about 12 minutes. Don't boil for more than 15 minutes, as you don't want them to get soft and start to split. Drain and set aside.

Preheat the oven to 350°F.

Pick a large roasting pan and add the carrots, leeks, and celery, with their cooking liquid. Sprinkle with the nutmeg, cinnamon, and pepper. Arrange the pheasant meat with the breast upside down on the bottom and the dark meat over it so that the juices run into the breast meat instead of draining away from it, again adding pepper as you layer.

Bake, covered, for 25 minutes, then remove the pan from the oven and add the potatoes. Cover and bake for an additional 20 to 25 minutes, depending on the size of the bird.

To test for doneness, insert a fork or sharpened stick into the thigh joint on the thick side of the bone. The juices should have a pleasing caramel color with the only red coloring coming from the Bordeaux sauce. Pheasant blood is a light red, cast towards the orange, unlike Bordeaux, which darkens to purple.

Serve hot from the oven.

Turkey

The easiest way to hunt a turkey is with a shotgun. My method is considerably harder, but it has the advantage of leaving the meat free of shotgun pellets. Turkeys are strong fliers. If cornered, they will take to the air over your head, but they also run pretty fast, and they're just as likely to dash into the brush. To this end, you and a couple of friends (who know how to keep quiet in a pinch) can catch turkey with a couple of lengths of old seine. The truth is, you can do this trick three or four times and still not come up with a turkey, but if you get good at it, you cut down the odds. To my mind, it makes the game sweeter if I use my head instead of a gun. We already know that man can kill any damned thing he wants to—I don't have to add my arm to the wrestling match to prove it.

Pick yourself a spot where turkeys feed now and then. This would be a spot with water nearby, preferably with a shallow stream and a sandy bed. Turkeys, like chickens, need to swallow a bit of sand and gravel now and then so they can break down the seeds they eat. You should pick a spot that has a healthy grassland near a sandy stream and enough trees and scrub brush scattered about to afford cover. Now and then during the day, turkeys like to roost off the ground a bit to survey the area. They nest in the spring in hollows on the ground, where the chicks are raised entirely by the hen. (I threw in that little bit as a subtle reminder not to hunt hens in the spring. You don't want to go killing somebody's mother.) Set up your nets out of sight by stringing them between low bushes. Make sure that the bottom of the net is close to the ground. The best way to do this is to weave in and out between three or four small bushes that are no more than a foot and a half from one another. Take the net in front of one and behind the other to give it strength. Do this in a couple of spots around a central area where the grass still has plenty of seeds to attract the turkeys.

Don't go off and leave this stuff in place or you'll catch all sorts of innocent animals who will then starve to death all tangled up in your trap. When you're done for the evening, take your nets down. It doesn't take that long to set them up again if you want to come back.

Turkeys bed down for the night, but they get up early, so if you want to try for day two success, get up before dawn and keep quiet about it. This is where you and your friends come in. Position yourselves opposite your nets. By opposite, I mean at least fifteen feet away, on the other side of that succulent grass. Squat on the ground and keep quiet, but be sure and leave yourself a little peephole where you can see straight through the brush to the nets. I like to take a couple of big canvas bags with me that I can throw over my head and back. Not only will the bags come in handy for wrapping up your turkey, but they help you to blend in with the grass. If you're lucky, a turkey will happen along to feed. Part of this luck depends, naturally, on your ability to pick a good place to set up—namely, a place with hungry turkeys in the area.

Turkeys are even less likely to fly to escape you if they have a mouthful of seed. I don't know why. Good question. So watch, and when you see him close his beak on a head of grass, stand up and say, "How ya doin', buddy?" It may sound friendly enough to you, but the turkey will take it as an affront and run into the bushes.

A turkey knows what a gun looks like, and if you keep your hands in your pockets, he's clever enough to know that you don't have one. He also knows that he can outrun you in the brush. He's seen you stumbling around and marked how clumsy you are. He can outrun you and your doofus dog, too, so most of the time, when you pop up and start talking to him, he'll run into the brush, thinking he can lose your clumsy carcass easier that way—just in case you have a gun hidden somewhere nearby.

This is where your nets come in. It doesn't matter how fast a guy can run. If his head is caught in a net, he isn't going anywhere in a hurry. Work fast and get to him before he can hurt himself or tear up the net. Throw the canvas bag over his head and wrap rags around his feet. Those feet can give you a real shock if the turkey gets one into your soft parts, so keep them away from your stomach, etc. Generally, in the dark confines of a canvas bag, the turkey will lie quietly and await further developments. Tie his feet together to insure that he doesn't wander off to the privacy of his nest to think about what happened to him.

Once you've caught one turkey in a given location, it's not going to work there again for a while. There are seldom more than three gobblers whose territories overlap, and the survivors are smart enough to read the signs of a struggle and steer clear.

In the fall, turkeys break up into social groups. Young toms, born in the spring, will hang together in groups of three to five. With any real luck attached to all your careful planning, you could get more than one in your nets and not risk any hens in this business.

Field Dressing and Preparation

A young tom weighs about 15 pounds. Cleaning and dressing are relatively easy. Gut, pluck, and scald as you would any game bird (see page 19 for instructions on cleaning a pheasant if you are new to this sort of thing) and store the meat for a day in a glass or glazed ceramic bowl in the refrigerator.

✶—✶—✶—✶ Bringing Down the Sky ✶—✶—✶—✶

As you might well imagine, there are folks out there who purely enjoy doing things the hard way. Offhand, I'm tempted to say that these are way smart folks who don't get enough challenge out of life unless they give themselves a handicap, but I can't say that with a straight face, due to the fact that I know a couple of these hard-heads personally. They were one and all born with enough handicap to set any honest soul back far enough to level even the most slanted playing field. I hesitate to tell this story, since everybody whoever met this fella will guess who it is I'm talking about, even if they haven't heard this tale before. (Okay, Bob, forgive me, buddy, but besides writing up recipes, I gotta give all due warning to folks reading this who might not know what for.)

Every time I get a chance to extol the virtues of hunting quiet-like, without a gun, I just have to do it. I showed my friend Bob that trick for hunting pheasants with a cardboard toilet-paper roll. I even took him with me to show him how it was done, though we missed the first three volunteers when he piped up louder than a politician at a fundraiser whenever he felt the need to ask a question. He asked such fool stuff as, "Now? Now's when you break the twig?" If I didn't know better, I'd swear he was pulling my leg and running off the game to tease me, but he also shot his mouth off at inopportune times when it came his turn to hide under the blanket and spring the trap. As if he hadn't asked enough questions when I was doing it, he had to repeat them all, every one, to check his list off, when I handed the reins over to him.

I shoulda been warned off by the fact that he didn't wear any boots or shoes that laced up in the years after he moved out from his folk's house and before he got married. These little markers are important, and you want to keep a notebook of such observations before you go out into the woods with somebody unawares.

We did eventually get us a pheasant that day.

About two months later, Bob showed up at my place to invite me on a turkey hunt. He was packing suitable firearms, and he leaned in close to confide to me that turkey weren't to be fooled by my tricks. To begin with, the trick I showed you of trapping pheasant with a cardboard toilet-paper roll won't work with wild turkey. For one thing, their heads are too big and for another, they pack a lot of brain into a small space and they are not about to fall for such a low trick. Friends, I went off with that boy anyway, despite the evidence that my life was about to get really interesting. I noticed in passing that he was carrying boxes of #2 shot, when I would've thought that #4 was plenty, but I didn't say anything at the time.

We set ourselves in the brush, near a sizable mesquite tree that allowed us plenty of cover. The field before us had patches of high grass crossed by sandy pathways. Since turkeys like to dine on the seed heads of grasses, I deemed it pretty good turkey country and settled in with my back against the mesquite to wait.

We hadn't been there long when a gobbler and a couple of hens made an appearance. They were walking along one of the trails, helping themselves to the seeds. Presently, the two hens fanned off and we lost sight of them, but that didn't matter anyway. Bob was dead set on taking down that gobbler. He was full size, sure enough, a good four feet long and at least thirty-five or forty pounds of him.

Bob broke cover and bore down his double-barrel at that turkey, making enough noise to scare off a rhino. The gobbler, no fool to this game, took to the air and flew over Bob's head. Some birds will break away from a threat, but a turkey is smarter than your average game bird. He knows that even the most determined predator is put off his feed when the prey makes a rush for him.

Bob didn't manage to squeeze off a shot until the turkey was just over his head, and then he let go with both barrels. Trouble is, the mesquite had already claimed that bit of growing room, and there wasn't a spare corner for Bob and his shot without there being a fight over territory.

This is one you don't want to win. Bob did, and the mesquite gave up the field, dropping the wounded limb on Bob's head in the bargain. Now mesquite is a dense wood, not to mention that it is covered in sizable thorns that can get up to four inches long. I hugged the trunk with my back and escaped with a few ugly scratches for my trouble, but we had to take Bob in and get him stitched up in half a dozen places. Plus, the weight of the limb broke his collarbone. Well, at least that kept him away from guns for a few months.

The turkey made his getaway clean. I thought, under the circumstances, that he might fall out of the sky laughing, but he was a gentleman through and through and just left the area without gloating.

Bob took up deer hunting after that 'cause he heard a rumor that deer don't fly. Course, that little decision on his part helped me make one of my own, namely that I intend to take one of my infrequent visits to town on the day he takes his gun out and starts oiling it up for the hunt.

Breast of Turkey Stuffed with Artichoke Hearts and Lemon Carrots

Serves 6 to 7

You can stitch up the cavity of a bird using plain, neutral-colored carpet thread. I know that there are fancy gourmet shops out there that want to sell you a packet of special thread for this job, but the truth is, you don't need it. Cotton carpet thread works just as well—it won't poison you, it's cheap, and you don't have to make a special trip to France to get a spool. Unbleached thread is best; otherwise, choose white.

This recipe is also very good using almost any poultry, even chicken, if that's what you can get your hands on. But wild turkey, domestic turkey, or game hen is best.

> *4 cups cooked wild and white rice, mixed about equally*
> *1½ cups seasoned croutons (garlic and onion work nicely)*
> *¾ cup chicken stock*
> *The breast meat from a turkey, boned*
> *3 tablespoons fresh lemon juice*
> *1 teaspoon garlic powder*
> *Freshly ground black pepper*
> *6 artichoke hearts*
> *10 young thin carrots, cut into 2-inch lengths*
> *Peel of 1 lemon, grated*
> *Butter*

Mix the rice, croutons, and chicken stock together. Spoon into a large roasting pan, and spread to cover the bottom.

Using a very sharp knife, cut a pocket in each of the turkey breast halves, starting from the thick side (the one that you cut away from the breastbone) and stopping short of piercing any of the other three sides. Rub the cavities with the lemon juice, garlic powder, and pepper.

Sprinkle the artichoke hearts and carrots with the lemon peel and stuff into the breast cavities, arranging them with all due artistry. Stitch the cavities shut, using large generous stitches that you can see and remove later.

Preheat the oven to 400°F.

Place the turkey breasts upside down on the rice mixture and press into it. Smear the backs with a little butter.

Bake, covered, until done. This varies depending on the size of your bird. Generally about 20 minutes per pound is the rule. To brown the turkey, turn it right side up a scant 10 minutes before the meat is done. Baking it upside down prevents it from drying out. I can't see going to all this trouble just to dine on a piece of bird-flavored cardboard. Test for doneness by inserting a fork or a stick into the meat. The juices should run clear. Let rest for 10 minutes, then slice and serve.

Note: If you want a fancy presentation, then whip together 1 egg yolk, $1/4$ cup melted butter, 1 teaspoon lemon pepper, and a few drops of lemon juice and brush this mixture on the breasts when you turn them. It'll make a succulent, tangy brown glaze that is not only toothsome looking, but good to eat as well.

Roadrunner

Roadrunners are impressively fast, agile, and intelligent birds, happily gifted with a sense of humor but very little modesty. They're about 20 to 24 inches in length, with a head comprised mostly of a wickedly strong bill and a lot of fluffy feathers that stand up from its skull a bit like a fancy hairdo on a rock star. They can run up to 15 miles per hour and make sudden sharp turns without slowing down. They can run so quickly that one occasional addition to their diet is small birds that they snatch right out of the air. The roadrunner will run very quickly and launch himself at the victim by bouncing upward and snatching the other bird with his beak. In their desert home, roadrunners are rarely quiet but produce a variety of sounds from harsh clacking, a bit like a scolding sound, to soothing coos, rolling chuckles, and triumphant crowing. They feed mostly on lizards and snakes, which they render edible by holding firmly in their beaks and bashing the unfortunate reptile against a rock. They also love grasshoppers, scorpions, spiders, and crickets.

Roadrunners know that they are smart, and they know that they are fast. If they see you watching them, they'll often turn and chuckle at you and run away, clacking their beaks as if to say, "You'll never catch me and you know it"—a behavior made famous in the cartoons. Sorry, I've seen lots of roadrunners, and I never in my life heard one say, "Beep beep." Not once.

Field Dressing and Preparation

No special rules apply to cleaning and dressing a roadrunner, other than the fact that you should use the smallest knife you have available to you, and it should have a fairly long blade. Be sure and pack in a triple load of patience because the job will take twice as long as a bird twice as big would. Roadrunners are the largest ground bird in the U.S., but that's still allowing for lots of room to fudge. Fact is, a roadrunner can get up to 2 feet in length, but a third of that is tail feathers and near another third is head and neck.

Gut, pluck, and scald as you would any game bird (see page 19) and allow to rest in a glass or glazed ceramic dish in the refrigerator for 24 hours.

─✳─ Making New Friends Somewhere South of Tucson ─✳─

One of the side benefits of hunting roadrunner is that they tend to hang out in places where there are healthy stands of prickly pear cactus, and if you don't succeed in catching yourself a couple of birds for dinner, there's usually a snake or two handy to fit the bill. Roadrunners are remarkably hard to catch. That cartoon with the roadrunner and the coyote is unfortunately pretty accurate. Shooting one won't really do you any good, since you'd have to hit it square in the head in order
to have enough meat left to eat. Sounds hard? It is. To make matters worse, they have proportionately small heads, and they're wickedly clever for characters with such small noggins. So unless you're pretty good at shooting cockroaches off of the wall, then don't even think about trying to hunt roadrunners with a gun. A big waterbug roach is only slightly smaller than a roadrunner's head, and they dart about—up and down and back and forth— with the same kinda traffic patterns.

Roadrunners are fast, and they know it. They're so fast and so clever that you can use that knowledge to let them outsmart themselves. They're cocky. Let that work for you. Snares work pretty well with them because you can sit close by and watch your traps, and the roadrunner is so confident that you can't get up fast enough to catch him that he is willing to come pretty close to get the bait.

I should mention here that I don't like snares. They're cruel, and unless you can get to your quarry in the first minute after they're caught, they suffer unnecessarily. The roadrunner's cocky self-confidence makes it possible for you to do just that. You don't need to hide under a blanket or anything hot and sweaty like that. The roadrunner'll know you're there no matter what devious plan you try to devise. So don't go to any special trouble to hide. Knowing you're there sweetens the game for the bird. Plan on losing at least two out of three of the birds your bait attracts. Roadrunners are both quick enough and smart enough to snatch your offering and get away with it.

A couple of fat grasshoppers with their back legs tied together with a bit of sewing thread makes a fine bait for roadrunner. One of those little birds can hear a hopper struggling to free itself from a hundred yards away, and, believe me, he's perfectly willing to run all the way over there to provide a handy escape route right down his throat. Another good bait is a small lizard. You can secure this to your trap by looping a bit of stout thread around his belly, just in front of his back legs. If you tie it to his tail, he'll just pop that expendable little item off right where your string runs around it and take off running into the brush. Sure his friends will laugh at him for it, but then so will yours.

Roadrunners hunt snakes for a living. They also hunt lizards and grasshoppers and stuff like that, but the very fact that they are not at all intimidated by the rattlesnake and his formidable reputation oughta tell you something about all due caution when you mess around with this bird.

It's not such a hot idea to grab a roadrunner around the neck or legs and expect to come out on top of the battle. In case you haven't checked lately, you don't have no poisonous fangs on your hands, and your one good weapon, your thumb, is noticeably occupied in holding on to the bird in question. This leaves him free to use his weapon, that long, wickedly hard beak of his, on the exposed flesh of your wrist. Even if you're wearing heavy gloves, it's gonna hurt and hurt bad. When you take a roadrunner out of a snare, always throw a canvas bag over his head. Wear those gloves I mentioned earlier, and get a simultaneous grip on his ankles and his neck. This allows you the freedom to twist his head sharply to one side, breaking his neck and ending the battle before he can put some holes in your hide.

In case you're thinking of going for the stealth method, despite all my words to the contrary, I should warn you, sitting under a blanket in roadrunner territory comes with serious drawbacks. Roadrunner territory is also scorpion territory, and the last thing you want is to sit still enough long enough to attract the attention of a scorpion or two. Whether they opt to slip inside with you or climb to the top of your mountain and get into your hair, the results are not something you want to actively pursue. My advice is to use the blanket technique in a place where these pesky little creatures aren't a problem, and be satisfied with sitting quietly twenty or thirty feet from your snares. In scorpion country, it's best not to sit on the ground too quietly for too long as they will take this behavior as an open invitation to familiarity.

Lemon Roadrunner with Almonds

Serves 4

I'm sorry to have to tell you that boning a roadrunner is a truly time-consuming (read: annoying) experience. The meat has a pleasantly nutty flavor that can't be duplicated, although to my mind, pheasant tastes good enough (and it is much easier to bone) so that I find myself substituting it whenever I get an undeniable hankering for this recipe, and the memory of my last encounter with a small knife and a roadrunner carcass is still fresh in my mind.

In the conspicuous absence of a roadrunner, you can substitute poultry—any variety except domestic duck or domestic goose. Pheasant or Cornish game hens work really well. Chicken is truly memorable.

Serve with rice. This dish is at its best when served with basmati rice.

3 tablespoons peanut oil

3 roadrunners, skinned, boned, and cut into manageable pieces, or 3 pounds of boned poultry of your choice

1 large onion, finely chopped

2 cloves garlic, finely minced

½ teaspoon peeled and finely minced fresh ginger

½ teaspoon ground turmeric

⅛ teaspoon ground cardamom

1½ cups water

¼ cup golden raisins (substitute dried cranberries if you prefer a sweet-tart dish)

½ cup almonds, blanched

2 tablespoons fresh lemon juice

1 teaspoon cornstarch, dissolved in 2 tablespoons water (optional)

Heat the oil in a large skillet over medium-high heat. Add the roadrunners and onion and sauté until the onion begins to take on a golden color. Add the garlic, ginger, turmeric, cardamom, water, raisins, and almonds. Cook over low heat for about 35 minutes.

Add the lemon juice. The sauce should have thickened as it cooked, but if it proved to be contrary, add the cornstarch mixture when you put in the lemon juice. Cook for an additional 10 minutes. Stir occasionally to prevent sticking.

Serve hot from the pan, since this dish doesn't reheat all that well.

Goose

The common Canada goose tends to feed on patches of land that are relatively accessible to folks who don't swim so good; namely, they like places where corn, wheat, rice, barley, oats, and soybeans grow. They're easier to hunt than ducks and don't require the assistance of a dog who can swim out and retrieve the bird.

If you're looking for the best spot to hunt for geese, then pick out a place where there's such a field within a mile of a small lake. Half a mile is even better, but though the geese are good at finding such places, it's not always so easy from the ground to pick the one field that'll suit their needs best. They like it to be near a handy source of water so they can roost on the float in the evening, and they'll pick a field that's a short flight away in the morning where they can pick up a hardy breakfast. The best idea is to scout out bodies of water and make yourself comfortable there just before dawn one morning. When the geese take off at first light, mark the direction.

A Canada goose has a wingspread of between 5 and 6½ feet and weighs 8 to 10 pounds. By the time you dress the bird out, it will weigh closer to 5 pounds. Brants and some of the subspecies of Canada goose are a bit smaller, weighing closer to 3½ to 4 pounds. Females are slightly smaller, but like I've said before, you don't need to be hunting the ladies, so their particulars are of no real concern.

Field Dressing and Preparation

For cleaning and dressing, refer to the instructions for pheasant (see page 19).

Raising Cousin Hiss and Auntie Flap

If you have a place to raise geese, the work is well worth your efforts. Geese are cheap to feed, requiring much less than either chickens or turkeys to put on ample weight, and their eggs are better tasting than chicken eggs, richer and fuller bodied, not to mention larger. Two goose eggs will make a hearty omelet for three or four people. Their meat is fatty and requires a few extras in the cooking to keep some of that fat off of your plate, but to honk their horn once again, the flavor can't be beat.

As an added bonus, geese tend to be a bit sour tempered—namely, they bite and they bite hard when they take a mind to. This may not sound like a benefit at first, but just remember, the biggest battles you ever fought in your life were the ones waged with your kids over the impending death of a lamb, turkey, or rabbit that they've become attached to. It only takes one or two bites on the behind or the back of the leg from a contrary goose to turn a kid away from the idea of befriending his ornery ass. With geese, you'll never have to suffer those long faces the kids favor you with at table when somebody they named only last spring is on the menu today with carrots.

I began to win the battle of the spring goose when my son was seven, and a goose bent on taking a hunk out of him chased him around the house half a dozen times, narrowly missing him as they made the bend at each corner. The door to the porch opened outward, and the kid didn't have the spare second to stop and open it without sacrificing that precious bit of flesh. I've been accused of laughing too long and too hard on several occasions. This, I'm told, was another such time. It never ceases to amaze me how a goose can run at top speed, flap his wings ominously, and hiss like a five-hundred-pound snake the whole while. Don't they ever run out of breath?

Folks in the know never serve up "family"—they trade with someone in the same situation and wait a day. Even bona fide farm families trade animals before slaughter. One guy I knew bought a suckling pig to raise and deliberately named it "Pork" so his boys would get the idea, but it didn't work. The kids went along with the gag until they saw Dad sharpening his knife, and then, friends, the war was on. That little ruse never works. Children are incapable of looking at an animal and seeing food. The use of the food name just makes them think that their progenitor has a poor sense of humor. The last I heard, "Pork" was eight years old and still living with his family. He has an old quilt in a box in the garage, his own personal tube of arthritis cream on the shelf above the washer, and he eats from his own bowl on the back porch with his kids around him. He's fat and spoiled, and any threat to his life is more likely to come from too much affection rather than from the knife.

The trouble with raising pigs is that they're too cute for your future good; namely, if you have a kid in the house, you're never gonna reap your just culinary reward without you have to live the life of a cruel and unusual monster in the eyes of your offspring. Stick with geese. Sure, they're cute when they're little, but they'll grow outta that before it's neck-wringing time, and a goose will actually help you to teach your kids not to protest too loudly.

I love a goose myself and will gnaw it down to the bone before I'm convinced that not another succulent bite can be found to savor. Wild goose has a much better flavor than domestic and the meat is not so fatty, though the truth is there are plenty of folks who horde up goose fat and use it for cooking such delectables as sautéed mushrooms. If you feel up to trying this, then use only fresh goose fat that has been kept refrigerated and treat yourself to a glass of red wine along with the meal—your heart will love you for it.

Sliced Breast of Goose with Sautéed Mushrooms in Brandy Sauce

Serves 4 to 6

If you want to use this recipe for a wild goose, a couple of changes have to be made. Wild geese don't put on nearly the amount of fat that their farm-raised cousins will. For wild geese, dispense entirely with the rack, bake the bird upside down in the roasting pan, and lay a couple of strips of bacon over the back to prevent it from drying too much, or else you'll need to inject it with butter and stand over it basting until your face is redder than a barn door.

Also, be sure to avail yourself of a young goose, preferably under one year of age. Older geese are, to use a kind word, chewy.

If you don't have goose, then try duck. Again, domestic duck should be cooked on a rack, while any wild duck can be treated as you would a wild goose. If you use chickens, remember that all chickens are domestically raised and tend to be fat, so the rack method it is with those boys.

> *1 young goose, 4 to 6 pounds*
> *3 tablespoons butter*
> *1 tablespoon peanut oil*
> *1 pound mushrooms, halved or sliced, if large*
> *½ cup brandy*
> *1 tablespoon rice flour*

Preheat the oven to 400°F.

Roast the goose on a rack to keep it out of the fat. Prick it with a fork often to allow the fat to drain away. Roast for about 20 minutes per pound. It should be slightly pink, a coy blushing pink, in the center of the breast when it's done. The juices will run clear with only the palest blush of pink visible. If you like your meat well done, cook for 10 more minutes at this stage.

When the goose has cooled sufficiently (you should be able to touch it without stress to your skin, but don't let it get cold or cutting it into neat slices will be difficult), cut away the breast and slice with a sharp carving knife.

Heat the butter and the peanut oil in a pan over medium-high heat. Toss in the mushrooms, shaking the pan continually for about 3 minutes to keep the pieces moving and prevent overcooking.

Decrease the heat to medium-high. Mix 2 teaspoons of the brandy with the rice flour in a small bowl. Add the remaining brandy and the dissolved rice flour.

Decrease the heat to the lowest simmer your stove will allow and continue to cook for another 3 minutes, stirring constantly. If the sauce sticks, it'll clump up into ugly, overcooked lumps, so keep that spoon moving.

Arrange the slices of goose on individual dinner plates and pour the hot sauce over it. Serve immediately.

—✳— Taking Careful Aim at Something Besides Tea —✳—

Along the Mystic Lakes, in the Cambridge to Arlington, Massachusetts, neighborhood, they have a subspecies of Canada goose that has forgotten the way home. Now they probably have these boys elsewhere in New England, but since I can't swear to that, I won't. It seems likely, since such a well-established breeding population implies the existence of other flocks close to hand, but more stomping around is required on my part before I'll put my name to it.

As a rule, these geese are a fat and friendly bunch, with nary a grudge to hold against a living soul, except maybe the occasional eagle that's been drawn to nest in the area by the presence of a year-round stock of ready dinner.

The story that the natives offer is a strange one. They claim that their forefathers raised or trained these geese not to migrate—the exact details of this particular portion of the story are a tad vague. I'm telling you everything they told me, the main difference being that you're getting it in one straight narrative, whereas I felt like I'd been picking up pennies for lunch money before I'd gathered all the facts laid down here.

Anyway, New Englanders claim they had a hand in teaching those geese to stay close to hand all year round. The point to this exercise, apparently, was to use the trained geese as decoys to lure down flocks of wild geese in migration. Now this is where the story frankly sticks in my craw and won't quite go down. Was there a shortage of wood at the time? Not so, the history books mention. Perhaps the tax on good steel knives was so high that they didn't feel up to dulling them by carving wooden decoys. There were plenty of folks who were handy wood-carvers. They left some right pretty examples of their work that are still about today. Okay, so maybe they simply had too many other tasks that took up all their free time, and they didn't have a spare minute for carving decoys that they could get some other way. Colonization is not an occupation for sissies, and I hear that it is some terrible time-consuming. Even if all these things are true, the question still stands there begging: Once you've trained them to stay, why not eat the resident population? Why hunt the migrating geese at all if you had the wherewithal to teach the meat to stay close and not fly away with their brethren?

It would have served New Englanders well to eat a few of these boys. They've been so successful hanging out on the Mystic Lakes throughout the year that they're now the closest thing to a nuisance you can get short of pigeons. Since waterfowl use open water as their toilet, a great deal of money is spent keeping the water clear and clean. Still, folks continue to feed them, and I gather that they don't look too kindly on the enterprising poacher who would presume to thin the population by a couple of choice members.

All and all, I suspect this story to be true if for no other reason than that the character of New Englanders goes a long way to support it. They did some pretty remarkable things in their time, and, in general, they are not given to telling whoppers. By and large, if they're gonna pull a stranger's leg, they'll give him bogus directions to Logan Airport and not fun around with history. They take their history way yonder too seriously to fool with it just for the sake of a good laugh.

Of late, I was wondering if maybe they hunted the wild geese as a way to get in some target practice. After all, there was a lot of squabbling going on with the British at about that time, and King George's boys might've entertained more than a smidgen of suspicion if the colonists had set up a row of oblong red targets to take potshots at.

Saffron Goose

Serves 4

You don't want goose too well done, so check it often. With game birds, it's better to err on the side of slightly underdone than overcooked, since all you can do with an overcooked bird is try to convince the dog that it's edible.

Lacking a goose, you can always substitute duck. Use wild goose or duck with this recipe. If you can't get either of those, then stick to either chicken or game hens. If you really want to try it with domestic goose or duck, then steam the meat for 10 minutes and allow it to cool on a rack before you rub it with turmeric and slip it into the clay baker. It'll be a bit oily, so you should also remember to keep a bit of red wine handy during dinner.

2 teaspoons turmeric

Breast of 1 goose, skinned, about 2 pounds

1 pound green beans, trimmed

A rash of pearl onions (I don't know how many you like, that's entirely up to you)

2 teaspoons saffron

Preheat the oven to 350°F.

Sprinkle the turmeric on the goose and commence to rub it around with your hands until it is spread evenly.

Arrange the beans and onions in a clay baker.

Lay the goose breast side down on top of the arrangement you've made and sprinkle the top with the saffron, dabbing at it with your fingers if you need to be sure that it gets all around.

Put the lid on the clay baker and put the whole thing in the oven. Bake until a sharp stick or straw in the goose comes out shiny but clean. If it's streaked with pink, put it back in the oven for a few more minutes. Generally, 45 to 50 minutes is plenty of time, but if you were lucky and scored a particularly large goose, it could take longer.

Remove from the clay baker. Thinly slice some of the breast meat for presentation and arrange it on a generous platter with the beans and onions beside it. This looks really pretty if you have remembered to cut the breast meat with a really sharp knife.

⚡———⚡——⚡—Waltz Me Around Again, Willie ⚡——⚡——⚡——⚡

The tastiest domestic goose that I ever put a tooth to was that particularly angry gander that chased my son around the house.

My boy had a special fondness for cornbread. He also truly loved a piece of fresh baked bread smeared with honey. On that score, he and that gander were in perfect agreement, but after that, their personalities parted company.

My boy was especially prideful of the fact that he enjoyed a special place in the favor of the cook who made both the cornbread and the bread. I could see that he was destined to be tall, and I didn't want to slack him so much as half an inch, so he was free to graze in the kitchen whenever the mood took him. For his part, the gander spent many an hour plucking at the handle of the screen door, but he never did make his way to the source of the goodies that my son paraded around the yard with.

Early in their acquaintance, my son trained the gander to cast an eye to the door now and then and to come on the fly, as it were, whenever he appeared with a treat in his hand. When they first knew one another, crumbs were forthcoming from my boy's hands, and the gander praised his generosity with a chorus of honks you could hear clear over at the stock tank.

It's like your old grandpa will tell you: you never had a worse enemy than a friend who thinks you slighted him. There was no two ways to think about it—when my son turned from sharing his crumbs to teasing his friend with them, that gander knew without a doubt he'd been slighted, and his cowl began to rise every time he laid eyes on that child. He didn't have nothing against the boy just because he was a man and not a goose, but he didn't hold with hoarding food, especially when food had been the core of their prior friendship.

Well, friends, I saw it coming, but I guessed that words would have less effect on the situation than a cup of water on a dry cornfield, so I deemed it well deserved if the gander got a bit of his own back. In other words, my boy was being a brat, and if he earned himself a just, if painful, reward for his troubles, who was I to interfere with providence?

The gander tested my boy's mettle with many a short skirmish, flapping his wings and making short rushes to see if his adversary would run or stand his ground. More than once, the inevitable was avoided when my boy started away from the menace so quick that he dropped his cornbread on the ground. The gander was not fooled, though; he knew that fear and not honest friendship had landed that succulent morsel in his grasp.

I was sitting at the kitchen table, watching my dough rise and enjoying a cup of good honey-sweetened tea, when the first shots of the real war were fired. The gander let loose with a salvo of honking and flapping that left no doubt as to his intentions. My boy, armed with inferior ammunition—for some reason, there wasn't a stick anywhere in the yard that day—shrieked and threw his bread down on the ground between them. This time, the gander wasn't taking the bait. He had his heart set on biting that little boy's butt, and nothing less was gonna satisfy him. Friends, the race was on.

The gander stuck his neck out and hissed, the noise fairly rattling in his angry throat. Truly, you could hear the anticipation in his voice—he could already taste the succulent morsel in his grasp. My boy, quick to grasp the true nature of his situation, took off running for dear life. My boy is long limbed and fleet of foot, but the gander's righteous indignation carried him along at a right good clip. There wasn't more than a couple a spare inches between the end of that gander's bill and his vengeful intentions. The two of them hove out of sight together around the corner of the house, and presently, I could hear them cutting the corner by the bedroom window. After a bit, they pulled into sight under the kitchen window again. My boy called out, "Open the door!" That's when I started laughing. The effort of yelling for help took a bare edge off of his advantage, but the gander's hot breath on his legs lent him wings of his own. They tore around the house again, and I rocked shamelessly back in my chair to the tune of "Open the door!" that sailed in through the window every couple of minutes.

Course, it wouldn't have helped him much if the door had opened in instead of out, since that would just have transferred the race indoors—the gander was too close on his heels to allow for something like a door to get between them.

I never did get that door open. I was laughing so hard that my legs wouldn't carry me if I'd tried. They were beginning to dig a rut in a circle around that house when my boy finally came to the conclusion that he was on his own. I suspect that the telltale sounds of raucous laughter tumbling out of the kitchen window gave him his first clue. Maybe he weighed the fact that it was a good three hours until sunset when that gander could be counted upon to nest for the night. Anyway, he stopped dead under the kitchen window, turned on his heel quick as thought, and kicked the gander a solid clout in the chest. By this time, the gander was a good two feet back in the race. He had been losing ground for the last couple of trips around the house. Geese aren't designed for long-distance running, and his wing power took him on long out-of-the-way curves going around the corners.

Not to be outdone by such a blatant sinner as my boy, the gander stuck his neck out and plucked at the toes on the end of the offender's weapon. About this time, my boy remembered that he had hands, so he slapped the gander upside his head a good clout and shouted some unprintable curse on him and his family. Then my boy screwed up royal—he turned his back on an enemy who wasn't quite so defeated as he thought. That's when the gander got his just revenge.

In time, my boy's injured hindquarters healed up good as new, and the gander found his way into the roasting pan.

Now, I don't want you getting the wrong idea here. Neither me nor my son blamed that creature for what he did. Geese are intelligent creatures and make tolerable good friends if you don't rouse their tempers, but they are mindful of teasing and won't tolerate it. So long as he was nursing his injured butt, my son was apt to be a bit harsh on the subject, but in time, he saw that he got what he was asking for.

Farmyard politics, not human tempers, signaled the end of that particular gander. It is the nature of male animals to fight over mating rights, especially where the number of available females is limited. The truth is, we didn't have enough geese to go around, and our gander made up his mind that he was gonna have to kill a couple of the older guys if he wanted to gain the respect of the women. He was all grown up and anxious to try his mettle in the mating wars when I made up my mind that enough was enough.

Roast Goose Stuffed with Apricots and Quince

Serves 6 to 7

The mix of flavors in this recipe ranges from the subtle to the divine with each bite a new presentation unto itself. The rich taste of the goose almost overwhelms the quince and would if all the quinces were included in the stuffing. That is why there is quince both in the stuffing and in the dipping sauce. Lemon helps bring the quince to the forefront and subdues the juices of the goose just enough to create a pleasant balance. Enjoy.

You can substitute duck or game hen. Chicken will do in a pinch, but it just doesn't satisfy as much. Pheasant is alright, better than chicken, but nothing tastes so good as a goose.

1 goose, about 8 pounds
½ lemon, plus 2 tablespoons fresh lemon juice
5 quinces
½ pound dried apricots
2 teaspoons ground cinnamon, plus a pinch
1 teaspoon freshly ground black pepper
2 tablespoons butter
Pinch of ground allspice
1 tablespoon honey

Preheat the oven to 300°F.

Put your goose breast side down in a deep roasting pan with a couple of inches of water in it and cover. Bake for about 20 minutes, then remove the pan from the oven and allow to cool for 30 minutes.

Pour off the water and discard. Score the goose with a very sharp knife in a crosshatch pattern, being careful to make your cuts very shallow and not pierce the meat too deeply. Rub the goose all over, inside and out, with the lemon half, squeezing the juice mostly inside the carcass.

Peel 2 of the quinces, core them, and cut into thin wedges. Set aside. Cut the remaining quinces into quarters.

In a large bowl, mix together the quartered quinces, the dried apricots, 1 teaspoon of the cinnamon, and ½ teaspoon of the black pepper. Stuff into the goose.

Preheat the oven to 400°F.

Place a rack in the roasting pan and set the goose on the rack breast side up. Sprinkle the skin with the remaining ¹/₂ teaspoon black pepper and a spare pinch of cinnamon. Bake for about 1¹/₄ hours. The skin should begin to look crispy when the goose is done. Remember to test by inserting a sharpened stick in the joint. The juices should be clear with just a hint of blushing pink.

About 20 minutes before the goose is ready to serve, melt the butter in a saucepan and throw in the wedges of quince. Sprinkle with allspice and the remaining 1 teaspoon cinnamon. Sauté for about 5 minutes, stirring constantly. Decrease the heat to a simmer and add the 2 tablespoons lemon juice and honey. Simmer for 5 more minutes and remove from heat.

Serve hot. Slice the breast meat and cut the dark meat into chunks. Serve with the stuffing on the side and the dipping sauce ready to hand.

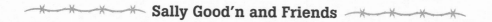

Sally Good'n and Friends

One reason that I hesitate to hunt geese is that most species mate for life. Often as not, the survivor will prefer to mourn rather than take on a new mate.

I never hunted Canada geese, but many years ago, I was with friends along the coast of South Carolina where one of our party fired into a flock and brought down a brant. The brant is a related species of goose that is hard to tell from the Canada goose unless you've a good eye. The brant has a smaller patch of white on the neck than the Canada goose, whose white patch extends upwards and includes a dash of white on the cheeks as well. Brants tend to be about twenty to twenty-four inches in length, whereas the Canada goose has so many subspecies that its size can range up to forty inches in length.

At the time, I didn't know that they mated for life. My friend brought down a young hen, and right away, another of our party took a second. Both birds hit the ground not far from us, and the rest of the flock turned together and flew out of our range.

All but one. A lone gander broke from his friends and circled back over our heads. He landed near one of the downed hens and shoved at her hopefully with his bill. When it was obvious that she wasn't going to rise up and fly away with him, he threw back his head and sent a series of mournful honks skyward. He stayed by her and mourned for a full five minutes, alternately pacing and honking his sad protest at the passing clouds. Nobody had the heart to shoot him, though I see now that maybe we should have done so.

Another time, a friend in Virginia rescued a brant hen from certain starvation when he took her home with him and cut away a twisted mass of plastic that was cutting into her bill. She had gotten tangled up with one of those plastic carriers designed to hold a six-pack of cans, and it was looped around her neck and head in such a way that she was dying from it.

She was pretty poorly, so he set up a pen in his yard with a roof of chicken wire so that she couldn't defeat his best interests and get off on her own again. She was with him a scant three or four days when he went out one morning to feed her and found a gander nesting in the grass nearby. My friend added a foyer to his pen, with a handy opening for the gander and a wire door that could be closed if he chose to go inside. In a couple of days, the gander ventured in to taste the offered food and share a few moments with his lady friend. At that point, my friend shut the door and removed the partition between the two cages. After that, he found himself inadvertently raising brants in his backyard.

As it turned out, the hen had also suffered some damage to her wing structure, probably during her futile attempts to free herself from slow death by plastic. She could fly, but only for a few feet. Her beau seemed perfectly content to live out his life on the ground with her. They had probably been together for several years, and he already knew that she was a good one.

Sautéed Goose Liver

Serves 6 to 7

Don't forget to remove the gall bladder from the underside of your goose liver. Not to worry, if you forget it once, you'll never do it again. Course, if you do it once, you'll likely lose any and all interest in goose liver. You won't have to take a bite of it to know you screwed up; the smell of a goose's gall bladder cooking will set you to opening windows and planning a long vacation right quick.

Sorry, there is no substitute for goose liver.

> *Goose liver*
> *1 tablespoon freshly ground black pepper*
> *1 tablespoon ground ginger*
> *1 tablespoon sugar*
> *½ teaspoon salt*
> *2 tablespoons butter (use the real stuff with goose liver—it makes a difference)*
> *1 pound mushrooms*
> *1 tart apple, cored, sliced into thin rings, then cut into ¼-inch slivers*
> *Garlic, peeled and minced*
> *4 shallots, cut into 3 or 4 pieces each*
> *¼ cup chicken stock*
> *3 tablespoons dry red wine*

Soak the goose liver in cold salty water (about 2 teaspoons salt per 2 quarts water) for 2 hours. Drain thoroughly and pat dry with a cotton towel. Lay out flat on a cutting board or in a large glass dish. Rub it gently with the pepper, ginger, and sugar and allow to sit for 30 minutes. It is a genuine goodness when the flavors have been given time to grow accustomed to one another and get friendly, so don't rush this step.

Scatter the salt in a sauté pan and heat over medium-high heat to a count of 10, then decrease the heat to medium and lay the goose liver in it. Sear on both sides quickly until the liver begins to turn a handsome golden brown. Decrease the heat to low and cook evenly. The whole process should take less than 3 minutes; take great care not to overcook it, lest it taste leathery. Remove the liver from the pan and arrange on a serving plate with deep sides.

Add the butter to the pan and sauté the mushrooms, apple, and garlic in it, keeping the pan moving all the while to prevent scorching. When the apples begin to turn golden, add the shallots. Sauté for a scant minute. Add the chicken stock a few teaspoons at a time. Add only so much as you need to prevent sticking. Most of the stock will be absorbed, so you will be left with only a couple of tablespoons of liquid.

Spoon the sautéed mushrooms and apples over the goose liver. Sprinkle the dry red wine over it, using your fingers to prevent the wine from choosing a favorite spot, as it is like to do if you use a spoon.

Serve quickly before everything starts to cool off.

Duck

Wild ducks sometimes have a slight marine flavor, like as if you laid the bird down next to a bit of fish and they swapped odors. Some folks claim they like that, but for me, fish is fish and duck is duck, or should be. To reduce the fishy taste of wild duck, rest the carcass breast side up in a glass or glazed ceramic dish with a good-sized peeled potato inside for about an hour. This actually works even better if you have the patience to cut the potato into thick french fries and stuff the lot in there for a bit. Don't forget to throw the potato away before you cook the duck.

Generally, a large duck, like a mallard, will dress out at about 1½ pounds. And a small duck, teal and the like, will only yield ½ to ¾ pound at most.

Roast duck is an acquired taste, and some folks, to be honest, never successfully acquire it. To my mind, it's better tasting if it's a tad under-done. Overdone is far and away a cruel thing to do to a bit of wild duck flesh. A large duck should be roasted at 350°F for about 20 minutes, then cool the oven down to 325°F and continue to roast, checking every 5 minutes or so for a maximum of 20 more minutes. For a smaller duck, start out with 15 minutes and then, after the cool down, resist the urge to roast it for more than 20 minutes more. Wild duck will dry out so bad that even your dog won't eat it if you overcook the thing. Have a little respect and leave off cooking the meat while it's still edible.

Field Dressing and Preparation

Clean and dress duck the same as you would pheasant (see page 19). Be sure to search the cavity and pull out any little stray fat deposits you find there.

 **A Good Dog Is Hard to Find**

Ducks won't do something so stupid as stick their head into a tube or their neck into a trap. Nor will they fall for any other sly trick you want to advertise to them because they tend to clear the area when they see a man and his friends approaching, unless they're the kind of ducks that live in a park and are used to haunting benches on the shoreline and begging for handouts.

I hate hunting ducks myself. The only way to do it is with a shotgun, which makes an ear-splitting racket and fills the intended meat with devious little pellets of metal, whose sole purpose in life (once their primary target, the duck, is dead) is searching for a man's tooth and lodging in it. Besides, hunting for ducks is wet and uncomfortable, and if I wanted to spend an afternoon standing in dank-smelling water, then I could visit my cousin after a hard rain and take myself down to his leaky basement—at least there it's quiet and free of snakes.

Now don't get me wrong here, I love snakes. I purely love to come across one slithering through the grass or trying to hide hisself under a rock. I can't help myself, but I've just got to pick him up and have a good look at him. Snakes are cool to the touch, and their skins are the finest bit of glitter that the sun ever illumed for the pleasure of man.

Now a snake in the water, that's a different kettle of goods altogether. I never heard of a snake that couldn't swim if he needed to get from here to there and a stream crossed his path, but some snakes live in and around water. One in particular comes to mind that makes water his home, and a foul-tempered piece of work he is, too. I'm talking about the cottonmouth, a snake who's born with an itch to bite something and spends his whole life trying to satisfy hisself about it.

Maybe at one time God wasn't so sure that the mud he shaped man from wouldn't melt away if man went swimming, so God set the cottonmouth in the water to keep his pet on dry land. The plan works real good with cowards like me, but as a general strategy, it didn't take into account the fact that no matter how ornery you make a snake, man can and will out-stubborn him in a head-to-head battle. There are plenty of guys who will squat in the marshes and tempt fate to bite them, and sometimes, it surely does.

Guys hunt ducks by hiding in the reeds near a pond or lake where the ducks come down to feed and socialize. Once the ducks have settled on the water, the guy and his buddies stand up and shout something rude and personal to get the ducks to fly again and then try to shoot as many as they can before the quarry is out of range. Apparently, the rules frown on the hunter opening fire before the ducks are duly warned that the game has indeed commenced, though it's considered well within the spirit of the thing to set out phony lady ducks, seductively carved and painted enticingly, to lure prospective paramours within reach of the shotguns.

Since the ducks are shot out over the water and they're not too likely to float obligingly within reach of the guy with the gun, a dog is brought along to swim out and bring them back. A dog also serves as rear guard and will bark and break up the fight if he sees a snake sneaking up on his friends.

A good dog will, anyway.

I knew a fella who was bit on the thigh by a cottonmouth that took exception to him and his friend. The man's leg swelled up as thick as his waist, and we thought we'd seen the last of him. He was in so much pain from the bite that folks in the other room were shivering in their chairs from it, but he pulled through in the end, so I'm guessing that the guy was about as tough as he looked, which was saying something. The guy is a retired cop from Denver, and I heard that he never once had to pull his gun on anybody. He just stared folks into a corner until they melted. In that, the snake had the drop on him, 'cause he was looking at the other end when he bit the guy.

Seems it had been raining, and the water level in their duck blind was a tad higher than it had been the day before. It wasn't high enough, though, to wash into the tops of their boots when they squatted, so they stuck it out. They had not been there long, less than half an hour, when the man who was about to get bit noticed his dog slinking away. He called to the animal, but the dog kept his own counsel. With his ears pulled back tight against his head, he hunched into his shoulders and slunk off. Naturally, the fella took a caution from the dog's behavior and twisted around a bit to see what was what. He was just turning back to his friend when he felt the telltale lightning bolts of hot fire hit his thigh. Lucky for them both, his friend had seen the snake at the last minute and had his knife out. He grabbed it and cut off its head quick, but the damage had already been done.

Walking is the worst thing you can do after a snakebite, but there wasn't any other way around it. He couldn't stay where he was without a dog to keep the snakes off him, so he had to lean on his friend and walk over a mile out to his truck before they could get him to a doctor.

When they got to the truck, that worthless, low-life dog was laying in the back waiting for them. The man's friend took a double handful of that ragged no-good and threw him out into the road. Wouldn't you know it, the one talent that animal had was a knack for finding his way home. Two days later, he showed up at the backdoor, expecting somebody to feed him.

Well, soft hearts and all that. The guy gave the dog to his niece as a pet. After all, he wasn't any good for anything else. Who wants to put their faith in a dog that won't even bark and warn his friends when an enemy is sneaking up on them?

If it had been me, I'd have barbecued that dog and made sure that all the other dogs for miles around saw me doing it.

Last I heard of him, the worthless rag used to run down to the school and walk the man's niece home, but then one day, a stray took it into his head to run after them both and bite somebody. The niece made it safely to the fence and over, but her pet showed his true colors to one and all. He ran away to save himself, and I guess this time that shame must of weighed him down, because he didn't dare show his face at that house after that.

Duck Marinated in Smoked Peppers

Serves 4

Chipotle chiles (smoked jalapeños) are hot. Some people get real annoyed when they bite into one and the roof of their mouth goes a bit numb. To my mind, the taste goes real well with the dark richness of duck. But if you're the sort that don't like to find yourself poking at your gums for sensation and wondering if it will ever return, then go ahead and use a mild green chile. Don't try banana peppers though, because they just won't do. They'll disappear under the flavor of the duck like they weren't even there.

I don't want to be accused of plugging anybody's kitchen products especially, but if you have one of those handy grills that big heavyweight boxer fella is selling, it works great for this recipe. It cooks the duck from both sides in 2 to 3 minutes.

Lacking a duck, you can substitute almost any poultry in this recipe. Chicken, goose, or game hen are the best choices. If you're the type who really prefers mild peppers, then chicken or game hen are the birds for you.

> *½ cup olive oil*
> *2 teaspoons minced garlic*
> *3 to 4 chipotle chiles*
> *1 duck, boned and cut into strips about 3 inches wide*
> *Indian flatbread, such as onion kulcha (available in most Middle Eastern food stores)*
> *Scallions, trimmed and halved lengthwise*
> *⅔ cup feta cheese, crumbled or sliced*

Mix the oil, garlic, and chipotles in a shallow glass dish and roll the duck in the mixture. Allow to marinate in the refrigerator for at least 4 hours. Lay the meat on a rack to drain for about 10 minutes before cooking.

Preheat the oven to 350°F.

On a hot grill, griddle, or skillet, sear the duck strips for 3 minutes, and turn and sear for 3 minutes on the other side.

Meanwhile, warm the kulcha on a cookie sheet in the oven.

Lay the cooked duck strips in a single layer on a piece of warm kulcha and top with scallions and feta. Serve immediately.

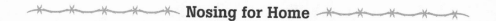

Nosing for Home

There's a guy just outside Bayfield, Colorado, who raised him up a dog what's legendary in those parts, though if truth be told, the dog worked so hard trying to grow into his title that he caused the man no small amount of grief with his efforts. Seems Carl overtrained his animal and had to do a little tromping around in the mud before things got straightened out to everybody's satisfaction.

Carl started that dog off as a puppy, teaching him to take hold of stuff with extra care for just what he had a grip on. Hang on. Me and you will let Carl teach us what to do and not to do if you wanta try raising your own duck mutt extraordinaire.

First, get yourself a couple of hairbrushes. Cut the handles off and glue the backs together. This gives the dog something tricky to pick up that requires he think about it a bit, instead of just making a rough snatch at it, as dogs are wont to do. A dog will develop a real tender touch learning to bring back a throw toy that he can't bite down on without it's liable to prickle the roof of his mouth.

Right there's where Carl shoulda left well enough alone, but he was so proud of his dog's soft touch that he used to show folks just how careful Dudley was. Carl'd roll a raw egg across the grass, and Dudley'd pick that baby up and return it unharmed to Carl's hand every time. The trouble came when Dudley tried to pick up a duck in the water without breaking it.

Carl took down a mallard drake not too far off from the blind. The duck landed just at the edge of the water, and Dudley took off, proud to show his stuff. Soon as he got to the duck, Dudley opened his mouth big enough to allow for a slow creep-up on the quarry and gently lifted it out of the water. Trouble is, he was so careful not to break it that it kept falling out of his mouth. In the end, Carl had to wade over to his dog, dragging his legs through mud and algae, and rescue the duck. Seems Dudley figured that rather than break it, he'd just nose it home through the mud. To this end, he busied himself shoving the duck through the mud with his nose, rolling it over in a slow march towards Carl. By the time Carl got to them, that two-and-a-half-pound duck weighed in close to eight pounds—most of it mud.

The way I heard it, it took some doing to convince Dudley that it was alright to take a firm grip on the duck in question. Carl worked at it pretty steady for a couple a months, but in the end, a nearly, but not quite out of the picture, soon-to-be-dead duck got the message across.

Carl started taking Dudley to places where they could communicate the lesson without either of them having to haul hisself through the mud to mull over the finer points.

The duck in question was one of a pair that Carl got, the first on purpose and the second because he was in the wrong place at the wrong time; namely, he was hanging out real close to a guy what had a bead drawn on him. So Carl ended up with two ducks on one shot. One killed outright and one lying on the ground wondering what the hell just hit him. Long about the time that the duck figured somebody owned him an explanation, Dudley strolled up and commenced to give him a ride back to Carl.

Poor Dudley. He had reasoned out pretty well that Carl didn't have any interest in the duck's heads, seeing as how every time he got back successfully with an unbroken duck, Carl would dump the duck in a bag for safe keeping, but the minute they got home, he'd take out his knife and cut the duck's head off. In a valiant attempt to do his duty by Carl, Dudley opened his mouth wide so as not to break the duck and picked it up by the head.

For his part, the duck figured he had no interest in gettin' a up-close and personal look at the inside of Dudley's mouth, so he reached out and made his opinion known by clasping hard on the likeliest object to hand— Dudley's tongue.

Well, of course, Carl saved the day, for Dudley anyway. The duck came off the worse for the whole encounter. He was so mad at Dudley for picking him up in his mouth that he refused to let go until somebody apologized. Shot and bit was just more than that creature was gonna put up with without somebody owning up to responsibility. Dudley tried to get a grip on the problem, but the duck had such a grip on him that all he could do was stand there blinking and crying with a mostly dead and justifiably aggravated duck hanging out of his mouth. Carl had to cut the duck's head off with a pocketknife to end the standoff.

After that, Dudley always bit the ducks in the neck a good swipe before he picked them up by the head and carried them back to Carl. You just can't be too careful.

Dudley's pretty thoughtful for a dog. I expect he wouldn't have tried to pick the duck up while he was still alive if he thought it was an issue. Pretty much, he takes his cue from Carl's opinions, and I guess Carl didn't think to mention it.

The other day, a couple of guys stopped by and told me of a grand way to hunt ducks without a dog or a gun neither. Before I get any further, I should point out that the praiseful adjective above was employed entirely by my visitors and does not reflect my own views.

Seems this guy they knew invented a kind of floating ring held up by phony wooden ducks. The ring was supposedly some six or seven feet across and floated a few inches below the surface of the water by means of posts coming down from the bellies of the phony ducks. Inside the ring, the guy had strung an old piece of fishing net that he tied off tight so it couldn't tear lose from the ring.

The way I hear it, the idea is that the ducks come down and land inside the ring and get their feet caught in the net, which of course they can't see from the air. Then the hunter simply pulls the whole contraption to shore and picks out his ducks.

The only thing I find wrong with this plan is everything. Ducks rarely land that close together so that, at best, you'd get one or two—that's if the game warden didn't take it into his head to wonder what that contraption was hanging out the back of your truck.

Maybe it works and maybe it doesn't. I have yet to meet anybody who claims to have actually seen it in action. I did notice that my leg looked a tad longer when those boys left, and I don't remember pulling it myself, but don't let me get in your way if you want to believe it. I am not one to interfere with the genuine pursuit of knowledge. Even if all you find out is that it's a cockamamie idea, that in itself it worth something, and if you get yourself arrested trying it, think what infinite pleasure you are bringing to your friends and family when they get to recount the story at every family gathering from now to eternity. You never know, you may be that one blessed individual in your family who is destined to provide object lessons to the young. How else are you gonna find out if you don't poke around and try stuff?

Roast Duck Glazed with Pomegranate Sauce

Serves 4

You can do this one with goose, chicken, or game hen, but duck is best. Don't try it with turkey because the dark flavor of turkey meat fights with the sensitive taste of pomegranate.

If you are doing two ducks, it will take about 5 minutes longer per side.

> *2 ducks*
> *1 lemon*
> *Freshly ground back pepper*
> *½ cup pomegranate molasses or thickened pomegranate*
> *juice (see Note, page 63)*

Rinse the duck carcasses thoroughly inside and be sure that there are no lumps of fat clinging to them. Rub the cavities with the lemon and sprinkle with pepper if you prefer your duck spicy. Prick the skin with a fork, but don't abuse the privilege. If you're cooking a domestically raised duck, place a sacrificial peeled potato in the cavity to absorb excess grease—throw it away when the duck is cooked. Use a loop of string to tie the legs together; otherwise, the duck has a tendency to dry out in some areas, while not cooking through in others—namely, the breast is bloody when the legs begin to want for a cooler environment than the oven.

Preheat the oven to 375°F.

Smear the entire carcasses with the pomegranate molasses and place on a rack in a roasting pan, breast side up.

Place the ducks in the center of the oven and roast for about 15 minutes, then remove from the oven, smear with more pomegranate molasses, and turn the ducks on their sides. Turn the oven down to 350°F.

Return to the oven and roast for an additional 20 to 25 minutes (the bigger the ducks, the longer the roasting period). Repeat this step for the other side of the duck.

The duck is done when the legs are loose in their sockets and the juices run a clear, pale yellow. Allow the pomegranate glaze about 5 minutes to cool before serving.

Note: To make thickened pomegranate juice (or pomegranate molasses, as it is usually called), pour 6 cups bottled pomegranate juice into a nonreactive saucepan. Stir in 1 cup sugar and 1/2 cup lemon juice. Bring to a boil, then decrease the heat to a simmer, and allow most of the water to boil off until the remaining liquid amounts to no more than 2 cups. It is imperative that you use either a stainless steel, glass, or enameled pan in this process, since aluminum spoils it horribly and will leave you with a bitter, aggressive mess. You can keep this stuff in the refrigerator for months, so don't worry about making it fresh every time you want it.

Early Morning Duck Chute

What with my general dislike of hunting ducks from a blind, it seemed natural to me that I should raise a few ducks of my own and save myself the grief of going out in search of them.

Well, it seemed like a good idea at the time.

Experience is a great teacher, and I'm here to tell you of my experience because you have to learn from the mistakes of others, if you expect to get ahead in this world. The truth is, you don't have nearly enough time in one lifetime to do every possible stupid thing yourself—you have to let somebody else do some of it. I did this one, so listen up and I'll tell you where I went wrong.

Two things, actually: I introduced the dinner to my son, who was about six at the time, and I picked their feeding times in the summer when the days are long and I'm up and about early.

I found out late in the fall that ducks do not care from sunlight. They have a built-in clock that tells them when breakfast time is, and they don't give a hang one way or the other that it won't be daylight for at least an hour. By this we know that domestic ducks don't have half the smarts of their wild cousins.

Seasons are real important to me. In the summer, I'm up and running with the sun and generally keep busy all day, excluding a rest from the late afternoon heat. In the winter months, whether it's cold outside or not, I tend to lay abed real late, stay up all day, regardless of the weather, and tarry way into the night before bed begins to look inviting.

Ducks don't do anything of the sort. Ducks are intractable and unvary-
ing. If breakfast is at six o'clock in July, breakfast better damned well be at
six o'clock in December as well. At best, they'll wait until a few gray streaks
appear in the east before they start complaining. They are quite willing to
get vocal on the subject, and they were issued adequate equipment for raising the dead if they so wish.

Innate laziness being the powerful master that it is, I tried leaving
them extra food at night, but ducks don't eat when it's time to sleep—
their invariable routine won't let them help you out in any way. The extra
food succeeded in attracting raccoons, who then scared the ducks into
raising a racket. Thus, I ended up getting up twice in the night for a couple
of weeks running and found myself parting with a few beloved dollars in
support of extra fencing as well.

It takes a lot of fencing to keep a raccoon away from a free feed.

By the time I ate one duck (over the miserable protests of my son), I
figured out that I had spent better than three times the price per pound of
ducks at the store on each and every one of my flock and that, in any event,
the one that met me and my hatchet behind the barn was the only one my
offspring was going to allow me to consume.

You'd think I'd butchered and ate his Great Aunt Betty.

So now I had a flock of "friends and relatives" living in my yard who
were dead set against the concept of sleeping in and who enjoyed the
protection of a powerful inside agent.

The eggs they laid were good, and to their credit, the ducks never
made a scene when I took them, though my son pressed his luck and tried
to convince me that he would perish from neglect if I didn't allow at least
one generation of baby ducks to bring cheer into his miserable life. By that
time, he had begun to wear out his welcome on the subject of ducks, and I
made it pretty clear that nothing would be done to encourage any more of
those noisy quackers to enter my domain. We were negotiating a decrease
and nothing else would be taken under serious discussion.

An impasse had been reached by the end of the second year, and the
ducks ruled supreme in the no man's land in between. Here I was, with
some dozen ducks demanding food and fencing, and I was buying duck
from the market for my dinner.

One warm August afternoon, I lit on the happy idea of eating in the yard to see if the ducks would be scandalized by my choice of cuisine and run away from the scene of the crime, but the impudent squatters stole my bread instead. Perusing the offerings, their leader leaned over the body of the fallen and helped himself to an entire loaf of French bread. Before I could react, they had dragged it over to their pond and dipped it, which is just one of the disgusting habits ducks cultivate—they dip their food in their swimming pool/toilet to soften it—and then they shared out the booty between them. They didn't seem to mind that the meat on the plate was probably a cousin. I pointed this out to my son, but he was not moved by the powers of logic.

In the end, frustration led to invention and ingenuity, and I solved my problem (though my appetite was left unsatisfied) with a device I call "the early morning duck chute."

Using an old piece of plywood as a friend, I constructed a ramp from my bedroom window to the lip of a large metal dish in the yard where the ducks were accustomed to feeding. Thereafter, when the ducks woke me, all I had to do was roll over and pour a premeasured bucket of duck feed out the window, where it rolled down the chute and into the dish. Once, I forgot to push up the glass before I dumped the contents of the bucket and got duck feed all over the floor, but the commotion outside alerted me to the problem pretty quick, so no worries on that score.

That's the way it generally goes in my house. I no sooner screw up then some helpful soul points it out to me. What else is family for?

Cardamom Duck

Serves 3

Surprisingly enough, this recipe works very well with strips of lamb. Cut the lamb into strips about 2 inches thick and 5 or 6 inches long. Besides lamb, it will work well with any poultry. A friend told me he tried it with beef, and it was very good, but since I have not tried it myself, all I can do is pass on the word. When using lamb or beef, change the white wine to a light red.

Serve with rice or couscous and a pita bread or kulcha (Indian flatbread).

> *¼ cup walnuts, pounded into small pieces*
> *1 teaspoon ground cardamom*
> *¼ teaspoon ground turmeric*
> *¼ teaspoon ground cinnamon*
> *¼ teaspoon ground nutmeg*
> *2 teaspoons freshly chopped dried red chile pepper (see Note, below)*
> *2 tablespoons dry white wine*
> *Breasts and legs from 2 ducks*

Grind the walnut pieces through your spice grinder or process in a food processor until you have a coarse powder. Mix with the cardamom, turmeric, cinnamon, nutmeg, and red pepper. Stir the white wine into the spices and blend into a smooth paste. Don't be afraid to add a little more wine if it seems too dry. If it's too runny, it will slide off of the duck and be lost in the bottom of the pan, but it has to be some runny to do that, so don't be shy.

Preheat the oven to 350°F.

Dredge the pieces of duck through your spice mixture.

Roast skin side down in a clay baker or a roasting pan with a rack for about 45 minutes, or until the juices run clear yellow with no hint of pink.

Serve hot.

Note: Those red chile peppers should be chopped into submission. If the pieces of chile are too large, it will detract from the delicate flavors of the cinnamon and nutmeg. If this seems like a task you are destined to mess up, no shame and no worries. Just get some of those crushed dried red pepper flakes available in stores and put them through your spice grinder. The flakes are far superior in flavor to the preground red pepper for this particular recipe.

Quail

Quail are small birds. The desert or gambrel's quail never gets bigger than 10 or 11 inches in length and dresses out at about 6 ounces. The scaled quail, only slightly larger, might get up to 12 inches in length and yield as much as 8 ounces.

Since most of the meat on a quail is in the breast, if you roast the bird whole, there is some danger of the legs becoming too brown before the breast is done. Take a strip of cheesecloth, smear one side with lard, and wrap it around the legs. Remove the strip of cheesecloth about 10 minutes before the bird is to be removed from the oven. The lard will keep the dark meat soft and tender while the breast cooks. If the idea of lard is offensive to your palate, don't worry, it won't be absorbed by the bird, and whatever remains on the skin will roast away before you serve the quail at table. If you still don't want to go there, either substitute butter, though this will scorch a bit and leave the legs an odd color, or you can remove the legs before roasting and add them at the proper time. Notice I didn't mention the proper time. I don't know it, since I've never opted for this method. I knew a lady who removed the legs and baked them inside the quail cavity. This seemed to work fine. She removed them about 10 minutes before she took the bird out of the oven and no one was the wiser for her ruse.

I have included in this section a recipe for quail eggs, which are very tasty morsels. Quail eggs often can be bought fresh at a goodly number of Asian food markets, which is a good way to acquire them, since if you are hunting quail when they have eggs on the nest, then you are doing a bad thing. It's called endangering the future of the species. If you are one of those fortunate souls who can root around in the grass and locate quail nests with little or no trouble, then I take my hat off to you. Since you don't want to take the eggs more than 24 hours after they are laid, and you certainly don't want to take more than half of the eggs in any one nest, this takes some doing.

Trouble is, even if you're doing it right, it's not a good deal for the species in the long run. Since their habitat is shrinking daily, the least we can do is let them raise their broods in peace. There are folks out there with the patience to raise quail in pens like chickens, and they can therefore harvest the eggs pretty easily without endangering the future of the birds. I like the idea of keeping these enterprising folks in business, and I also like leaving the quail parents in the wild alone to tend their brood without my bootprints raising their feathers or otherwise causing any undue consternation.

Field Dressing and Preparation

Clean and dress quail per the instructions for game birds under pheasant (see page 19).

⚹—⚹ Learning to Laugh on an Empty Stomach ⚹—⚹

I got my one and only fine for poaching using the cardboard tube trick to hunt quail. I still don't know how that happened except that I had the bad luck to run into a warden who had less of a sense of humor than most . . . and that is saying something.

I was sitting on the ground, nodding off. I'd had no takers; my bag was empty, and I was thinking about giving up and calling it a day. My stomach was growling, and I was beginning to think good thoughts on a bowl of beans and cornbread.

Off behind me, I heard a pair of boots making their way through the grass, and I managed to scatter most of my corn before I deemed the head attached to the boots could catch sight of me. (For this reason, it's a good idea not to carry too much corn. Bait is bait, and there's not much you can argue about that.) I made myself presentable for company and sat back to wait. I must have cut it close, because he broke into the clearing pretty quick after I'd settled. Naturally, he asked me what I was doing. Manners being a good thing to start off with, I answered "sitting" just as politely as I could and tried to look friendly without giving the man the impression that he was talking to a smart-ass.

Apparently, my face doesn't do that trick all too well because he took exception to me almost from my first word. One woulda thought that he came up behind me looking for somebody to argue with—he was that testy.

"You tryin' to tell me you're just sittin' out here in the dirt doin' absolutely nothin'?" he inquired, kicking at my little cardboard roll with the tip of his boot just as if he meant to prompt me into a tearful confession with a combination of acknowledgment of the facts to hand and a hint at the power of the law. He was none too happy with my response is all I can guess. Some folks have high expectations, and when those designs prove to be unreachable, they get their back up in the air over it.

I pointed to the bit of cardboard and told him that I was out for a stroll when I came upon the pitiful evidence of man's ability to leave his mark in even the most out-of-the-way places, and I was thus compelled to meditate on this sorry fact before I could move on.

Next he prodded my canvas bag and asked me what it was for.

At this point, I was glad that there were no quail in that bag. I was under the mistaken impression that, lacking evidence, there was nothing he could do to me. As it turns out, this particular warden had never meditated on anything in life, excepting the possibility of arresting persons unknown whenever and wherever the urge took him.

I didn't get any quail that day, but I did manage to meet Dudley Do-Right with an attitude.

He retrieved the bag from the ground and turned it inside out, inspecting the fibers closely, then he repeated his question.

"I'm a potato salesman," I told him, determined not to be intimidated by his boots.

"This bag is empty," he informed me, skinnying his eyes down in anticipation of his fondest dreams coming true right there in that field.

"Well, that's because I'm a very good potato salesman." I smiled at him to lighten his load in life, but I shoulda known by his shiny buckle and the creases in his clothes that he had no more sense of humor than a cedar fence post.

He asked to see my hunting license and my driver's license, in that order. It didn't do me any good to point out that I was neither hunting nor driving and, therefore, had no use for either license.

By now, he was plainly annoyed, though I had tried my best to appease him. He cited me for contentious behavior and poaching even though I had no gun, no weapons of any kind, and no ill-gotten game in evidence.

He gave me a ride into town, though in truth I wasn't going that way and didn't need his help. Conveniently, the ride provided me with the opportunity to pay my fine immediately and get on with my life. I thought I had been getting on with my life pretty well before he invited me to partake of his company, but by now I had figured out that talking to these boys was about as productive as trying to reason with an avalanche, so I just went with the flow and dug myself out when they had passed me by.

Sometimes, that's all you can do.

They even appropriated my canvas bag. They turned it inside out and shook it like a terrier with a rat trying to find a feather or two. In the end, when they didn't find any, they took that absence for evidence: only a poacher would go to so much trouble to clean a canvas bag so thoroughly.

With logic like that for evidence, there's no use in arguing about it. Pay up and make yourself scarce before those boys think of some other entertainments.

Quail in a Bowl of Spaghetti Squash

Serves 4

Pheasant works really well here, if you don't have quail handy. If you can't get either quail or pheasant, then try turkey. Chicken loses a bit in the translation and both duck and goose overwhelm the squash. I tried the recipe once with store-bought ground pork and it was a big hit at table, though you have to brown the pork a bit and drain the excess fat off before you put it in the oven to bake.

This recipe is also very good with acorn squash, though if you go with the stronger-flavored winter squashes, the artichokes clash a bit. Mushrooms make a good substitute for artichokes, and their flavor resonates better with acorn squash. Duck and goose go better with acorn squash as well, so if that's the bird you have, then try it with the acorn squash and mushrooms.

> *4 quail, boned, about 1½ pounds*
> *2 cups heavy cream*
> *2 tablespoons honey*
> *2 teaspoons ground nutmeg*
> *1 large spaghetti squash, about 2 pounds*
> *5 tablespoons melted butter*
> *½ cup balsamic vinegar*
> *1 cup port*
> *¼ cup rice flour, dissolved in ¼ cup water*
> *6 artichoke hearts*

Coarsely grind the quail meat through a meat grinder, or mince it with a sharp knife (see Note, page 72). Mix the meat with the cream, honey, and nutmeg.

Preheat the oven to 350°F.

Cut the spaghetti squash in half lengthwise and scrape out the seeds. Abuse the flesh with a crosshatch of knife cuts (do not penetrate the skin), brush with 4 tablespoons of the melted butter, and wrap in aluminum foil. Bake for about 30 minutes. A fork should slice into it easily. If it doesn't, then bake for another 10 minutes.

Meanwhile, mix the vinegar and port in a small saucepan and boil until you have reduced its content by half, stirring regularly unless you want to pitch it and start over. Add a few drops of the reduced sauce to the rice flour mixture, then pour it back into the saucepan. You don't want the rice flour to react to the heat and clump. Stir it in thoroughly and when the sauce appears to be thick and smooth, add the remaining 1 tablespoon butter and remove the sauce from the heat.

Remove the squash from the oven and increase the oven temperature to 375°F.

Stuff the cavity of the squash with the quail mixture. This is where the size of the squash becomes crucial—you don't want the quail mounded up over the edge of the squash. Push the artichoke hearts into the quail mixture, leaving only the upper halves exposed.

Place the stuffed squashes in a baking dish. Cover and bake for 8 to 10 minutes. Test for doneness by inserting a clean, wooden chopstick in the center; it should come out clean—slightly oily but free of bloody residue.

Using a large stew spoon, transfer your creation to a serving bowl that is large enough to accommodate the squash easily without allowing it to tip.

Dribble the sauce over it and serve immediately.

Note: If you don't have a meat grinder for this recipe, you can get in much needed practice with a knife. Cut the meat into thin strips, like you were trying to invent spaghetti only outta meat. When you have a pile of strips on one side of the cutting board and no large chunks on the other, turn the strips sideways and commence to cutting them into the littlest bits off the end that you can manage. Don't fret if it's not perfect. Whatever you get will do fine. Variety in life is always a notch better than perfection. Trust me.

If you're still not happy with it, then spread the pieces out until it resembles a patty and hack the knife up and down a bit until you think you've done your duty. Even if you only do this for a minute or two, you'll end up with a collection of smaller pieces than you started with.

⚡——Bagging It on the Plains of Eastern Colorado——⚡

I got an extra surprise quail hunting one day. It was a fine warm day, with just enough clouds to keep everybody from roasting where they sat—me especially in that alpaca poncho of mine. I'd had six birds in less than two hours. Such luck could not be denied, and I couldn't drag myself away from that spot till I'd got another . . . and then another. You get the picture. I hesitate to use the "g" word where my own modest appetites are concerned, but the truth is, greed kept me glued to that spot long after leaving time.

Seems my profitable little pastime had attracted a spectator. Patching together later events and revelations, a picture comes to mind that begins to explain the why and wherewithal of the thing that otherwise might want for a reasonable explanation.

I expect he was hiding in the cornfield behind me some and off to the west. He could see me clear, apparently, though I had no notion he was even there. All the while I was sitting on the ground taking quail and stashing them in my bag, I was checking my supply of corn, and never once thought something besides the bait I brought with me intentionally could maybe be bait for something.

That other one was sittin' off there in the corn field watching me hunt and thinking how good one of those birds would taste. Now he probably didn't set out to get hisself a bird for dinner. Like as not he was tracking a deer mouse that slipped away from him, and the chase brought him nearby to where he could see somebody, namely me, having considerable more luck at the hunt than he himself was having.

I can't say how long he watched before he took it in his head to help himself. I didn't spend enough time with him to be able to tell you whether or not he was the kind of fella who could put two and two together and act on four before it got too big to handle, but I can tell you that once he had sorted out the players, he went straight for the prize.

Somewhere in the watching, he made up his mind that the birds in the bag were considerably easier to catch than the ones flying over his head. He came up behind me, slow and sure and so quiet that I never heard so much as a grass blade holler. Right into the bag he went and commenced to help himself to a free meal. Not being a glutton, he swallowed just the one, and that's when he messed up. He could have made his getaway, and ever after I always woulda thought that I had miscounted— none the wiser for my new friend's full stomach. But it was warm and dark in that bag—a good place to digest and take a little nap, and that's what he did.

Sometime later, I decided that enough was enough and got up to leave. I tied a string around the neck of my bag and headed for home, lugging a befuddled interloper with me.

At home, I laid the bag on the workbench in my shed—no use in taking a mess of feathers into the house with me, since once in, you'll never clear them all out. No sooner had I got the string off and prepared to stick my hand in there after a bird or two than the bag hissed at me in a way that no bag had ever threatened me before. It set me to thinking, I can surely tell you. I let the canvas fall away slowly, and a powerfully angry rat snake, some $3^1/_2$ to 4 feet long, revealed himself, coiled amongst my birds.

He still had a sizable, bird-shaped lump about midway down his belly so the reason for his visit was about as clear as it could get. He postured and hissed just as if I had been whacking on him with a stick or somewhat, which stuck in my craw, since I figured I was the one who had a right to feel injured here. I explained to my visitor that he could just put his tempers where they belonged, thank you very much, since I wasn't running a rat-snake soup kitchen here and didn't think much of his blaming me 'cause he got caught stealing.

Well, of course, the logic of the thing escaped him. He was way yonder too shook up to put reason to the thing. When he climbed into that bag, he had thought it was a stationary object and for certain, he hadn't gone in there intending to take a long, bumpy trip on the floorboards of a truck. Adventures are all well and good if you've got your gear with you and you know what's coming, but it don't do to take a fella by surprise like that and expect him to shake your hand all agreeably afterwards.

In time, he calmed down, and I retrieved what remained of my birds. He was too full to want to fight. Snakes need to take it easy and kick back for a few hours after they eat such a large meal, and this one was so stuffed that he bulged in the middle. My new friend acquainted himself with the shed for a couple a days, and then I went out and caught him again, on purpose this time.

I had some neighbors down the road who had a terrible problem with rats in their barn. I put my bag on a pillow and set it on the seat beside me to make the trip over so my snake friend wouldn't give the neighbors the kind of greeting he gave me and put them off him. It's always advisable to put your best foot forward, as it were, when meeting new folks, so I was just doing my bit to help things along.

Well, I shouldn't have worried. They hit it off like old pals. The snake took one look at their barn and moved right in. He set up business around the stalls mostly, but he made his home in the hayloft. After a while, he joined a dating service to help him find a wife, and by the next year he'd lit on the right girl and the two of them were living happily ever after and raising a brood of younguns that would grow up to be the terror of every mouse and rat in that end of the county.

Rat snakes will take baby chickens, but since my neighbors weren't raising anything but horses, a couple of milk cows, and some geese, everybody got along fine, and they didn't have any "why I oughta's" happening between the various families that called the barn their home.

Sweet Lemon Quail with Pine Nuts

Serves 2

This is one of my grandfather's recipes that I changed only a bit. He had rough old hands and didn't mind a bit the kind of abuse you have to take to harvest piñon nuts. He used them in this, but along the way, I figured that I'd rather save the ends of my fingers for work other than donating scraps to the piñon pine, so I changed it to pine nuts.

Pheasant, game hen, chicken, and turkey also will work with this recipe, though turkey is a bit strong for the spices and tries to overwhelm things generally. Pine nuts are a truly unique experience that can't be duplicated, but I find that some folks just purely don't like them and no amount of creative cooking will get them to go down. If that turns out to be the case with you and yours, then by all means, substitute almonds and *bon appétit.*

¼ *cup fresh lemon juice*
¼ *teaspoon ground nutmeg*
¼ *teaspoon ground cinnamon*
¼ *teaspoon ground cardamom*
6 *quail, about 2 pounds of meat*
Pita bread or a couple of new potatoes, sliced paper thin
2 *tablespoons peanut oil*
Pinch of freshly ground white pepper
½ *cup pine nuts*

Mix together the lemon juice and ¹/₈ teaspoon each of the nutmeg, cinnamon, and cardamom. Rub the quail with the mixture, inside and out, place in a glass dish, cover, and refrigerate for at least 8 hours.

Preheat the oven to 375°F. Place a roasting rack in a roasting pan. Cover the rack with the pita bread or potatoes. Brush with oil.

In a large skillet, heat the peanut oil over medium-high heat. Brown the quail lightly, being careful not to scorch it.

Remove the quail quickly from the heat and place, breast sides down, on the pitas or potatoes on the roasting rack. Sprinkle with the remaining ¹/₈ tea-spoon each of nutmeg, cinnamon, and cardamom, and the pepper. Cover tightly.

Roast for about 10 minutes.

Uncover, flip the quail over on their backs, and continue to roast for another 10 minutes.

About 5 minutes before the quail are done, toast the pine nuts over medium heat in a scant tablespoon of peanut oil remaining in the skillet, until golden and fragrant, about 2 minutes.

Remove the quail from the oven and transfer to a serving dish.

Scatter the toasted pine nuts over the roasted quail and serve immediately.

Quail Eggs in Black Tea

Makes 4 quarts

Every year my family used to put up a dozen jars or more of hen's eggs with this recipe. Done that way, it's just as colorful and right tasty on its own, but it's not quite the same. Quail eggs are better. If you try this with hen's eggs, pick the smallest eggs you can find.

The eggs are canned in black tea and cushioned with beets and spinach. The beets are a crunchy, tasty extra, and after you've munched up all the eggs, the spinach is great sautéed with leftover roast goose tidbits and pistachio nuts. Garnish these gourmet leftovers with feta for a special treat.

½ cup black China tea leaves
3 medium cubes crystallized ginger
1 medium cinnamon stick
4 medium beets, peeled and sliced into rings
1 (12-ounce) bag fresh spinach leaves (more is also good)
2 dozen quail eggs

Fill your canning jars with water and place them on a wire rack in a pot that is large enough to allow for at least 2 inches of water covering them. Bring the water to a boil and boil for at least 10 minutes.

Secure the tea leaves in a tea strainer or a square of cheesecloth, and steep for 5 minutes in 5 quarts of boiling water, along with the ginger and cinnamon stick. Meanwhile, strain the tea, but keep it simmering as you don't want it to cool.

Pour off the hot water in the canning jars and place a layer of sliced beets in the bottom of each jar. Add a layer of fresh spinach leaves on top of them. This is to cushion the eggs from the cruelty of glass jars. Stand the eggs on end in the jar (you should be able to fit three to a layer) and place more spinach and beets to cushion them from their cousins above. Continue this process until you have six eggs in each jar, each with its requisite layers of beets and spinach. Leave the top open for now—if you put the beets on just yet, you'll splatter hot tea on yourself.

Fill the jars with the hot tea, distributing it equally among them and topping the jars off with boiling water, if necessary, to cover the contents completely.

Now you can add that last layer of beets and spinach. Screw the lids down tight on the jars (see Note, below). Process in a boiling water bath for about 15 minutes, then seal the jars tightly.

Stand the jars in the refrigerator and leave them alone for at least 2 days. If you did it right, when you peel the eggs, the whites will be nearly black with a velvety red hint and the yolk will be a rich maroon.

When you open them to serve, the jars should make an audible popping sound when you free the lid. If they don't, then there's air in the jar. Don't ever eat any preserved foods that have been sitting in the jar and allowed to mingle freely with air. You can't trust it and you shouldn't.

After the jars have cooled, place them in the refrigerator. You should eat all of the eggs within 2 weeks, and at all times, they should remain in the refrigerator for storage. There is no genuinely safe way to preserve eggs, even if you use a ton of salt and generous quantities of vinegar. Eggs have a porous shell that allows the young chicken developing inside to breathe. Unfortunately for us, when we harvest the eggs for ourselves, this shell allows all sorts of bacteria to make a home in the egg. So ... if two weeks go by and you haven't finished off your eggs, kiss them goodbye and toss them out. Canned eggs are a fragile commodity and ideally should be eaten within a week.

The taste is heavenly with a mixture of sweet beets that is elusive but present all the same and an ethereal mix of ginger and black tea, all highlighted with a pervasive strain of cinnamon.

Note: Waterbath processing is simple and easy. You will need a pot big enough to allow for a wire rack on the bottom (this keeps your jars off the bottom of the pot and provides a little distance from the metal), plus the height of the jar, plus about 2 inches of water. After the canning jars have been filled, screw on the lids but do not finishing tightening them. They should be tight enough that they won't come off but not so tight that the contents of the jar can't breathe. You need to allow any trapped air inside to bubble out. Set the jars on the rack with the pot about half full of hot water, then pour more hot water over the top until the jars are sufficiently covered. Bring the water to a slow boil, decrease the heat, and allow the water to simmer for 10 to 15 minutes. All the bubbles should be coming up from the bottom of the pot and not from the rims of your jars. Turn off the heat under the pot and allow to cool for a few minutes. While the jars are still hot, remove them from the pot. Dip out some of the water with a ladle or a Pyrex measuring cup, then lift the jars out carefully. Screw the lids down tight and allow the jars to cool completely. If the center portion of the lid doesn't pull down into a dimple, then you didn't get all the air out. Return the jars to the pot, cover with hot water, and boil a bit longer.

GAME

Deer

Venison doesn't necessarily mean deer. It refers to the meat of any of the members of the deer family. Deer, elk, and moose are all very good in the recipes in this section, though I prefer the tenderness of a Texas white-tailed deer. Whitetails are small, not much bigger than a big dog, and persist in large numbers in the wild.

A mature white-tailed buck will weigh in between 75 pounds (if he's a yearling) and 300 pounds (for a wily oldster). Does rarely exceed 150 pounds. A mule deer can weigh up to 400 pounds, with yearlings weighing in around 125 pounds. Does range between 100 and 150 pounds.

White-tailed deer are one of the wild creatures, along with raccoon, opossum, and a host of smaller animals, that thrive in populated areas. Ask anybody with a garden in the suburbs of Houston how well fed the deer are. In some places, there are so many of them that they don't even bother to skulk around, but come right up and help themselves in the middle of the day.

Bucks have those impressive racks so they can compete with each other for the attentions of does, but they are anxious and quite able to use them on you if you get presumptuous. People have been killed when run through by an antler spine. The most common way to get yourself hurt is to presume that the animal is dead when actually he's just in shock. Always prod the animal first (using a stick or the tip of your gun, whatever will keep your soft spots at a safe distance from his antlers), before you lean over him. Folks tend to lean over things head first, which puts your neck in perfect range for his antlers. Not good at all. Also, I should mention that the hide of the mule deer in the Colorado Rockies sometimes transports the ticks that carry Rocky Mountain spotted fever. It's a good idea to protect yourself from ticks when hunting any animal that is subject to them. That's pretty much all of them except fish.

Field Dressing and Preparation

Position the deer on its back. Cut off the scrotum and the penis and toss them away. Find the arch of the ribs in the middle of the chest. Make a small slit with your knife at this point, big enough to slip in the blade of the knife and two fingers. Straddle the deer, facing the tail. Girdle the blade of your knife with two fingers and slit open the belly. By protecting the blade with your fingers, you lessen the risk of overcorrecting and nicking the intestine. It won't kill you if you do nick something, it's just more work rinsing later on.

Turn and face the deer's head. Split the skin over the chest area all the way to the base of the throat and pull it back, exposing the rib cage. Cut through the cartilage on either side of the sternum. Get a firm grip on the sternum and pull it up and out. It'll break free of the body easily if you have cut through all the cartilage. The cartilage is much easier to cut through than the sternum itself. Cut through the esophagus at the base of the throat and pull it out. Now, make a circular cut around the rectum, being careful only to cut through the skin and not to puncture it. Pull it free from the body a spare inch and tie it off with a piece of string or a stout rubber band. Turn the carcass on its side and scoop out the organs with your hands. You'll have to work your fingers carefully into the pelvis and encourage the intestines to let go. Don't puncture the bladder. Rinse the cavity and allow it to drain. By now, it will have accumulated a lot of blood so let that drain out. Next cut through the exposed diaphragm and remove the heart and lungs. If you like hearts and liver, transfer those to a bag that will allow you to carry them out without undue bruising. Rinse the cavity again and allow it to drain once more. That done, don a pair of cheap rubber gloves, such as you would use to protect your hands from cleaning fluids, and pull back the skin over the inside of the hind legs. Locate and remove the tarsal glands sitting on top of the muscle tissue and throw them away. Put your gloves into a plastic bag and carry your trash out with you.

Debunking the Bambi Myth the Hard Way

I served venison one night to a couple of guys that were best left unenlightened. They were cousins of a friend, and I didn't know them that well personally, but I figured out later that some people are best left sleeping since waking them up sets all sorts of events in motion. While the momentum they build up can be good for a laugh later—in the safety of your own home—the grin on your face kind of hurts, too.

Seems these two guys bought the Bambi myth and decided that deer were nothing more than sweet, harmless huggy toys with big brown eyes. That and the fact that venison tasted better than anything these guys had ever chewed on previously got them thinking. The fact is, with the brain size we are talking about here, it was only a matter of time before trouble got involved with their schemes. The good news is that neither of them owned a gun, or a license to try to use one either—that much is a genuine blessing—but between them they did own a van and that turned out to be enough to get the ball rolling.

Fate played out the rest of the hand for them.

One night, about two in the morning, these two were returning from a late-night drinking and sports evening with buddies. They were doing the smart thing and following a big rig the better to keep an eye on that tricky road—the one that kept weaving back and forth under their tires. I guess nobody amongst their friends had enough sense to put them up for a few hours till they sobered a bit, more's the pity. Lots of grief could be avoided if a man's friends would show him half the consideration that they would show to a stray dog. Of course, a stray dog, if fed proper and trained a bit, can be counted upon to make hisself useful sometimes, which isn't always the case with a man's friends.

Anyway, the guy driving the big rig caught an impressively healthy mule deer buck in his headlights and clipped him a good one before the deer could recover and dart back into the bushes. Our boys in the van saw the whole thing and threw the brakes on hard, sliding halfway off the road in the process. They climbed out and inspected the hapless buck in the glare of the headlights and deemed it edible extraordinaire.

Either they didn't realize that the deer wasn't quite as dead as they thought, or they didn't think that little detail would cause them any trouble. Just goes to show you how much trouble a guy can get himself into when he tries to think through a situation when the equipment he's been issued isn't quite up to the task—even before he numbed it silly by having way yonder too much fun.

Those two took that deer by the legs and hauled him around to the door of their van and laid him out inside. I hear that that was a pretty nice van before they did that. Now these two boys were not bad-looking fellows, just a tad simple—slow out of the gate, as the saying goes. Fact is, they considered themselves two of the front-runners in the ladies' man competition, and I honestly can't argue with that, so long as the ladies in question are only interested in a man's appearance. Those boys had fixed up that van to entertain ladies of that caliber, and by all reports they were reasonably successful at it.

The night they dumped that mule deer buck in there, they changed all that irrevocably.

Well, they had shut the door and made it a couple of miles down the road before that deer began to stir. He put his head up and looked around him and decided that he didn't want to see the world from the inside of a van.

Naturally, that deer didn't know what had hit him, but right then and there, he was prepared to blame all his troubles on those two boys. There was just enough room in the back of that van for him to get his legs tucked under him and start slamming the walls and roof with his head. In other words, he had just enough room to let his temper fly and, brother, it flew.

He was a big buck, though over the years and many retellings of this tale, his antler spread has grown from ten points to proportions that don't rightly exist on an earthly deer. From what I heard, he'd have to be some bigger than an elk to have a rack that big.

Needless to say, he had the ammunition to shoot down that van in short order. He broke out the windows, tore up the upholstery, and did more than a little redecorating generally. Our heroes drove into the ditch and rolled their van trying to drive away from the ruckus behind them, and while the three of them were sequestered so intimately on their backs in the ditch, the deer redecorated those boys a bit as well before he lit on the right approach and sprung the door. With the promise of freedom only inches away, he decided to forgive them and lit off for home with only a couple of solid kicks to the head of the nearest culprit for old time's sake.

Fortunately, a passing motorist happened upon them before they bled to death, and neither spent more than a few days in the hospital, though they nursed broken bones and an array of truly impressive scars for much longer.

The scars are now part of a long hunting story that has nary a mention of a van in it and, like I mentioned earlier, the deer appears in that story in proportions that would terrify a grizzly bear. In all fairness, he probably looked near about that big in the close confines of that van.

Since then, some well-meaning but misguided fool has taken those two fishing and taught them somewhat of the art. I guess they can't get into too much trouble in a fishing boat, unless they take up fishing with dynamite, but then, that's a whole 'nother story.

Venison Stroganoff

Serves 3

This recipe can be adjusted to accommodate almost any red meat or game bird. My first choice would be beef, followed by moose, lamb, goose, turkey, duck, or rabbit. Don't try it with pork as the flavor of pork tends to squabble with the cardamom and nutmeg. Serve with your favorite pasta.

4 tablespoons butter
¼ small onion, very finely chopped
2 pounds venison fillets (steaks cut into strips about 2 inches wide by 4 to 6 inches long)
1½ cups sliced mushrooms
2 tablespoons all-purpose flour
¼ cup dry white wine
Scant pinch of ground cardamom
Scant pinch of ground nutmeg
Large pinch of freshly ground white pepper
1½ cups sour cream

Melt 2 tablespoons of the butter in a large deep skillet. Before the butter begins to brown, throw in the onion. Stir for about 1 minute, then add the venison to the pan and brown on both sides. Don't cook the strips through, just brown them a bit and then take them out of the pan and set them aside.

Add the remaining 2 tablespoons butter to the pan and when that begins to sizzle, toss in the mushrooms and sauté them for no more than 2 minutes, then shove them to the edge of the pan to keep them out of the way. They'll keep cooking, so don't take too long with this, just shove them around a bit, and get on with it.

Stir in the flour and mix it in well with the butter. Remove the pan from the heat and allow it to cool for a minute, but don't let the flour clump up, which it will do if you hesitate too long.

Add the wine to the pan and set it back on the fire. Stir to incorporate the butter and flour and then return the venison to the pan. Sprinkle the cardamom, nutmeg, and white pepper over the venison. Let it cook for about 3 minutes.

Turn down the heat to a simmer and add the sour cream. Simmer for a minute or so. Don't let the sour cream boil or it will curdle. Poke the meat with a fork and if it doesn't stain the sour cream pink, then it's done.

Serve hot, as reheating tends to mess with the flavors.

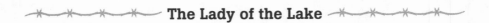

The Lady of the Lake

If only those boys with the van had given up on venison and stuck to fishing.

I promised you the rest of that story, though, in fact, I'm not sure that it's truly over yet. Any two guys that work that hard to get themselves into trouble constitute an ongoing concern. If we've heard the last of them, then I'll be the first to express surprise.

Apparently, fishing was way too tame to suit their hard-living intentions. The same well-meaning fool what taught them to fish went and lent them his nice bass boat and an almost new Evinrude motor. They had had time to buy their own gear, so some justice was served up in the interest of yet another hard lesson, though I've no doubt that the gist of this one flew right over their heads just as quick as the last one did. I can't even rightly blame this bit of tomfoolery on drink. True, they'd had a couple of six-packs between them when they took that first fatal step, but the way those two suck down the brew, a couple of six-packs would hardly be much of a mitigating factor.

Well, fishing turned out to be one thing they were fairly good at. They had just about caught their limit and a fine, healthy batch of volunteers they had in their bags by all accounts, when the next deer to enter their lives swam in at stage left.

Deer can and do swim sizable lakes and rivers if they have business on the other side, and they don't feel up to walking all the way around. This one fancied she had a good-looking buck to rendezvous with on the other side, I expect, and had no mind for those two ignorant busybodies in the boat.

The boys spotted her head bobbing in the water, noted the considerable splashing she was making, and convinced themselves that she was drowning. Perhaps they felt bolder by the fact that here was a deer who lacked the dangerous rack they had come up close against in their earlier fray. That smooth, unthreatening female head lulled them into thinking they were stronger than her.

Don't you believe it. Bambi is a work of fiction, okay? Deer have big eyes so they can see in the dim light of dawn. The fact that they look help-less is an accident of nature.

The boys got their engine started in short order and maneuvered up beside the doe, who was rolling her eyes and snorting at them, trying to warn them off—to no avail. Keeping the boat along her flank, they then grabbed her by the neck and forelegs and dragged her into their boat.

Less than five minutes after this part of their imperfect plan had been accomplished, all three of them were swimming for shore, the doe to one side and the boys to other. They had lost interest in her company by this time. I'm betting that, excepting any five-minute period that they spent trapped in that van with the mule deer buck, that the five minutes in the middle of the river with an angry doe in their boat was the longest five minutes of their sorry lives.

I guess her mother taught that doe pretty well not to accept rides from strangers, because, friends, she no sooner got her bearings than she began to stomp the daylights out of anything her hooves could reach and, brother, they could reach quite a bit in those cramped confines. I have never seen a bass boat that was built to accommodate an angry woman, and that doe was some angry, by all appearances. She made pretty quick work of the situa-tion. She not only stomped those boys black and blue, she stomped a num-ber of holes in their boat, sending it, that good Evinrude motor, and all their fishing gear to the bottom of the river.

I hear that they eventually paid back the well-meaning, but misguided fool for the loss of his bass boat and motor, but by that time I'm sure that they had found some other mess that they could drive into headlong. History may not repeat itself exactly, but in some cases it generally presents a close facsimile, and those two knotheads are predictable, if they're nothing else.

Those two boys may not be up to snuff in the learning-from-your-mistakes department, but I have certainly learned the error of my ways. In the future, I will pay closer attention to whom I introduce the taste of venison. Apparently venison meat has addictive qualities that I hadn't sus-pected before. I can't think of any other reason why a man would risk life and limb—twice—for a taste of it.

Venison in a Cup of Rice

Serves 6

I came up with this one one year when my son and I were so poor that we were sick to death of venison and rice and that's very near all we had. Some friends gave me some beets and I came up with the idea of concealing some of dinner's ingredients underneath them. Adding mushrooms and putting the little cap of rice on the top came later.

Since this recipe is baked in individual dishes, and it is practically impossible to transfer it to a serving dish without destroying the presentation, some accommodation needs to be made in order to avoid subjecting your guests to hot dishes. To this end, I've acquired a collection of small baskets just a hair larger than the Pyrex baking dishes I use. Small baskets are available at a variety of kitchen stores and import houses and come in so many sizes that no matter what size baking dish you choose, you should be able to find a few little baskets to accommodate them. Remember, they don't have to fit exactly, so long as the baking dish slips into it, and the basket prevents the sides of the hot dish from coming in contact with your guests' hands.

This recipe is also very good if prepared with beef. It can be made with lamb, but you will need to substitute carrots and red onions for the leeks, beets, and mushrooms. Also add a dash of cardamom and grated orange peel to the lamb while it is browning.

1½ cups chicken stock

1 cup water

½ cup milk

2 tablespoons sugar

1½ cups rice

2 leeks

2 tablespoons butter or peanut oil plus 2 tablespoons butter, melted

2 pounds venison, cut into small cubes not more than 1 inch square

1 cup sliced mushrooms

White pepper (optional)

2 tablespoons rice flour

¼ cup light cream

2 small beets, sliced into thin rings

In a saucepan with a lid, bring the chicken stock, water, and milk to a boil. Stir in the sugar, then add the rice, decrease the heat to a simmer, cover, and cook for 15 minutes, until the rice is tender and the liquid is absorbed. Set aside, uncover, and let cool.

Wash the leeks, cut away the tough, dark green stalks, and slice lengthwise, then into short rings.

In a large deep skillet, heat the butter over medium heat. Add the venison, mushrooms, and leeks. If you want to season it with white pepper, this is the time. Sauté until the venison is browned, about 2 minutes.

Blend 2 tablespoons of rice flour into cream until it is free of lumps. Remove the venison from the heat and add the rice flour mixture to it.

Preheat the oven to 400°F. Grease six individual-serving ovenproof dishes with butter.

Scoop out some of the cooled rice and press it into each dish to about a $^3/_4$-inch thickness all around—forming a cup. Fill each cup with the venison mixture and top each one with a thin slice of beet.

Turn the remaining rice out onto a greased surface and press it with oily hands until you have a reasonably flat slab. Cut it into circles big enough to cover each baking dish and lift it off with a greased spatula. Cover each of the dishes with a cap of rice. Brush each with the remaining melted butter.

Bake for 8 minutes.

Remove from the oven. Slip each of the dishes into its own serving basket. Serve hot.

Put the Gun Down and Back Away Slowly

I've had run-ins with guys in the woods who know less about guns than your Aunt Tilly likely knows about fusion energy.

Spooky, ain't it, how easy it is for a guy to plunk down a few bucks and head off into the hinterlands with a loaded weapon. Having some idiot suffering from deer fever shoot at you goes a long way towards engendering serious thoughts.

After considerable thought, I'm thinking that maybe a fella ought to prove that he knows more about his weapon than how to start it up and run somebody over the first jump out of the chute before society turns him loose on unsuspecting folks whom fate might throw into his path. Having been one of those unsuspecting folks once or twice, I'm here to tell you that I'm beginning to suspect that it's a damned sight safer to be a poacher than to brave the field during deer season when the woods are awash with folks who've been bit hard with the deer fever.

If you're dead-set on being a law-abiding citizen, then get going on the first day or two of the season. Unless you are a long-time seasoned hunter and know a bag of tricks from way back, you aren't likely to get much after the third day. Some real lucky guys bring one in, but luck and fate often work the other way late in the season.

A funny thing starts to happen as each day goes by—the deer get smarter and the hunters get stupider. At one time, I was ignorant of the reasons behind some of the things that ranchers did—like buying a can of spray paint and marking the broadside of their stock with the word "cow." Over time, I have come to understand all too well. Guys will start to shoot at anything that moves—on the theory that the deer in their sights went mad, killed a hunter, and stole his coat, that's why he's dressed in red.

You think I'm kidding, friend. I wish I was. More than once, bullets zinged by me, way yonder too close for comfort, but the pièce de résistance that turned me into an incurable poacher was as close as I want to get to shot.

Nowadays, I know that part of that was my own stupid fault. Deer season was gonna be over in two days, and the guys who were still out there were the ones packing new guns and itchy fingers.

Lord, what a combination!

The one who found me waited until I had brought down my deer and gutted it before he scared the daylights right out of me. To this day, I'm hoping the fool was truly aiming at the deer and not trying to save himself the trouble of hunting by killing another hunter.

Anyway, I had brought down a medium-sized eight-point buck with a goodly amount of meat on him. I had him hoisted over my shoulders with his legs dangling down over my chest and his head resting on one side. I was just coming over the top of a hill when a loud "crack" pulled my head up just in time for the side of my face to be splashed in blood and fragments of skin. I put my hand up and felt around, shaking down to my toes when I realized that my deer had a fresh hole in his chest, not a full inch from my ear.

I dropped that buck quick and slung my rifle up, hitting the dirt fast and bawling out as many words as I could think of that only a human would know so as to identify myself. I was careful not to say anything that might sound like it came from a smart-ass talking deer.

As another shot rang out from a line of trees ahead of me, I took a good look at my situation and came to the conclusion that the best defense might oughta involve a little offense, so I set about figuring the best way to make myself too offensive to shoot at.

They were making plenty of racket, this particular idiot and his buddy, so I took aim low, about where their knees ought to be and fired into the trees. I did warn you that hunting late in deer season is fraught with bad luck. Well, the truth is I missed both of those two boys. Bad luck had me coming and going that day.

By the time I made my way to the scene, they were long gone and nary a drop of blood marked their passing, though one of them had dropped his shiny new rifle in his haste to save himself. It had been fired twice. The barrel was hot and the spent shells were still lying there in the leaves. I stopped and vomited a couple a times before I decided to keep the weapon I was nearly killed with.

Mind you, I learned something from all this. I've never carried a deer out on my shoulders since. From that day to this, I have taken the time to lash together a travois and pull my kill out that way. My right ear still quivers and tries to fold up whenever I hear somebody in the woods with a .30–30.

In lighter moments I can kid around with this story saying something like, "Those boys had probably never seen the rare crab deer before. He climbs up the hills sideways some six feet in the air, bobbing along with his head down." But it generally takes at least two shots of Jim Beam and a damned fine dinner before I can laugh about the possibility of my head being mounted on some idiot's rec room wall.

Sesame Venison

Serves 5 to 6

This stuff tastes real good all on its own, but you have to have a few starches and veggies with a meal, so a good choice here would be rice and steamed Brussels sprouts.

If you don't happen to have venison, you can use beef or chicken. If you choose chicken, then add ¹/₂ teaspoon ground orange peel (see page 23) to the dipping paste.

> *3 egg whites, lightly beaten*
> *2 tablespoons soy sauce*
> *¼ cup cornstarch*
> *1 cold leftover venison roast, about 3 pounds*
> *½ pound sesame seeds*
> *Peanut oil, for deep-frying*

In a large wide bowl, stir together the egg whites, soy sauce, and cornstarch until you have a smooth paste. It should be smooth and fluid, but not runny. If it's too thin, it will not hold the sesame seeds to the venison and the whole exercise loses some of its original intention.

Slice the cold venison roast into longish cubes, roughly 1 ¹/₂ inches square by 3 inches long or thereabouts. If the pieces are smaller than that, they get crunchy; if they're much bigger, the center doesn't get the full benefit of the heat when you fry it.

Dump the cut pieces of venison into the mixture in the bowl, mix well, and refrigerate, covered, for at least an hour.

Roll out a long strip of waxed paper, then dump the sesame seeds onto it. Roll the venison pieces in the sesame seeds. Then stick it back in the refrigerator again for another 30 minutes.

In a deep heavy saucepan, heat 3 to 4 inches of oil to about 325°F. If you don't have a thermometer, you can test the oil with a piece of white bread. Take a piece about 1-inch square without crust and throw it into the oil. If it begins to pop and hiss, the oil is too hot; if it soaks up the oil and sinks, it's too cool. You want the piece of bread to float and begin to stir the oil around it into a slow foam. Slip a few pieces of venison into the hot oil so they are not crowded too closely together. They should look like a collection of bumper cars on a crowded lake. Fry for 2 to 3 minutes. If the sesame seeds start to turn too dark, get them out of the oil immediately—either the oil is too hot or your clock has stopped. Drain on a rack or paper toweling. Continue until all the pieces are cooked.

Serve hot.

✳━━✳━━✳━━✳ A Little Game of Tag—You're It ✳━━✳━━✳━━✳

Me and a buddy were out doing a little poaching in April one year and had the luck to come up behind two other hunters with the same idea. Small world. Trouble was, a singular hunter, the kind who always hunts alone, was out that day and before sundown, all our paths crossed.

There was a light dusting of snow the day before, not more than a couple of inches, but it made tracking a piece of cake. We'd been out since about 5 A.M. and had seen nothing but does. April is a bad time to take a doe. She is either due to deliver any day, or she has a youngster who is still depend-ent on milk. Either way, it's bad business to shoot a doe in the spring, so we were holding out for a yearling buck who'd wintered well. If we didn't find ourselves one, well, then we'd had a nice day out of doors and that's a goodness unto itself.

Long about 11 A.M., we came across boot tracks that didn't match ours, so we followed the tracks offhand-like, thinking that maybe we better see if this was the game warden or just a couple of boys out stomping around in the woods on a fine day.

A half hour later, we marked where the two guys had come across the path of a cougar. Their boots prints overlaid the cougar's with no new snow in between, so we knew that they had found her trail that morning and were following her. That sounded a lot like a game warden to us, so we made up our minds to follow him for a bit and determine his business that day. We were doing our bit as citizens, you understand, to help the man avoid undue aggravations. We had it in mind that if he came across us, that he'd consider us an aggravation, and we were dead set on sparing him that confrontation.

We hadn't gone more than thirty yards before we found where the cougar had taken off into the rocks on a sloping hillside, and the boot tracks we were fol-lowing had followed them. This part of the woods was dead familiar to both of us, so we skipped that part of the party and skirted the hill by means of a cut less than half a mile back. We came through on the other side not far from where the cougar had descended into the creek bed that runs beside the rocky hill, and that's where things got really interesting.

Again, the boot tracks of two men came up alongside and overlaid the cougar's and the two of them took off along the creek, but after a bit, we noticed that the cougar had gotten tired of the game and slipped off amongst the rocks again. This time, when she came down, she was behind her trackers, following the tracks that were following her tracks. She was now between us and the guys up ahead.

Cougars resent having their movements marked, and this one was showing all the signs of getting her fur up over it. Likely, she had a pair of kittens in the rocks thereabouts and had made up her mind that the men following her were a threat to her family.

We followed a bit faster than we had been before, trying to catch up the distance between us. We were moving along about as fast as we could trot without risking losing sight of the tracks. We came over a rise about half an hour later and saw the whole tragic comedy laid out before us.

The two guys who were following the cougar tracks were leaned over studying the confusing patch at their feet. Maybe they had come up to the place where she had circled back, because one of them pointed off towards the rocks from time to time. The cougar who was following the men who were following her was crouched in among a couple of boulders, shielded by a low fir tree. Her back was shivering and her hindquarters twitched as she prepared to teach these upstarts a lesson.

Like I said, cougars truly hate to have their movements marked. They're predators and they know predator behavior in others when they see it.

My buddy fired his weapon into the air, and we started yelling and throwing rocks, screaming our lungs out and launching everything we could reach as fast as we could lug it up and shoot it off. The cougar took offense to this obscene behavior and made herself scarce. She howled a string of perfectly applicable insults, laced with a few well-placed threats, and took off up the mountainside, spitting and hissing, just in case we had missed the meaning in her first speech.

My friend and I were glad to notice that neither of the guys below us in the flats took aim and fired at her. The lady had every right to be angry, so we let her go about her business, and we gathered our forces and retreated in the opposite direction.

A mixture of caution and respect kept us moving for a while until we all agreed that lunch was in order, so we stopped and shared all around. After a while, we were all laughing about it, but not too loudly. The naked power in a cougar's muscles is a lovely thing to see, but I'm none too happy to see it when the cougar in question is justifiably hot and bothered.

Cougars, by nature, will not attack a man unless they are threatened. The few exceptions have been very old cougars who've decided that hunting a human child or wounded adult was easier than chasing after game. Human children have high, screeching voices that sound like wounded game to a cougar's ears, so if you happen to be in the woods with small children, it's best to keep them close by you and teach them not to run in amongst the trees screaming. Games that are safe for kids to play in a city park have a way of attracting a different audience if you're out in the mountains a long way from city lights.

I've seen cougars in the wild several times, once when my son was with me, and we've never had any trouble from them, nor them from the likes of us.

Cities have hazards, and the people who live there learn them as children or they don't get along well. There are hazards in the mountains as well, and the people who live there learn the habits of folks around them, like the bear and cougar and snake and deer, and respect those habits. That's the natural way of things.

If you go there and you're not familiar with the ways of the animals, go with somebody who grew up in the country. I don't want you getting hurt any more than I wanted that cougar or her kittens to get hurt that day. You may not be as pretty as she is, but you've got a certain familiarity about you that I find comforting.

Braised Venison on a Bed of Loquats

Serves 6

I'm partial to the use of venison in this one. You can use any red meat but pork or any game bird that suits you, but my first recommendation, if you can't get venison, would be either beef or lamb. Both are delicious.

I introduced this recipe to some of the older members of my family and got accused of fancifying the vittles, but I did notice that they all cleaned their plates and the rest of the stuff on the platter didn't want for attention neither.

> *1 clove garlic, crushed*
> *½ teaspoon ground coriander*
> *¼ teaspoon ground cinnamon*
> *¼ teaspoon ground nutmeg*
> *A strip of venison, about 3 pounds, cut into 3-inch cubes*
> *8 loquats*
> *Sesame oil*
> *¼ cup pomegranate juice*
> *1 tablespoon fresh lemon juice*
> *¼ cup water*
> *2 scallions, chopped (optional)*

In a bowl, mix the garlic, coriander, cinnamon, and nutmeg. Roll the venison in it to coat and place on a plate. Do not discard the spices—set them aside for later.

To prepare the loquats for broiling, halve each down the center, scoop out the seeds, and trim the rough bits off of the ends. Be sure to get the membrane that surrounds the seed casing. You will likely need a big spoon to dig that out as it resists being removed from the fruit.

Arrange the prepared loquats and the chunks of venison on a broiler pan. Brush lightly with sesame oil. Yes, I mean the loquats too. If you don't brush them with oil they'll burn black and taste like charcoal briquettes. Not good. Stick them in the broiler and brown on all sides by turning and brushing with oil every few minutes.

When the venison is browned and turning crispy at the edges, remove the pan from the oven.

Heat a large frying pan over medium heat (brush lightly with sesame oil if your pan is not a nonstick variety) and transfer both the loquats and the venison to it. Sprinkle with the remaining spices. Pour the pomegranate juice, lemon juice, and water over the loquats and venison and allow them to cook over low heat until the liquid has been absorbed.

Remove from the pan and arrange on a serving platter, with the loquats around the perimeter and the venison in the center. Top with the scallions and serve hot.

 **Calling the Kitty**

Lots of folks hang venison to allow it to age sufficiently before eating, but to my mind, it's way yonder easier to butcher and wrap the meat and allow it to age in the freezer for a bit. It's not possible to leave your deer hanging unless you have a stout shed and even then, though the deer may be securely inside, the smell of him is gonna get out and go roaming.

A friend of mine who lives down on the Ute Mountain Reservation in southern Colorado had been accustomed to taking himself a deer or two every year since he was a boy and never had a bit of trouble in the hanging and aging phase. Nevertheless, trouble eventually found him and even came back for seconds.

The first day of deer season, my friend brought down the buck of his choice, gutted him on the scene, and carried the parts he wanted back to his place. He had him a pretty nice smokehouse, but he was using that to smoke a couple of domestic pigs he had slaughtered, so he hung the deer in his tool shed and didn't think another thing of it.

Nothing much happened the first day, nor even the next, but the following night a ruckus from his dogs woke him up about 3 A.M. So he threw on his pants and ran outside just in time to catch sight of a big male cougar helping himself to the buck. The door to the tool shed hung open, and it looked like one of the rusty old hinges had surrendered without much of a fight.

My friend was so flustered that he started digging in his pants pocket for ammunition before he realized that he'd left his gun in the house. By the time he tore back in and got it, the cougar, the deer, and my friend's hopes for a bit of venison had hightailed it over the fence and hove out of sight. The whole kit and caboodle had vanished into the night. The way he tells it, he was so mad he couldn't even cry over it. That came later.

A couple a days passed. My friend drove to Cortez to the hardware store and bought a couple of new steel hinges and a bolt for his shed on the theory that if he was to hang another deer in that shed, that the cougar would surely be back for that one, too. It's a fact that once a cougar has found easy pickings somewhere that he'll check that spot again the next time his stomach commences to rumble and there's nothing easy to hand.

This one was no different from any other of his brethren. Near a week after the theft of his deer, my friend was again awakened by the yelping of his dogs. This time he was up and at it pretty quick. He'd been sleeping with one eye half open and his gun laid out on the bed beside him since that infamous night when the perfidious tool shed had handed over his deer to an intruder.

He got to the back porch just in time to stand witness to a thing he hoped he'd never see. The cougar, finding the shed securely locked, turned his back on disappointment and smacked one of the dogs across the side of the head, killing him instantly. A free meal is a free meal, and I expect that boy took something the dogs were saying as personal.

Dogs are an easy kill for cougars since they rarely have the good sense to back down. They got 'em a pretty clear picture of what a cat's supposed to be and by the time they adjust their attitude to take in new facts, the cougar has generally re-adjusted their neck somewhat.

My friend got off a couple of shots and buried at least one .30–30 shell in the cougar's hindquarters, but in the end, the dog went the way of the buck, and nobody in that neighborhood never saw hide nor hair of either of them again. Neither did anybody report coming across either a dead cougar nor even one with a noticeable limp. My guess is that the cougar figured out that my friend was possessed of some powerful temper and that, in any case, dinner at the price of a bullet in the behind was too expensive for his taste, so he took his appetite elsewhere.

For his part, my friend took his surviving dog in the house and taught him to sleep on the bed between the footboard and his master's feet. He was dead set against the idea of supplying another meal to a cougar, any cougar.

Spicy Venison Strips in Yogurt Sauce

Serves 4

If you're a bona fide city slicker and all of your friends do indeed live in apart-ments (as do you yourself), then I'm sorry to tell you that there are precious few places to buy venison, and this recipe is not as tasty with beef. It works fair to middling with buffalo, and a lot of specialty meat markets have begun to sell that. A friend told me that emu is a good substitute, but since I haven't tasted it, I can't swear to it here—you're on your own with that one. I had something similar done up with ostrich at a restaurant in Estes Park, Colorado, and I'm here to say that it was right good, but I should warn you that ostrich is a very strange sort of meat. After a couple of pieces, your brain wants to know what's what and fairly soon, you're coming to conclusions that don't set right with one another, namely that ostrich tastes like a red meat, but it has the tex-ture of poultry. Don't let me stop you trying it though. Might be you're the sort of person who finds that sort of thing real interesting.

Serve with the rice that you remembered to cook whilst you were doing up the venison.

2 pounds venison

1 small jar red chiles, juice drained

All-purpose flour

2 tablespoons peanut oil

3 tablespoons yellow curry paste

¼ cup slivered almonds

1 small can mandarin oranges, juice drained

1 small can diced pineapple, juice drained

1 teaspoon ground allspice

1 teaspoon ground cloves

2 cups vanilla yogurt

Cut the venison into strips no more than 2 inches wide. Place in a deep dish and pour the entire jar of red chiles over them. Allow them to get to know each other in the refrigerator for at least 4 hours, then remove the strips of meat. Save the red chiles for later, but you can pour out the juices and wash the dish.

Preheat the oven to 300°F.

Dredge the venison strips in a little flour to coat evenly.

Heat the oil in a large skillet over medium-high heat. Add some venison in a single layer and brown on all sides. Transfer to a platter lined with paper towels to absorb excess oil and repeat until all the meat is browned. Place the meat in the oven while you make the sauce.

In the same pan you just used to brown the meat, blend the curry paste with the remaining oil until it is hot and bubbly. Decrease the heat to a simmer and stir in the almonds, oranges, and pineapple. While you are stirring, sprinkle the allspice and cloves over it, then add the chiles. Keep stirring to prevent scorching, and cook until the almonds begin to brown slightly. Remove from the heat and add the yogurt, stirring briskly until the yogurt begins to match the temperature of the fruit.

Arrange the venison strips on a serving platter. Pour the yogurt sauce over them and serve immediately.

Moose

If the moose you bring home from the field is a big bull, then you're going to have to take the time to tenderize the meat before you can do anything with it other than make stews. Boiling in hot water over long periods of time can go a long way towards rendering it chewable, but the process is simplified if you slice it, pound it for a bit with a meat mallet to get its attention, and then allow it to rest overnight in a bath of either watered-down balsamic vinegar or thin tomato sauce. Champagne works wonders as a tenderizing agent as well.

Since once it is opened, champagne needs to be drunk up in a few hours or it goes flat, I always seem to have a half bottle of the stuff sitting around waiting for a bit of tough meat to drop by. The good thing is, it doesn't matter how flat it's gone. If you have the refrigerator room, you can save it for a year and it still works great.

Actually, unless you bring home an old bull who's all tuckered out from the mating season, then no tenderizing is necessary. Moose meat is remarkably tender and likely the tastiest thing you'll ever put a tooth to.

Field Dressing and Preparation

Dress a moose the same as you would a deer. It is built the same, only bigger. See detailed instructions under the heading for deer (see page 81).

Watching Somebody Else's Temper—
Up Close and Personal

The best time to hunt moose is in mid to late September when the bulls are in rut and not likely to listen to reason. I have no idea when the actual hunting season is sanctioned by any local government, so it might be a good idea before you head out to find out these things.

I'm not advising you to break any laws, I'm just telling you how I do it. In a free and fair universe, you have to decide for yourself how you want to take this thing on. So far as I've heard, hunting season is meant to keep tabs on guys who stalk with a gun; since I don't do that, it never occurred to me to find out when it is.

Stalking moose with a gun is a chancy business. Despite that huge, decorative rack of his, he can make impressive speed through thick brush with hardly a noise to warn you of his approach. A long time ago, in my innocent youth, I went with a guy who thought it would be good to teach me how to surprise a moose and the two of us damned near got stomped into the earth for our troubles—and he was good—so I went home and rethought the process before I headed out to the moose's stomping grounds again.

Yeah, surprise, you caught that—stomped. A moose doesn't ram you with his rack when he's got his dander up. The antlers he sports are to show off to other bulls, bragging as it were, about what a big tough stud he is. For everything from an insignificant annoyance like yourself to a seriously hungry wolf, the moose will strike hard and fast with his hooves—repeatedly until you get the point and sometimes long after.

Myself, I'm not the confrontational type. I like to try to exercise my brain whenever I can and save the muscles for running if I have to. Besides, a gun with enough pop to bring down a moose is an expensive item, and I figured out a long time ago that a really big rock was generally a lot cheaper.

Okay, bear with me and I'll get to the point. Most of the year, the moose is a pretty reasonable guy. He lives alone, wading in deep pools in search of the tender greenery he feeds on, or standing around placidly chewing and staring off into space. Not much activity.

Reason and the quiet life go out the window in the fall, when the women announce their breeding intentions. Every bull wants all of the women to himself, and he's perfectly willing to fight tooth and nail for the privilege.

You ladies, I know you've seen this kind of behavior often enough—no surprises here—and since a substantial proportion of men think that this attitude is perfectly reasonable, I won't belabor it.

Each bull has a familiar territory that he patrols, searching for ladies already within his domain and trying to lure others with his irresistible charms. Intruders are met with bellowing hostility. Trouble is, almost anything can spark his anger: the sight or smell of another bull, your doofus self wandering through with your head down, a train whistle (which he interprets as a challenge), or even a really big rock in the path that wasn't there the day before. This is also a challenge, and one that he cannot back down on if he's to go on believing that he's the studly hunk he's been saying he is.

Within his territory, a moose will stomp down pathways to his favorite haunts. Along or near the perimeter of his territory, he'll have a path that will allow him to survey his rivals and spy out the guy's yard for a lady he might entice to join him.

It takes some doing and some luck to hunt moose by using his temper and his habits against him. You have to be lucky enough to find a moose with a sizable hill in his territory—Vermont, New Hampshire, and Maine are great places for this. You also have to be lucky enough to follow his path and not run into him. It's best to do this in the spring, when he's standing in the water feeding.

Look for a spot where his path cuts close beside a hill, and then search the hill for a sizable boulder that you can dislodge. Mark the spot in your head and come back in late September or early October when your chosen moose is heavily into the mating wars. Dig around your rock carefully, mostly on the downhill side, and give it a little shove until it rolls freely down the hill and into the path. You want it to block the path, so if you overshoot, you're in for some heaving and grunting work. Good luck that the moose doesn't come along about now and take umbrage to this behavior, which he surely will. Oh, and never, ever, walk around the downhill side of your chosen boulder for any reason. It might decide to roll before you're ready. Even though it's got no evil intentions towards you, a big boulder can kill you dead as dead.

When you've got the rock positioned, get out of there and find a safe place to wait where you won't be attracting attention to yourself. Best not to light a fire or anything like that. Carry cold foods and tough it out. Don't wait near a path, any path.

Eventually, the moose who claims that territory will come along and find that uppity rock in the middle of the road. That's when the fight starts.

To the moose's way of thinking, that's his property and nobody, not even a rock, has the right to change a thing, applied for in triplicate or not.

He'll step back and display his rack to best effect, then he'll set his feet squarely and bellow some version of "Why, I oughta . . ." to that rock and wait a scant few seconds for it to hike up its skirt and get the hell out of the way. Of course, it's not going to—it's a rock. But like I said earlier, the moose has thrown both caution and reason out with the bath water, and he's in no mood to hear "can't." All versions of "can't" translate as "won't" and that makes him mad—really mad.

He may actually give the rock two or three serious warnings before he decides that there is no other recourse but to charge. In your little hiding place, you should hear this, but don't go look, not just yet. You don't want an angry moose adding your name to his current list of wrongdoers.

After two or three runs and as many vocal warnings, the moose will have done some serious damage to his skull, but that only makes him more determined than ever to win this fight. Eventually, he will break his neck in a fruitless battle to convince a boulder to move out of his way or else.

"Or else" seems to be one of the several simple and direct phrases that define a bull moose's life during the rut season.

By the way, before you come over the hill, knife and fork in hand, with dinner on your mind, pick up a branch and poke your prize from at least eight feet away just to be sure that he's dead. Those guys are way strong and you don't want to go putting yourself in striking range if he's not down and out.

The good news about this hunting method is that it never accidentally gets anybody else but your intended target. No female or calf would waste two seconds of thought for that rock, and once the guy who owns the territory has had and lost his battle, the rock in the path ceases to be an issue. For the new bull who moves in to take over the territory, it was there when he got there so it's not an intruder—no problem.

In a pinch once, I helped a friend fell a dead tree over a path, but my skin was crawling with nerves the whole time we were about it. Doing this with a live tree has two setbacks. First, I don't approve of taking down a tree just to prove you can do it. And second, it takes even longer to cut a live one than a dead one, so double the nerve factor.

Another guy told me that his uncle went so far as to dig a hole and plant a really stout cedar stump in a moose path, but just hearing about this sent me to the pantry for a drink. The amount of time that you'd have to spend standing there in the potential line of fire with your back to traffic asks a lot from one's personal angels.

Moose with Okra and Eggplant

Serves 4

Any sort of venison will make this recipe up proud, but if all you can get your hands on is a bit of beef, then cook it up and not to worry. Beef is real good this way. Split for the high-quality stew meat so it won't be tough. It can be made with lamb, but to tell the truth, it's kind of an acquired taste. Try it on your own before you serve it up to company.

Serve with basmati rice or couscous.

> 3 to 4 tablespoons sesame or peanut oil (sesame oil tastes better here, but either will do)
>
> 2 pounds moose meat, cut into chunks about 2 inches square
>
> 1 strip of marrow from a moose's thigh bone (see Note, page 107)
>
> 2 small onions, diced
>
> ½ teaspoon ground turmeric
>
> ½ teaspoon freshly ground white pepper or lemon pepper
>
> 3½ cups water
>
> 1 cup chopped tomato (canned is fine)
>
> Peels of 4 limes, dried and ground (see page 23)
>
> Splash of fresh lemon juice
>
> 1 cup dried yellow split peas
>
> ¾ pound okra, trimmed and sliced
>
> 2 small eggplants, peeled and cubed

In a large skillet or wok, heat a couple tablespoons oil over medium heat. Add the moose meat, the marrow, and the onions and brown. This will take about 15 minutes; moose meat is resistant to domestication at table. Add the turmeric and the pepper when the meat starts to look brown.

Transfer the browned meat and onions to a stew pot and add the water. Bring to a boil, then decrease the heat to a simmer. Cover and cook for about 30 minutes, then add the tomato, and continue to cook for an additional 30 minutes.

Add the ground lime peels, lemon juice, and split peas to the pot and cook for 20 minutes.

While the peas are cooking, heat a couple of tablespoons of oil in the wok and stir-fry the okra and the eggplant.

Add the stir-fried okra and eggplant to the stew pot and cook until the split peas are tender, 5 to 10 minutes (too much longer and the peas will get so mushy that they begin to liquefy, altogether a nasty business that we won't entertain here).

Serve hot or reheat when your guests arrive.

Note: If you don't have marrow, then substitute 2 cups stock derived from boiling a bone, preferably a moose bone. Reduce the water added to 1½ cups.

—✳—✳—✳—✳— **Ice Dancing in Maine** —✳—✳—✳—✳—

Moose are the only game animal in the U.S. to routinely hunt motorists. Deer do it half-heartedly, taking out a few cars every season in each locality where their numbers are plentiful. Moose are so dedicated to the sport that in Vermont, they keep score on a big chalkboard that hangs in the capital in Montpelier. Occasionally a moose will go so far as to challenge a train, but then humans have them on that score—the train usually wins, though I have heard of a contest that ended in a clear draw.

When my son was stationed in the Coast Guard in Rockland, Maine, he and a couple of friends made good use of their days off by beating a path into the hinterlands with all their gear and putting in a little ice fishing. On one such occasion, they slowed down for what they figured was a small truck stopped in the road ahead. Upon closer inspection, it turned out to be a whopping bull moose with an attitude bigger than his rack, though from the description my son gives of the size of this boy, he was bigger than a bread truck and made of sterner stuff to boot, so he had to be in some kinda bad mood to top that.

Anyway, one of the fellas in the vehicle with my son came from somewhere out in Oklahoma, where you're less likely to pass company with a moose than you are to stop for a herd of elephants to cross the road.

I only mention this so you'll know that he did what he did 'cause he didn't know no better, not 'cause he was looking for a fight. He wasn't driving, which provided him ample opportunity to grab the furnishings and pray when the moose took offense to his affrontery and commenced to chase them.

Seems the guy from Oklahoma thought that honking the horn would get the ball duly rolling, so he leaned over the driver and did just that. Fortunately, for all concerned, the driver hailed from upstate Minnesota and had some inkling of what they were in for. He had already slung the transmission into reverse before the fight started, and as soon as he caught wind of what his friend was up to, his foot hit the floor, squeezing the gas pedal for dear life.

Friends, the gauntlet had been thrown and the race was on.

The road was a tad icy, but like I said, the driver grew up with this kind of thing, so he managed to back them out of harm's way faster than the harm could chase them down. Just barely, by all reports.

They backed up more than a mile before the moose decided that they had demonstrated a sufficiency of submission to allow him to forgive them.

By that time, they had near a mile's worth of genuine respect under their belts, so they waited patiently where they sat while the moose took their measure and then wandered off the road and into the trees.

Moose Roast with Artichokes and Lemon Sweet Potatoes
Serves 6 to 12

Unless you can afford a sirloin tip roast of beef, then nothing you can substitute for moose will be nearly as tender. The flavor of moose meat agrees real well with lemon pepper in a way that beef doesn't quite match. Amazingly enough, a moose roast is so tender that you can frequently cut down a slice into bite-sized bits with a good butter knife. I find that this makes for good company around the table, what with those sharp implements in the kitchen.

> *3 to 4 pounds moose roast*
> *Lemon pepper*
> *Garlic powder*
> *4 to 5 sweet potatoes*
> *¼ cup fresh lemon juice*
> *7 to 8 artichokes*

Preheat the oven to 350°F.

Set the moose roast in a big roasting pan and sprinkle it with lemon pepper and garlic powder. Roast for about 1½ hours, or 20 to 30 minutes per pound, for rare to well done. (The internal temperature for rare should be 125°F.) Don't sit down and think you're through. Before the roast is done, you need to get your vegetables ready to add to it.

Meanwhile, split the sweet potatoes down the middle and make a bunch of little slits in the flesh. Rub 2 tablespoons of the lemon juice into the slits. Place the sweet potatoes in a steamer (lemon side up) and steam for about 30 minutes, until tender.

Bring a large pot of salted water to a boil. Trim the artichokes, leaving a bare h inch of stem. Throw away the tough outer leaves. Use scissors to cut those cussed little spines off the tips of the remaining leaves. Cut the artichokes in half lengthwise and scrape out the fuzzy stuff at the heart. Throw the artichokes in the boiling water and decrease the heat to a simmer. Cover and cook for about 20 minutes, or until the artichokes are tender (if they're not tender after 20 minutes, then you bought some *old* chokes). Remove the artichokes from the water and drain. Rub them with the remaining 2 tablespoons lemon juice.

About 30 minutes before your roast is done, arrange the sweet potatoes and the artichokes around it. Finish roasting. For rare, the temperature should be 125°F. Serve in a large dish with a small amount of the juices.

Wild Boar and Javelina

If you've ever hunted either the wild boar or the javelina, then I don't have to tell you how bright these animals are. Few humans are stealthy enough to sneak up on one. Your best bet is to flush a group that is feeding together and annoy one of the young males enough that he feels obliged to take a run at you, and then hope that your trigger finger is faster than his sharp little tusks. If he wins the encounter, all you get out of the deal is a pair of ripped jeans and a collection of stitches on the side of your unlucky leg. A blind won't do you any good, since their sense of smell is phenomenal, and they're clever enough to make a circle around any object high enough to conceal a predator.

A wild boar can get up to 5 feet in length and stand 3 feet at the shoulder. He's a bunch heavier than the javelina and can weigh up to 400 pounds. Don't be fooled though, he's just as fast and quick to turn as his smaller cousin. Other than size, the main difference is that the upper tusks of a javelina point downward and those of a wild boar point up. Both of the lower tusks point upwards, and it's these that they use to slash at you.

The boar prefers forested areas for his habitat, and the best hunting for them in this era of dwindling ranges is to be had in Arkansas, across

Tennessee, and on through North Carolina. A javelina, otherwise know as a peccary, ranges in the Desert Southwest of Arizona, southern New Mexico, and western Texas. They get up to 3 feet in length as adults and 2 feet high at the shoulder. Weight varies from 40 to 50 pounds generally. In good years, when the foraging has been favorable, the meat has a sweeter, lighter flavor than wild boar.

Field Dressing and Preparation

If you do get one, make sure that you remove the musk glands under the skin in the middle of the back immediately. Don't wait until after you've gutted the animal, since by then, the meat won't be worth eating anyway. The musk begins to permeate the meat within ten minutes of the animal's death. You want to be real careful not to puncture the glands either—the smell would drive off a skunk. Don't worry about losing any meat, just go ahead and make a wide cut in the back and come up on those glands with all due caution. The fatback on a javelina is not edible by anybody but a coyote, so just get down to business and quit worrying about saving something you're not going to eat anyway.

Gut and clean as you would for a deer. See detailed instructions under the heading for deer (see page 81).

All pork is subject to trichinosis, so be sure to protect it from overheating and cook it thoroughly (to at least 170°F). Pink might look good, but it's too big a risk to take. Trichinosis is incurable.

Scaring Up Lunch

At one time, my son decided to enliven my life a bit by bringing home the stupidest dog ever spawned. My boy picked out this mutt 'cause he was pretty. I guess that animal thought what with good looks on his side, he didn't have to engage his brain in any undue activity. That much about him I can swear to: he didn't warm his brain up nor take it out for a walk unless it was absolutely necessary. Often as not, he didn't presume to wake that august body up then neither.

One fine morning (well, it woulda been if I hadn't had this doofus animal in my life), I woke up to find that my son's pet had had an attack of shoe tooth the night before and my son's new sneakers were scattered about the house in bite-sized pieces. I had long since learned to hang my good boots from a hook stuck in the roof beam, but my boy persisted in trusting his perfidious pretty boy with such necessaries as foot coverings and jeans.

On this particular night, the dog had completed his meal by shoving open the door to the water-heater closet and chewing off the plastic knob that you push down to light the thing should it go out. I put on my boots and treated the other end of that mutt's body to a taste of good leather for a few rounds and then went outside to cool off before confronting my son with the concept that maybe we should consider chewing his dog. After all, it had been more than a month since we'd had a barbecue.

My boy was duly scandalized and countered by suggesting that perhaps the animal would straighten up if he got a chance to run more. Our yard at that time comprised near an acre, so naturally the reasoning on this one left my hair blowing in the wind, but the idea of taking that shoe-chewing fiend out somewheres where he might run off and get hisself lost brought an unbidden smile to my face that, try as I might, I couldn't put down so in the end, we packed everybody in the truck and took off for distant parts. To my way of thinking, the more distant the better.

Getting shed of that dog was the best idea I'd had in weeks, but I couldn't allow my son to see how genuinely gleeful the prospect made me, nor allow him to figure out that that was indeed the whole purpose of the trip, so I packed along some heavy gloves and a couple of big burlap bags and my tongs, and we went off hunting prickly pear apples.

We were living in Texas and, along the road, I found myself thinking about that dog and regretting that there weren't bears in Texas nor enough cougars to do any threat to a dog. Right there's the trip when I decided it was well and truly time to move back to Colorado or New Mexico. If that dog survived my concentrated efforts over the next couple of weeks, maybe I'd take him to Montana. Surely there was something big and hungry living in those mountains. Trouble was, I'd shelled out so much money on shoes and jeans and whatnot that I wasn't sure I could scrape up enough cash to move.

I found myself wondering if dog leather would make a fair pair of moccasins.

By the time we'd driven the back roads for a couple of hours, we found us a lovely stand of prickly pear that seemed to go on for fits and starts off into the sunset. A good spot by any standards. We piled out of the truck and let the dogs out to wander a bit.

Besides the worthless rag I was considering eating, my son had another dog, a Border collie that was smart as they come and better behaved than a preacher's wife. I couldn't see any way that I could leave this animal home when the miscreant was allowed to play so I brought him, praying all the time that he would have the good sense to let matters alone and not go rescuing doofus should he get hisself into a scrape.

He didn't . . . and neither did I, but things took a turn for the peculiar anyway.

The best way to collect prickly pear apples is with a long pair of wooden tongs. I mean long as in two to three feet in length. That way you can grasp them pretty good without the prickly pear grasping you. If you're good with wood, you can make yourself a pair of these from the kind of stuff you build a stout lattice from. If not, I think the nearest place you can buy a pair of tongs is in Portugal. You may not get your hands on a pair of tongs no matter where you go, but prickly pear apples are worth getting, so give them a try anyway.

We had us a good-sized bag of these delicacies and had even bagged us a fine, healthy rattlesnake. The thought of going home was strong in our minds. Wouldn't you know it, that stupid dog hung right by my side the whole day and wouldn't no way wander off and get hisself lost. Long about late afternoon though, he showed a true talent for moving the situation from bucolic to chaotic in record time.

In following the prickly pear, we had moved among them, picking only the young, tender fruits and moving the truck up now and again. I had just moved it and was getting out when I lowered my leg into the conflab.

The dog, it seems, had nosed his way along a low escarpment in my absence and woke up a gang of javelinas sleeping away the afternoon heat in sandy dugouts in the shade of the rocks. Pigs were running everywhere, looking for somebody to blame.

My son's Border collie knew a world of trouble when he saw it and jumped into the back of the truck even before I pulled to a stop. My son, on the other hand, was busy running in a wide loop around a stand of prickly pear, I suspect as a means of confusing the enemy into thinking he was some sort of berserker predator and not to be messed with.

It didn't work.

Three stout sows had already claimed that patch as a good-enough spot to stand their ground with their children lined up behind them. Enter my son, boots clomping the earth in a mad fever, gloved hands waving madly over his head, yelling dire warnings to one and all. I woulda swelled with pride, but I figured he was aiming to get his leg ripped open, so I lit out after him. Naturally, I followed his lead, yelling and waving my arms. I felt like a fool, but since there was nary a soul about to tell the tale on me, I did the business up proud. Besides, I figured this to be an important family-bonding experience, and I wasn't about to miss a minute of it.

Seeing the two of us stomping and waving like damned fools made those sows itchy. They didn't rightly know what kind of animal was on to them, and that's a fact. They were clicking their teeth something fierce to let us know that they weren't about to tolerate this kinda behavior; but all the while, they were stealing backward steps and casting covetous glances in the direction of every bush and stand of prickly pear within a hundred yards of our little passion play.

Soon enough, the piglets found themselves in the forward lines, facing an enemy that nobody had warned them about. My guess is that me and my boy came under the heading of daylight nightmares. Oh, yeah, and stupid dog was busy running in circles barking his fool head off, offending one and all, me included, with his tomfool good humor. I didn't even have time to stop and pray that some veteran old boar would hush him up with a good swipe of his tusks. I was that busy.

I thought I had my hands full, but that was coming up sooner than I thought.

Apparently, the little piglets hadn't learned to back out of trouble, 'cause all the gears I saw them using were of the forward variety. At an unseen signal, they broke and ran, straight for my son. That got me moving, I can tell you, 'cause the minute those little ones did that, one of the sows followed suit. Friends, the fight was on.

Well, I wasn't gonna just stand there and let that lady give one to my only child, so I reached down before I could think better of the idea and snatched one of her children up by the hind leg. I figured at the very least, we could exchange prisoners, and then we all go about our business with no more of these "Why, I oughta's" between us.

My son musta thought that this part was all of a piece in some grand plan of mine, so he did the same. We were wearing heavy leather gloves, so there wasn't much such a small-fry could do to us, but our legs were still standing out there on eye level with some good-sized pigs, so my knees began sending an urgent Morse code call for help. I don't know what my son was doing. He had the kind of grin on his face that made me wonder if he was seeing this thing with his brain plugged in or if he was starting to take after his dog—not the smart one that got hisself into the truck quick-like either . . . the other one.

I can't tell you how glad I was that we thought about the possibility of snakes and wore our good boots. Way too many vivid images were scooting in and out of my brain—none of them pretty.

Those little pigs squealed and wiggled like as if they thought the devil hisself had a hold of them, which from their viewpoint mighta been the gospel truth. Funny thing was, the rest of the gang heard that god-awful racket and turned tail and fled for their lives. Nary a mother javelina came to her baby's rescue, but run off into the bush to save herself.

I've since heard similar stories from long-time javelina hunters. It seems that if I'd taken to threatening one of the young ladies of the gang, then every mother's son of those pigs woulda come for me, but they're not up to risking their neck for a squealing infant. To that end, javelinas are way yonder different from wild boars. Those boys are just looking for an excuse to teach your nefarious carcass a lesson in manners, whereas javelinas don't mind taking a few insults so long as you don't hassle the womenfolk.

That's a real shame, too, 'cause if you're gonna partake of javelina flesh, the young females are the only members of the gang that are not only edible, but downright succulent. That is, if you don't count the piglets, which I'm here to tell you are tender and tasty.

We gave a couple of the bigger bones to the dogs and while the Border collie accepted the offer, gnawed it a bit, and forgot about it, that worthless shoe-chewing hound took the gift to heart. He carried the bones around in his mouth long after there was nothing left to chew. I'd come across him, now and then, lugging those pig bones around with an idiot's prideful grin on his face just like he thought he had done something truly wonderful. I expect he was reliving the day of the great pig hunt and congratulating himself for it.

He even took a couple of them with him when we moved to Montana the following month.

Thrice-Cooked Javelina Brain in a Crushed Pecan Coating with a Sweet Leek Sauce

Serves 2

Lucky me, most of my friends who are any good at hunting javelina are the kind of folks who scoff at the idea that the brain is worth eating, so I get this delicacy given to me sometimes, along with a funny sidelong glance I might add. I'm beginning to think that the only reason they save the brains for me in the first place is so they can see if the story is true—the one that goes, "I give her that thing, and she took it like I was handing her chocolate cake on a platter," followed by an eye roll and a rush of astounded breath. So far, I've played my side of this game very successfully, taking the offerings gratefully and carefully avoiding serving this amazing dish to the friends whose opinions might be altered by a taste of it.

If you don't have javelina hunters for friends, then try it with store-bought calf brains.

Chill the brain overnight on a bed of ice before slicing or you'll get a mushy mess. This recipe takes two days of preparation, one day to steam the brain and the next to prepare it for dinner.

1 javelina brain, about 1½ pounds

2 cups sweet red wine

3 tablespoons honey

2 large leeks, chopped

1 tablespoon butter

Extra light olive oil

1½ to 2 cups very finely chopped pecans (a bare step
above pecan flour, with the crunchiness retained)

Scallions, cut into 1-inch strips, to garnish

Wrap the javelina brain in cheesecloth and place on a rack in a steamer. Cover and steam for 45 to 60 minutes, until it is firm when you push down on it with a spoon. Don't push too hard because you don't want to mush it if it isn't ready yet. Steaming times may vary depending on the size of the brain and the altitude. Refrigerate overnight, or for at least 8 hours.

Pour the wine and the honey into a saucepan. Toss in the leeks. Simmer for 15 to 20 minutes, until most of the liquid has steamed away and the leeks are slightly crunchy when pressed with a fork. Stir in the butter. This gives the sauce an appealing glaze.

While the sauce is reducing in the pan, preheat the oven to 300°F. Oil a baking sheet. Remove the cheesecloth and cut the brain into thin slices. Some of the edges will crumble away, but that's to be expected. (Save the bits that take a dive and brown them with a few chopped onions in a pan of hot oil for inclusion in your morning scrambled eggs.)

Rub the slices with olive oil and sprinkle them liberally with the crushed pecans, turning to coat both sides with as much of the stuff as will stick.

Pan-fry the slices in hot oil for about 2 minutes a side.

Place the slices on the prepared baking sheet. Sprinkle with the pecans that fell off during the pan-fry process. Bake for 7 to 8 minutes, until the pecan coating is a rich golden brown.

Arrange on a platter and dribble the sauce over it. Garnish with the scallions. Serve immediately.

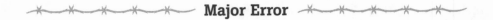 **Major Error**

As if my respect for pigs wasn't enough, along comes this fella who went to high school in Hawaii and tells me a horror story that the likes of Stephen King would shy off of.

Seems when this old boy was a youngster—seventeen or so—there was a wild pig living on the big island that purely owned the place, or at least as much of it as he took a notion to lay claim to.

Among other things, there's a sizable military presence on that island, so folks what knew of this particular pig nicknamed him Major. Of the few guys I've known who could claim that title for themselves, and the story this fella told me about the pig on the big island, I can see real easy how the comparison came about. Seems that Major was in the habit of ordering people the hell out of his domain, and more than one would-be hunter obliged with a quick march long before the guy in charge of the situation had to hand him his orders in triplicate.

Years went by, and lots of guys claimed that they "nearly had him" and showed scars to prove it, but Major was too well known for this kind of talk to wash. The thinking went like this, "If you've got a scar small enough that you survived it and his head is still on his shoulders, then you didn't no way nearly get him."

Hard heads being what they are, Major attracted a following of men who began to take his very existence as a challenge. Apparently, the sacred honor of the great apes was in eternal jeopardy if they could be bested by a pig. In the upshot, a lot of rash declarations of personal prowess were made that could only be affirmed if blood was shed.

One fine hot and misty morning, a delegation of guys set out to bring this old boy down or die trying. When their expedition had wound down and the smoke had cleared, it was easy for one and all to see that they had accomplished a bit of both. Myself, I could never see the sense of cutting off my own line of retreat, but these boys went to a different school where they all got A's in burning bridges.

Five guys and seven dogs set out to bring Major down. They slunk about in the brush, tracking his movements for three days before every-body's tempers got the better of them all at once.

Major probably had a young lady on his mind and was thinking about calling her up, because he didn't show much interest in fighting with the delegation of hunters and their dogs. Times are when even the boldest fighter would rather be a lover. He made a few feints to let them know that he was otherwise occupied, but all in all, nothing to write home about. After three days, he made up his mind that enough was enough, and the only way to get rid of these fellas and get back to business was to throw them bodily off his land and be done with it. For their part, the hunters and their dogs had decided that this old boy was turning slow in his old age, and they could take him easily enough if they closed in on him and made it clear what they had come for.

Some time after the fight started in earnest, the survivors straggled out to tell their story and to get a little help in carrying out the bodies of the fallen. One man lost his leg, another his life. They had shot Major once for each of the seven dogs he had gutted and flung into the bushes, and once again for the fella whose leg he ripped to the bone. By that time, shots were flying about a little wildly, and nobody remembers whether they had squeezed off another in defense of their downed comrade or not. The guy with the ripped leg and the three other survivors waited in the trees until Major bled to death on the ground. The one fella was already dead and not a man among them wanted to join him. They buried the dogs on the spot and carried Major out to stand for a few photographs, then they buried him as well, with a mound of rocks marking the spot. I expect they buried his tusks with the man who was killed in the hunt. If this story fits any of the others that I've heard, I'd bank on it.

The guy who told me this story seemed to think that the moral here was something along the lines of "live and let live," combined with a close reading of "I am not now, nor was I ever that hungry. If chicken's for dinner, I'll take chicken and be glad for it." I'm not going to argue with a word of that, though I'll add a couple of thoughts. I figure there are times when it's not such a good idea to take an imaginary insult so close to heart that it blinds you. Somehow, these guys got it into their heads that they had to prove they were superior to that pig and after that, there was no going back. No offense to the fallen, but I can't help but think that this philosophy is plum sideways. I never heard yet of a cougar, or a bear, or a coyote that had to prove his masculinity by killing something.

You want to hunt for the pleasure of it, that's all well and good, so long as you make use of what you kill and don't waste that creature's life, but if you buy a gun and are out stomping around in the woods because you need to prove something to the animals, then me and mine are planning to stay in the house with the door locked until you get it out of your system.

Roasted Boar's Haunch Stuffed with Crab Apples and Apricots

Serves 8

The truth is I've only prepared this recipe with wild boar ham one time. I confess, I get a case of the nervous jitters when wild boars start digging the ground and making out like they're going to run at me. Boars are smart enough to figure out right off what a gun is, so you can't actually raise your weapon until he's committed, and then you have to aim and shoot pretty quick. Most of the time, I manage to talk myself out of beating a path through the brush just so I can donate another piece of my leg to the wild pig population, so this recipe gets made with store-bought, pen-raised ham on a regular basis.

If you use domestic pork, don't substitute pork shoulder for ham since the size of the cut compared to the hassles of boning and the reduced cavity size make for more trouble than it's worth. This recipe is also quite good if made with breast of goose or duck.

¼ cup white wine
1 tablespoon honey
1 medium ham, about 7 pounds
¼ cup cranberry mustard (or honey mustard if you prefer)
4 to 5 crab apples, cored and quartered
1 tablespoon ground cinnamon
1 teaspoon ground nutmeg
1 cup dried apricot slices

Mix the wine and honey in a saucepan and simmer until the two are insepa-
rable, 3 to 4 minutes. While it's still hot, pour over the ham and marinate
overnight in the refrigerator.

Bone the ham. With a good sharp knife, circle the joint, feeling your way
along the bone for a clean cut, then follow the thigh bone down the length
and work your hand into the opening, nicking the meat along the length of the
thigh until it releases its grip. It sounds hard, but a little practice and the exercise of equal amounts of persistence and common sense will get the job done.

Rub the inside of the ham with the cranberry mustard and allow to rest
while you make the fruit stuffing.

Sprinkle the crab apples with the cinnamon and nutmeg.

Preheat the oven to 300°F. Position a rack in a large roasting pan so that
the meat will sit at least 1 inch above the bottom of the pan.

Layer the apricots and crab apples in the cavity and secure by tying the
ham with a piece of stout string.

Position the ham in the center of the rack in the roasting pan with the cut
side up. Pour an inch of water into the bottom of the pan and cover.

Roast for about 3 hours, or 25 minutes per pound. It's hard to cook this
too long. Check for doneness by puncturing the meat with a long thin knife
and then inserting a straw. To be safe, insert a thermometer. It should read
170°F. Turn slightly. If the fluid that runs up into the straw is pink, then cook
the ham a bit longer. When the juices run pale yellow, the roast is done.

Transfer the roast to a large cutting board with drainage grooves. Slice into
thick slices and arrange them in overlapping layers on a large platter. Some care
has to be taken to prevent the filling from falling out. If you don't think you can
do this, then transfer the roast to a long platter with high sides and slice it at
the table. That way, you can rescue the filling from each slice and arrange it on
the plate as you serve each guest.

Buffalo

You have to buy buffalo steaks. Sorry. There is no place that I know of where you can legally hunt a buffalo, though sometimes you can stand in line with a few hundred other hopefuls when one of the state parks decides they need to thin their herds before they eat themselves out of house and home.

If you shoot one illegally, the fine is many times greater than the price of the meat at a market, plus, they don't let you keep the meat after you've shot it.

Stealth is not possible since a bagged buffalo is way too big to carry out of the field with anything smaller than a truck the size of Wyoming, and if you've got such a vehicle handy, then you're not all that stealthy anymore.

Take my advice and don't try it. In the first place, buffalo tend to hang out in open country where the game warden (equipped as he is with a handy set of binoculars) can spot your nefarious carcass from miles away. Even if he does happen to be napping, the buffalo themselves will tell him what you are up to in no uncertain terms. Even before your quarry hits the ground, his buddies will thunder off in search of the law, pounding the earth with their hooves with enough force to shake rocks down from the hills. As if the noise they make isn't enough, the dust cloud they will raise is just about as good a marker as anybody could ask for who's trying to pinpoint your position.

If the buffalo don't run you over—always a distinct possibility—then you'll find yourself looking over a desk and some folks who'll take a dim view of your nefarious activities. It's probably safe to say that those boys will make it quite clear that they think less of you then they do of a dung beetle, and they're perfectly willing to help you empty your wallet so you can feel the proper amount of shame and make amends for your misdeeds.

Altogether a crummy way to spend an otherwise pleasant afternoon.

Fencing Lesson

There are a number of places now that have what they call wildlife parks, and some of these cater specifically to buffalo. The one I'm most familiar with is just over the first ridgeline, heading west through the mountains out of Denver, just by Chief Dan Hosa Park. The first thing you'll notice is how thick the posts are for the formidable fence they have around these animals. When you put your hand up to it, you'll realize that the wire is near as big around as your little finger. That is some stout chain-link, friends.

When I was living up that way, I heard a story about a couple of guys (not my two friends with the deer, although it truly sounds like something they would do—no, these boys were unknown to me, thank the Lord for small miracles) who decided that hunting animals who were so handily penned was something they could handle pretty easy.

To this end, they perused the fence, looking for a spot that they could scale. The plan was, so I've been told, that they would park their four-wheel drive near the fence, shoot one of the animals, and then make away with it before the game warden could show up to scope out the noise.

I said it was a doofus plan, didn't I?

The guy elected to climb the fence and do the butchering practiced climbing it several times before they showed up one morning before dawn to do the dirty deed.

They had brought along a couple of hefty skinning knives, a box of plastic garbage bags, and four Coleman coolers to help them in their task.

They only had two problems. First, the gun they were packing was stout enough to talk back to an elk, or even a bear, but you need special armaments to take down a buffalo. And second, the buffalo in question didn't seem interested in approaching the fence.

The sun was threatening to come up, and they were getting nowhere fast, so the one with the smallest brain jumped in the truck and started honking the horn to attract the attention of the intended prey and summon them to slaughter. Buffalo, I might add, purely hate the sound of a horn, any horn. If either of those two would-be hunters had read the signs posted around the fence, they would have noticed the warnings against just such rude behavior.

Well, the horn gambit worked, but it worked way better than anybody in his wildest dreams would hope. The buffalo not only approached the fence, they charged it, intent on putting an end to the racket.

They did, too.

You see, it's not really possible to put up a fence that can stand up to a herd of buffalo and maintain any integrity to speak of. That fence was there to prevent the buffalo from wandering away. They make materials that are strong enough, but the cost of putting one up that is long enough to enclose the kind of space a herd of buffalo needs in order to graze would exceed the national budget. Mostly, parks depend on educating people and put up helpful signs to this end. If you read them, they really are helpful.

This particular fence gave up pretty quick and came down on the man who'd been leaning against it. The guy in the truck survived, and I'm guessing that he's the one who's been telling the story around. He never did own up to what he and his friend were up to, but the stuff in his truck told that part of the story for him.

It's just not a good idea to deliberately antagonize a guy who weighs in near two thousand pounds. Especially if he's got all his buddies around him.

Braised Buffalo with Beets

Serves 4 to 6

This is especially tasty if the parts of the buffalo you use to prepare it are specific to the bull. There are a couple of restaurants in Colorado and Wyoming that serve buffalo testicles prepared in simple, straightforward ways, but none that I approached was willing to part with their stock and sell them to me on a regular basis from out the backdoor. Once seemed to be the magic number. I gather that you have to find a meat market that sells buffalo, and where the owner understands what is meant by "waste not, want not." Buffalo are raised and sold for the meat, but I fear that more often than not, this particular cut is tossed on the pile with the hooves and the tail.

Not to sound crude, but when you decide to throw away this delicacy, you are throwing away quite a bit of meat, not to mention that the meat in question is meltingly tender. A center cut is oval, very dark red in color, and can exceed the size of a beef sirloin. The dead giveaway is the even-grained texture and the fragile band of rippled skin binding it. If you order "mountain oysters" in a restaurant, and they bring you something with a recognizable grain, and you find that you have to cut this meat with a knife, then you've been duped.

Lacking buffalo, a really tender beefsteak will work wonders.

> *3 beets, trimmed, peeled, and cut into rings*
> *1 cup hot water*
> *1 teaspoon fresh lemon juice*
> *½ cup prunes*
> *2 buffalo steaks, 1½ pounds to 2 pounds each*
> *4 tablespoons sesame or peanut oil*
> *Freshly ground black pepper*
> *1 onion, sliced into rings*
> *1 teaspoon ground turmeric*

Place the beet rings in a steamer with sufficient water and bring to a boil. Allow to boil until a fork pushed into the center of the beets slides in easily. Remove from heat and allow to cool.

Mix together the 1 cup hot water and lemon juice. Pour over the prunes and allow the prunes to sit for about 1 hour. Drain and set aside.

In a large skillet, sear the buffalo steaks over medium-high heat in a couple tablespoons of the oil. Remove before they are completely cooked. You just want to brown them on both sides, not finish the process. You don't want them to get tough.

Sprinkle the steaks with pepper.

In a large wok or skillet, heat the remaining 2 tablespoons oil over medium-high heat. Add the onion and turmeric and stir-fry. Return the buffalo to the pan.

Arrange the beet rings and prunes around the buffalo steaks and add just enough water to cover the bottom of the pan, but do not cover the meat entirely. Cover and cook on the lowest simmer you can manage for about 45 minutes.

Remove from the heat and arrange on a platter, layering the buffalo steaks and spooning out the beets and prunes around the edges.

Shaking Hands with the Fog

I figured out long ago that I get in the most trouble when I decide to take a little vacation and get away from it all. Apparently the vacation venue trips some automatic setting somewhere in my brain that tells that otherwise trustworthy organ that it's time to slack off.

A couple a years ago, I took off to Yellowstone at the end of the season. The weather had been so truly awful that for once, the park wasn't awash with tourists. This was also the same year that terrorists hit the World Trade Center, among other things, and lots of folks who would normally have been on vacation that fall stayed home. I suspect that they didn't have much frolic in them after all that had happened, and the comfort of their own home sweet home looked pretty good to them.

I pulled up early in the morning and parked my Landcruiser in the first convenient lot that looked near empty. I was dead set on getting away from my fellow human beings for a day or two, and I had no intention of coming back to find a block party going on in the lot of my choice. Hence the search for a spot that other tourists didn't care for.

Tent and backpack in tow, I set out to do a little getting away from it all. When I found a suitable spot, namely out of sight of paths and persons, I put up my tent and set about gathering twigs and other natural flotsam that I could use to disguise my presence. I used a few longer branches and tied them together to support my other finds and set about stacking as much of it around my erstwhile domicile as I could manage. By the time I crawled inside and helped myself to a sandwich and a mug of cool water, I decided that national park or not, they'd have to drag me out by my ankles before I'd leave.

In the end, I was gone for nearer a week, but that's no matter. I wasn't expected anywhere so I forgot the world existed and truly enjoyed myself.

I shoulda stayed gone another day . . . at least.

The day I walked out to my cruiser, a fog set in that gripped the ground tenaciously. You'd a thought they hadn't seen each other since childhood. I got turned around once or twice on my way out of the park and that set me back to near dark by the time I recognized a line of trees that led to the parking lot. By this time, I was grateful for finding the place.

That feeling would pass soon enough. Sure as I hoped, nobody much thought that the lot I picked was the one they had a hankering for, and I could see clear—well, mostly—that my vehicle was sitting there all by its lonesome. That morning, I didn't have much interest in getting back in a car or driving anywhere, or anything like that, but after hours of stumbling in the fog, I began to have a soft feeling in my heart for that Landcruiser sitting there waiting so patiently for me.

I approached my old friend with a quickness in my step I hadn't felt all day.

It moved. Some five or six feet to one side.

I rubbed my eyes and marveled at how truly tired out I was. I changed direction and approached my vehicle again, only to find that it moved on beyond me one more time. I figured that the fog was messing with my brain, though truth to tell, if I'd had my brain with me that day, I wouldn'ta done what I did next.

Planting my feet square, I stiffened my back and commenced to abuse the perfidious vehicle for moving out of my way, when clearly it was time for the two of us to get our fannies down the road and out of this damnable fog.

Not to be spoken to that way, the dark shape in the fog snorted at me. I guess I was being told to keep my rude tongue to myself. Sometimes I listen to a warning fairly given. Not that day.

I took off walking towards my cruiser, mad as hell for being talked down to that way. I stomped through the fog without regard to where I might be planting my feet. Friends, I was determined not to let something so insignificant as a mode of travel get the best of me.

I got less than five feet from the object of my pursuit when a strong breeze tugged away a bit of fog in my path and cleared my view of a bull buffalo.

That big boy was none too happy with my uppity behavior and snorted a couple of times to get my attention. I guess he figured I wasn't in my right mind, and he was doing his part to wake up what few brain cells I possessed. This time, it worked and worked wonders I may report.

I backed out of there with many a sincere apology, which he graciously accepted. He turned out to be the kind of gentleman who suffered fools now and then, though I didn't want to hang around to test his limits. I had the feeling I was approaching them pretty quick.

A scant half hour later, I found my cruiser, which looked way yonder smaller in that fog than the bull buffalo did, but maybe by that time my brain was awake enough to begin elaborating.

I hear tell that a bout of genuine terror will do that to a body.

Buffalo Pastitsio

Serves 4

Mountain oysters work real well with this recipe. The tenderness of the meat goes a long way towards making the dish easy to break down at the table. If you opt to use beef oysters, then cut them into quarters. You can also use good-quality beef stew meat.

> *3 cups medium or large shell pasta*
> *3 tablespoons peanut oil*
> *2 small onions, finely chopped*
> *2½ pounds buffalo meat, cut into 1½-inch cubes*
> *½ teaspoon ground cinnamon*
> *¼ teaspoon ground nutmeg*
> *½ teaspoon dried oregano*
> *¼ teaspoon dried purple basil (or regular basil if you're feeling especially common)*
> *2 cups tomato purée*
> *6 tablespoons butter*
> *6 tablespoons all-purpose flour*
> *1 cup milk*
> *2 cups light cream*
> *6 egg yolks, beaten lightly*
> *1½ cups grated Parmesan cheese*

Boil the pasta shells in salted water for about 10 minutes, until they are tender but not mushy. Drain and rinse in cool water.

In a large skillet, heat the oil over medium heat. Add the onions and stir-fry until they are golden yellow, about 10 minutes. Add the buffalo and brown for about 10 minutes. Sprinkle the cinnamon, nutmeg, oregano, and basil over the meat. Add the tomato purée. Turn off the heat and allow the flavors to blend while you go on to the next step.

Melt the butter in a saucepan over medium heat. Stir in the flour. Add the milk and simmer until it thickens into a smooth sauce. Combine the cream with the egg yolks and whip together. Stir this into the paste and simmer for a few minutes until you have an even cream sauce with no visible lumps. Be careful not to scorch it or let it curdle. Keep the heat low and stir constantly. Be patient. If you scorch or curdle the sauce, then you just have to start over again and that takes even longer.

Preheat the oven to 375°F.

Arrange the pasta and the browned meat and onions in a large baking pan by alternating layers, first the pasta and then the meat, finishing with a layer of meat on top.

Pour the cream sauce over the whole works. Sprinkle the top with the grated Parmesan.

Bake for 45 minutes. If it is done correctly, it should cut into squares and lift out easily. Let it sit for about 10 minutes before cutting it.

Bear

Bear has to be field dressed immediately. If you carry it out with the skin on, then you run a serious risk of the meat becoming overheated and spoiling. Even if it's winter, the fur is so heavy that the meat will suffer from overheating. Besides which, it's much easier to carry a bear out in pieces, as a mature bear can easily weigh from two to four times as much as a large man. A black bear weighs up to 400 pounds, and a grizzly bear twice that much.

Field Dressing and Preparation

Cut away the genitals and throw them away. Then make a circular cut around the rectum, pull it out an inch or so and tie it off with a bit of string. Cut around the wrists and ankles and around the neck. Now, slit

the skin from the cut you made around the neck to the rectum and pull the skin away completely. Scrape off all visible fat and toss it.

Gut and clean as you would for a deer. See detailed instructions under the heading for deer (see page 81).

Bear meat, like pork, is subject to trichinosis, so you have to cook it carefully to 170°F.

Charades

Looking at bears and watching them from a safe distance is a rewarding way to spend an afternoon. Though their eyesight is not the best, they have an especially keen sense of smell and their hearing is excellent, so a safe distance generally means some ways off with a pair of binoculars or, if the landscape allows for it, uphill from the bear.

In mountainous country, the breeze is almost always from the lowest point to the highest. The chief exception to this rule being some god-awful run-for-the-hills storm with an unhealthy downdraft—in which case you ought to know enough to come in out of the rain anyway.

Uphill advantage carries the bear's scent to you instead of the other way around. Mostly, a bear who smells a man nearby will turn and seek entertainment and adventure elsewhere, both of which he considers to be greatly improved by your absence. If you think the bear smelled you, and he didn't turn away and start to make off or, worse, he tastes the air and heads your direction, then, friend, you are definitely up that proverbial creek. If you have to paddle with your hands to get your fanny out of there, then by all means, time's a wasting.

I should mention that you should paddle with as much stealth as you can manage, because running from a bear is not recommended as an activity designed to promote long life and good health. Bears, like most everybody else, humans included, interpret running as either guilt or cowardice. Either way, you've just sent up a flag that reads, "Victim! Loser! Come and get me!" Not what you want to say.

A buddy of mine bragged to me once how he bested a grizzly bear by running at him and screaming at the top of his lungs. The bear must of thought he was crazy—so do I. No matter what you do, your chance of it working out for you is roughly fifty-fifty. I don't like those odds. Especially if I'm being asked to gamble on predicting the behavior of a bear. If the fifty turns out to be in favor of the bear and not you, then it's one hundred out of one hundred that you're gonna come out much the worse for wear in the deal.

Bears are too much like humans for anybody, even a bear expert, to predict. Besides, the guy who told me that story is given to telling incredible tales.

Bear Ragout

Serves 4

I've heard a lot of folks complain that bear meat is dark and dank and frankly inedible. All I can guess is that those folks either dragged their kill out of the woods without field dressing it, or they tried to cook it without scraping away the fat first. Bear meat is a lot like pork in that it does not have to be basted. There's enough fat in the meat that it cooks up juicy and tender, but if you leave any of the surface layer fat on it, then it tends to spoil the meat somewhat. Too greasy is simply too greasy, plus, failure to scrape away the excess fat while field dressing will result in slightly rancid fat, which never tastes good.

If you don't have bear meat, then try this with beef, buffalo, moose, or other venison. All are very good and well worth the effort.

> *2 pounds bear meat, cut into 2-inch cubes*
> *2 onions, chopped*
> *6 carrots, chopped*
> *1 clove garlic, finely minced*
> *1 pound smoked bacon, cut into 4- to 5-inch strips*
> *Freshly ground black pepper*
> *1 tablespoon sweet paprika*
> *1 teaspoon dried marjoram*
> *1 teaspoon caraway seeds*
> *½ cup water*
> *1 tablespoon fresh lemon juice*
> *2 cups dry white wine*
> *1 pound mushrooms, halved*
> *2 tablespoons butter*
> *1 cup sour cream*
> *2 tablespoons all-purpose flour*

In a dry large skillet over medium-high heat, brown the bear meat. Set aside in a bowl. Wipe the skillet clean.

Return the skillet to medium-high heat and stir-fry the onions, carrots, garlic, and bacon until the onions turn a lovely yellow. Remove from the heat and add pepper to taste and the paprika, marjoram, caraway seeds, water, lemon juice, wine, and bear meat. Cover and simmer over low heat for about 30 minutes, or until the meat is tender when prodded with a fork.

Sauté the mushrooms in butter over medium heat until they give up their juices, about 8 minutes. Set aside.

In a saucepan, mix the sour cream with the flour and heat—very slowly—until it begins to thicken. Pour the sour cream sauce over the meat and cook over low heat for 5 minutes or less.

Top the whole thing with the mushrooms and serve.

Downhill Racing with a Friend

I've been fortunate (I think that's the word I'm looking for) to encounter bears in the wild twice when I was out walking and totally unarmed. Normally, I don't put much stock in firearms, but there's something about the naked power in a bear's physique to make you glad for the advantage of technology, even if you're not going to use it.

The first bear I ever came across was occupied with destroying the remains of a tree trunk to get at the honey inside. Bees were everywhere, fruitlessly trying to sting the bear through his thick fur. They'd have to be big as a small bird for that to work.

The noise should have alerted me, but I was a kid and thought I'd come across a friendly face chopping wood if I kept following that sound. Well, chopping wood was close to right, but the face with it didn't look all that friendly.

I remembered to look at the ground and not into the bear's eye. Bears consider a direct stare a challenge. She didn't have any cubs, and she was mostly full of honey and feeling pretty good about herself, so she turned back to her business and proceeded to ignore me. Not one to look a magnanimous gesture in the mouth, I took the hint and backed out.

Backing is good. It allows you to watch the ground for signs that the bear has changed her mind. Turn around and make quicker progress when you are out of sight, but don't run. Crashing noises attract curious onlookers and, with few exceptions, everybody in the woods who's possessed of enough curiosity to find out who is making so much racket is strong enough to demand respect and get it.

Bears and cougars scope out unusual noises. Cougars generally can be discouraged from coming after you if you make a lot of noise and wave a stick. Cougars don't want trouble, they want something to eat. Bears sometimes want trouble.

The second bear in my history of close encounters got a little hairier. I was walking the ridgeline, at peace with heaven and earth and soaking up the rich smells wafting uphill to my waiting nose. Since I was not raised in the big city, I have a pretty well developed sense of smell, though, truth is, even a piece of dead wood could smell a bear.

Ridgelines are a goodness—downhill in all directions and a clear view of the countryside. Too much confidence when you're alone in the woods is not all that good.

Seems that the bear's folks had tuned him in to the concept of uphill as well, because the bear I met was doing the same thing I was.

I hadn't stopped or even slowed down for a light for quite some time and the next corner I rounded brought me face to face (well nearly—my memory of the situation seems to want to make this part scary movie time) with a bear coming from the other direction. We both put on the brakes and veered to the right, but that left us eyeballing one another suspiciously. Since he had the bigger teeth, he won the staring match.

I remembered just before he put it in gear and charged me that if you have to run from a bear, run downhill. Bears have powerful hind legs and their center of balance weights them heavily to the rear. They start to roll head over heels if they build up too much speed running downhill.

I didn't know where I was going, but, friends, I was looking forward to getting there as quickly as possible. Ten yards from the path, I broke into a steep clearing and less than ten yards after that, the bear rolled past me, tearing up clumps of grass as he went. My feet took roots and a short time later (too short) the bear gained control over his situation and pulled to a stop.

I was happy to see myself uphill with respect to the scent business, though at this point he hardly needed to sniff the air to find me. What I found distressing was that if I intended to run downhill from the bear, I'd have to run straight to him first. Not good.

There was a fair-sized cedar shrub that came up to about my chin about four feet in front of me and a little off to my left. I wished it would hurry up and grow taller—like in the next three minutes. Hiding sounded like an enticing prospect just then.

Perhaps the slope of the hill fooled him because the bear stood up, stretching his neck and began feeling the air with his lips to locate me. He let himself down, and I thought maybe he would forget about me and go on his way, but no such luck. He took a few steps to the side and stood up again, guffing and blowing air through his nose when he spotted me.

I found myself wishing I'd done something sensible that day, like bungee jump off the devil's high bridge. It sounded positively bucolic by comparison to the adventure I was having.

I tried not to look at his face, but looking at his feet didn't help much either. My stomach didn't like it one bit when I saw that bear's feet moving toward me.

I tried to keep the cedar shrub between us, and at one point I actually tore off a branch and slapped the bear on the nose with it. Cedar has a strong scent of its own, one that is powerful enough to mask a lot of other sins, like the stink of man, which any animal that could speak would tell you is one foul odor. Rubbing cedar on yourself and your clothes is one way to hunt deer without alerting them to your presence.

Somehow, the cedar branch to the face gambit turned the bear's temper. I fell to the ground and rolled past him as he tore into that bush, slapping and tearing for all he was worth. He had to blame somebody for his temper, and a cedar shrub with self-aggrandizing pretensions would do him fine.

I slunk away towards the ridge above me while the bear reduced that poor shrub to a stalk and then tore the stalk out of the ground for good measure. I made the cover of the trees before he finished with his victim and remembered just who it was he had been chasing.

He looked around half-heartedly, returning now and then to the defunct cedar shrub as if to ask himself if that's all there was to it.

I stayed down until he made up his mind that enough was enough and lumbered away.

I can't tell you how glad I was that I didn't have to find out if it was true that bears can run uphill twice as fast as a human being. Right then and there, I thought I could probably fly if I had to, but I'm glad that particular skill wasn't put to the test.

Amazingly, I only had two small scratches on my forearm to show for my scare. Must be luck, because it can't be clean living.

Bear Stuffed with Ham and Mushrooms

Serves 6 to 8

Oddly enough, this recipe works really well with the breast meat of poultry. Chicken, goose, or duck works quite well, but I should warn you that turkey fights with the ham. Pork works best of all, but if you opt for pork, then leave out the slices of ham and simply stuff your roast with mushrooms with a few greens added for color and taste. Collard greens, spinach, or string beans work real well with it.

> *½ pound mushrooms, sliced or halved*
>
> *1 tablespoon butter*
>
> *3 thin slices smoked ham, cut into narrow strips no more than*
>   *2 inches in length*
>
> *1 egg, beaten*
>
> *Freshly ground black pepper*
>
> *½ teaspoon ground cardamom*
>
> *¼ teaspoon ground cinnamon*
>
> *¼ teaspoon ground nutmeg*
>
> *1 bear roast, approximately 6 inches thick and at least*
>   *10 inches in length, about 4 pounds*
>
> *½ cup red wine*

Sauté the mushrooms in the butter over medium heat until they give up their juices, about 8 minutes.

In a large bowl, combine the mushrooms, ham, egg, pepper, cardamom, cinnamon, and nutmeg.

Preheat the oven to 375°F.

Beginning at the center, cut a deep pocket in the side of the bear roast, continuing with this activity until the roast is held together on three sides by no more than an inch of meat. Fill the pockets with the mixed ingredients in the bowl. Stitch shut with size-eight carpet thread. Place on a rack in a large roasting pan and cover.

Roast, basting regularly with the wine, for 2½ hours. Test for doneness by slicing the meat near the thick part and inserting a straw. If red juice wells up, it's not done yet. Roast until the juices are slightly tan, while still retaining a faint pinkness. If in doubt, roast a bit longer. Bear is like pork in that it is very hard to overcook it, but risky to undercook it. For safety's sake, check with a thermometer. It should say 170°F.

Allow to cool for 10 minutes before slicing to serve. Remove the thread in the kitchen.

SMALL GAME

Rabbit

It's easier to raise rabbits yourself than it is to hunt them.

Jackrabbits, by the way, aren't worth eating unless you have a fondness for boot leather. If that is indeed the case, then avail yourself of a boot, since its nutritional value is roughly equal to the jackrabbit and easier to catch.

A rabbit will hold his peace, sitting as still as death under the cover of a hedgerow until he's absolutely sure that you know where he is, then he'll bolt and lay in a zigzag pattern across the grass. Some folks use a dog to help flush the rabbit early, but that smacks of cheating to me, so I've never done it that way. I like to wear heavy boots and make a good racket so the rabbit is afeared that I know more about his whereabouts than I do. It works pretty good. I find that if I stomp about like a leviathan was comin' and take a kick at a low shrub now and again, that the rabbits bolt early and leave me a clean shot.

Field Dressing and Preparation

Field dress a rabbit by making a small incision just under the breast-bone and carefully slitting open the belly, guarding the blade of your knife with two fingers in order to avoid puncturing the intestines. Make a small circular cut around the rectum, then pull it out a spare half inch and tie it off with a bit of string. Draw out the intestines, taking care not to rupture the bladder. Clean out the abdominal cavity completely and rinse with a bit of water. If you want to tan the skin, then save the liver.

At home, cut around the arms just above the elbow and remove the lower joint. Do the same for the back legs just above the ankle. Make a slit under the throat and come up over the top of the head just behind the ears. Check to be sure that the abdominal cut runs the full length of the body from the rectum to the throat. Now make light cuts in the underside of the legs from the abdominal cut to the end of the limbs. Grasp the skin firmly under the throat area and slowly pull it away from the body. Lay the skin aside. Cut through the cartilage on either side of the breastbone and pull the breastbone away from the body. Now you can remove the heart, lungs, and diaphragm easily. Rinse the body cavity with a little water.

Hunt for wild rabbits in the early winter after the first freeze to avoid tularemia, or rabbit fever. Rabbits sometimes have parasites that carry this flu-like disease. The parasites cannot survive the freeze, and rabbits that are badly infected can't either. If you hunt earlier, in the fall or late summer, then wear gloves when you clean and dress your kill, since tularemia is transmitted to humans via cuts and abrasions on the skin.

Herbed Rabbit with Plums

Serves 3 or 4

This is actually the only rabbit recipe I ever tried that can be successfully digested if the rabbit used is jackrabbit. Of course, the jackrabbit was very young and hadn't had time to develop those stringy muscles that his elders favor. If I had the teeth of a coyote, perhaps I'd be willing to sample jackrabbit more often. Lamb, duck, and goose also work quite well with this recipe.

As a side dish, choose either rice or couscous.

> 2 rabbits, about 3 pounds each, boned and cut into
>   3- to 4-inch pieces
> 3 tablespoons peanut oil
> ½ teaspoon ground coriander
> 4 leaves fresh mint or 1 teaspoon dried
> 2 tablespoons fresh lemon juice
> 1 bunch fresh scallions, trimmed
> 7 to 8 fresh plums, pitted and skinned
> ½ teaspoon dried tarragon (I prefer the Russian variety)
> Freshly ground black pepper
> 2 cups water

In a large skillet, heat the rabbit in the peanut oil over medium-high heat for about 5 minutes per side, until brown. Decrease heat to low. Sprinkle the coriander over the rabbit and let them get to know each other for a few minutes. Then sprinkle it with the mint and lemon juice. Lay the scallions over the top, keeping them well clear of the bottom or the sides of the pot. Cover and allow the scallions to steam for a scant minute.

Add the plums, tarragon, pepper, and water. Cover and cook over low heat for about 40 minutes, until the rabbit is tender and can be separated with a fork. Uncover after 30 minutes or so to allow most of the water to steam off. Watch it carefully so it doesn't stick. If you walk away and let it look after itself, it could take a notion to burn on the bottom.

Serve hot from the pan as this dish does not do well when reheated.

✳—✳—✳—✳ **Kicking up a Foul Smell** ✳—✳—✳—✳

When I was young, I used to like a challenge considerably more than I do now, so rabbit hunting was something that I did now and then—both for the aggravation and for the target practice.

Wild rabbits have an elusive flavor that is not duplicated in their pen-raised cousins. Nowadays, I know from the sort of traps that catch the beast alive, but back then, a hot afternoon stomping around in the bushes with a pistol was the only way I knew how to go about hunting rabbit.

My son prefers bow hunting and always did, so we had but few years in which my interest in hunting rabbits and the age at which he could safely come with me overlapped. Besides which, if you get him out in the country, and he is not himself doing any hunting, he is quite capable of making way yonder too much racket and otherwise mucking up the day for his companions.

I learned long ago that my boy's ability to focus on the business at hand is entirely dependent on it being his own business. Consequently, I only took him along if I figured that lollygagging was an entirely acceptable way to while away a day.

He was about thirteen and already showing quite a talent with the bow when I agreed to take him and a friend from school along with me one day. The two boys came along for the fun of getting out of the house in spring. My boy left his bow at home, since hunting rabbit with a bow is a fool's errand, and his friend was a city kid and didn't know the first thing about what he was looking for or what to do with it if he found it.

That last bit came home to haunt me.

We took off from the house around 5 A.M. so as to catch the rabbits rooting around for breakfast. Only a fool with plenty of time to waste hunts rabbit in the middle of the day, so we set out planning to do a bit of walking and get back by midmorning.

At least part of my day was a lucky one—I'd taken three rabbits, all fine, young bucks and didn't even come close to shooting myself in the foot whilst I was doing it. I was feeling no small swell of pride, so I guess I deserved for things to take a turn for the grisly.

My boy and his friend had been lagging behind, and I hadn't seen anything to snag my attention, so I turned back to gather the kids up and make for home. I guess I'd gotten a bit farther from the boys than I thought 'cause I'd been backtracking for about ten minutes when I came across my son actively engaged in looking out for me. His friend was another fifteen yards farther on and still about the same business he'd been on to all day—scuffing his shoes on the ground and staring off into the sky. He happened to look down just in time to get us all into trouble, more him than the rest of us, but with what he found, nobody in the radius of a mile is left unscathed.

Now, in my own defense, I hadn't caught a hint of this character my boy's friend had found because I'd been walking into the wind while I was hunting and this fella was coming up behind us.

By this time, of course, he was close enough that his scent was fanning out around him pretty good, and I had an idea that we maybe needed to get our tails on towards home. Too late. My boy's friend spotted the skunk making his way between clumps of grass and—for private reasons of his own that we have never to this day figured out—he took two long steps forward and kicked the creature in the fanny.

When I asked him, he told me he'd never seen a skunk, but I suspect that by the time the spraying he got wore off, he had that particular image pretty well ingrained in his thick skull for life.

We took him home, pushing him ahead of us with a juniper branch. Even though my boy and I mashed the fragrant tips of that branch with our boot heels before we deemed it a worthy prod, the sweet smell of juniper just couldn't compete. We walked the whole way with tears in our eyes, though in truth, I couldn't tell you how many of those tears were squeezed out from the smell and how many from stunned amazement for what'd we'd witnessed. I can say that there isn't anything more purely amazing than to see a truly talented doofus finding his form, but I don't recommend that you get so close to the event—binoculars were invented for just such historical moments as this one.

My son and I took our brainchild home, stuffed his clothes into several successive plastic bags, and washed him down in cider vinegar. Cider vinegar helps, but only time cures all smells, so my boy and I took his friend home in the truck and made our getaway before his mother could mark our approach and come after us with her broom.

Up until that morning, he had been planning to spend the weekend at our place, but with all our efforts washing him and changing his clothes, all we ended up with was cider skunk for our troubles, so I gave him back to his folks. I didn't raise an idiot and wasn't looking forward to spending the weekend breathing next to one.

For the life of me, I have never been able to figure out why that boy walked up and kicked that skunk like that. It'd be my first guess that he's used to kicking his dog and getting away with it; if so, then maybe it was a lesson well learned. I just wished he had learned it somewhere besides under my nose.

Years later, my son taught me how to deal with skunks without getting sprayed. I was over at his house of an evening, standing out in the garden while he did the watering when a skunk wandered into the corner of his yard, making his way towards the tomatoes. Apparently, he had been helping himself to them and figured he may as well get an early start on dinner. My son twisted the nozzle of his hose to a hard stream and aimed it dead at that skunk's broadside. Friends, he bowled that animal over, end over end, taking aim at him and knocking his wind out every time the creature regained his feet. In the end, the skunk took off running for the trees and never hesitated to look back. That's the only time I ever did see somebody spray a skunk.

Rabbit with Juniper Berries

Serves 3 to 4

This recipe came to me one night while I was camping out under the stars in New Mexico. I had dined that night on a rabbit that I roasted over the coals, and all I can guess is that my disappointed stomach stayed up all night drinking in the smells around me and came up with a list of improvements. It took a couple a rabbits and some perseverance to perfect it, but in the end, it turned into one of our favorites. Me and my stomach both like it.

You can substitute any variety of poultry that suits you, but only rabbit works really well. If you can't get your hands on juniper berries, then try garlic. Garlic changes the flavor of the finished product, but in no way diminishes it. Using both makes for a truly spectacular dish.

This recipe can be served with rice, roasted potatoes, or a host of other side dishes. A good, firm bread with a substantial crust is a must. Have patience—this recipe takes a couple of days to prepare properly.

> *3 cups water*
> *2 cups red wine*
> *1 cup red wine vinegar*
> *½ cup honey*
> *1 teaspoon grated lemon peel*
> *¼ cup juniper berries*
> *½ teaspoon lemon pepper*
> *1 medium onion, diced*
> *2 rabbits, about 3 pounds each, back legs removed, saving the saddle meat for another time*
> *½ pound thinly sliced bacon (preferably smoked)*
> *2 tablespoons rice flour (I prefer it but you can use whatever you have except rye)*
> *¼ teaspoon dry mustard powder*
> *½ cup sour cream*

Mix the water, wine, vinegar, honey, lemon peel, juniper berries, lemon pepper, and onion in a large saucepan. Bring to a boil and allow to boil. for a couple of minutes, but stir it to keep it from foaming. Foaming will scorch the flavor of the wine.

Put the rabbit into a large glass or glazed pottery bowl and pour the hot wine mixture over it. Cover and allow it to sit for 2 days in the back of the refrigerator. Wait for it. It really does make a difference. Turn twice a day to ensure equal exposure to the marinade.

Preheat the over to 325°F. Place a rack in a large roasting pan.

Remove the rabbit from the marinade but don't throw the liquid away. Wrap the pieces of meat in the strips of bacon and bake on the rack, basting frequently with the marinade. Bake for about an hour or until the rabbit is tender. Naturally, you have put a catch pan underneath to keep the drippings and the marinade off the floor of your oven. The rabbit drippings and the marinade are especially tasty and you're going to use it later, so don't forget and stick your rabbit on a barbecue grill. If you do, you'll lose most of the flavor you've worked so hard to attain.

In a small bowl, mix together the flour, mustard, and 2 tablespoons of the sour cream.

Pour the pan juices into a saucepan and add the flour mixture to it. Bring to a boil, stirring constantly. Decrease the heat and continue cooking until nearly half of the liquid has boiled away, then add the remaining sour cream.

Arrange the baked rabbit on a platter, lace with the sauce, and serve immediately.

✳──✳──✳──✳ Digging In and Digging Out ✳──✳──✳──✳

I went with a guy once whose idea of hunting rabbits included a shovel.

Now I've always thought that if an animal makes it home, that that's sort of like King's X and you should respect that manner of thing and take your business elsewhere, but this old boy was the world's worst shot and, like me, he didn't think much about snares or jaw traps that's fit to repeat in company. He learned the shovel method to even up his odds.

Unlike prairie dogs, rabbits will stick it out if you run a little smoke through their burrow. They get paralyzed by fear so that their limbs freeze up and they couldn't run if they wanted to.

Me and this guy made us a bet that I couldn't get the first rabbit we spotted in two shots or less. If I did, we'd hunt my way; if not, I'd stand back and let him employ the shovel method.

Now I took the bet partly because I didn't want to stand there and admit that the thing couldn't be done and if I did do it, then we should declare a miracle, and partly because I was sure that there was something blasphemous in the idea of digging up a fella's house and home. To that end, I took the bet because I was sure that I'd get divine help and take down my quarry with the first shot.

In my own defense, let me just say that I'd had a piece of apple pie and a bowl of pistachio ice cream for breakfast, and my brain was so happy on sugar that I couldn't have thought in a straight line if you'd stuck a ruler to my head and tied it to my ears with twine. I took that bet of my own free will, and free will means that you're free to screw up as often as you want.

If God has a sense of humor, then he probably also has a Polaroid and a pile of family photos a mile high that would make you laugh so hard it would bring tears to your eyes. I know there's one or two choice ones of me in there, and I expect that one day I'll be able to laugh at them just as freely as everybody else surely does. Right now, it's too close to home, and when I think of some of the stupid stuff I've done, it rightly gives me a powerful headache.

Well, that morning, half a dozen rabbits popped up in front of us and, naturally, I took three or four shots at each one before I conceded defeat.

Sugar also makes me notably hardheaded, aiming high for purely stubborn. After a little give and take on the subject, we changed tactics to the shovel method and started chasing the rabbits instead of shooting at them. We spotted a likely candidate that didn't run more than three or four yards from us and then dove down a hole. We scouted around and found two other holes that we plugged up with rocks and set to work digging out the one our rabbit had gone into.

My friend had done this part before so he leaned into his work and made good time, building up the sides of the hole with the dirt he was digging out. He was coming near about the right depth and took a breather to wipe the sweat off his face when a young buck came dashing out of the hole, barring his teeth and screaming insults.

Yes, rabbits scream, and it is something else to hear, too.

This one was acting like he'd seen way yonder too many *Rambo* movies. He flew around, throwing his body into the most macho Kung Fu poses he could muster and smashing our ears with power screams to back up his intent.

I had a feeling this wasn't supposed to happen.

My friend just stood there with his mouth gaping, and I couldn't help but notice that he held his shovel in what could only be described as a defensive position. After a couple of rounds, the rabbit declared victory over the barbarians, ran up the flag, and disappeared back inside the burrow.

We thought things over for a minute and changed our tactics a bit. He was still doing the digging, but now I was running interference with a leafy branch that I kept brushing the opening of the hole with to confuse the issue.

What we found in that burrow was surely a pitiful sight. There was just the one buck and by now, he was cowed by the opening, standing his ground in front of the women but too purely beat down to fight. Behind him, there were three does waded up in a lump over their kittens. One looked too old to be raising younguns, and the other two looked like they should still be huddled next to their own mothers.

One look and we figured out where that buck learned to fight the way he did. These folks had been living a life that would make a *Rambo* movie look like a Disney cartoon. Rabbit Armageddon must've hit nearby, and these four had escaped this far, dug in, and begun to rebuild.

No words needed to be said for us to come to the conclusion that these people did not deserve us in their life at this time. A rebuilding thing was happening and our digging had set them back a ways.

While I stood guard over the burrow, my friend backtracked to a dump we had passed about a half a mile back. Presently, he returned with a defunct front-loading washing machine panel that he had kicked the little round door off of and a couple of pieces of scrap tin. We put the washer panel up against the burrow opening to close it off safe and built a little tunnel with the sheet tin, shoveling dirt back over the whole works until the little family was safe back underground and their doorway was functioning like it oughta again.

On the way home, we stopped off at the store and bought ourselves a couple of chickens and some greens and chowed down at my house with the family smiling and telling jokes around us.

The next time we went rabbit hunting, I hit the first three we came across—two on the first shot and one on the second. Go figure. I guess my accuracy felt the need to improve itself in the presence of a guy who was such a terrible shot that he was as like to shoot me as he was the rabbit.

Desire for self-preservation can make an average shot into Annie Oakley pretty quick.

Ginger Rabbit

Serves 3 to 4

This is such a colorful dish that it is a pleasure to look at it while you eat. In my enthusiasm to add yet more color, I once adorned this piece with three kinds of sweet peppers: red, yellow, and green. Still, experiments with brightly colored veggies paid off, and an alternative recipe that uses a judicious sampling of red chiles turned out to be quite a winner. As a side benefit, ginger rabbit with red chiles does a bang up job of clearing your sinuses. Add 2 red chiles and 1 banana pepper to the ingredients below. Approach with caution.

This recipe is so versatile that it can be prepared with almost any variety of poultry, beef, lamb, or pork. Rice makes a good side dish.

> *¼ cup white wine*
>
> *½ cup soy sauce*
>
> *1-inch piece fresh ginger, peeled and thinly sliced*
>
> *1 cup hot water*
>
> *1 rabbit, about 3 pounds, boned and cut into slices (2 by 3 by ½ inches works pretty well)*
>
> *2 tablespoons fresh ginger juice*
>
> *2 tablespoons sugar*
>
> *3 tablespoons peanut oil*
>
> *1 red bell pepper, cut into narrow strips*
>
> *1 small crookneck squash, sliced diagonally*
>
> *½ small head purple cabbage, cored and very thinly sliced*

In the morning, gently heat the wine, ¼ cup of the soy sauce, and half of the ginger slices in a saucepan. Add the water, bring the whole works to a boil, and immediately remove from heat. Pour the hot marinade over the rabbit and allow to rest in the refrigerator until you are ready to cook dinner.

Mix the remaining ¼ cup soy sauce, the ginger juice, and the sugar in a small bowl and stir until the sugar dissolves.

Remove the rabbit from the marinade and pat dry.

Heat the oil in a large skillet over medium-high heat. Throw in the remaining ginger and the rabbit and sauté, stirring constantly, for about 4 minutes. Add the bell pepper, squash, and the soy mixture. Cook for another 3 minutes; continue stirring constantly to prevent scorching. Add the cabbage and cook for 2 more minutes. The rabbit should be tender, but don't allow the cabbage to get soggy.

Serve immediately.

Marmot

Woodchucks like to lounge around outside their burrows in pleasant weather, although catching them napping is not as easy to do as it sounds. They have an excellent sense of smell, and they can hear you walking a goodly ways off. Their eyesight isn't too bad either—they can detect movement as far away as 500 to 600 feet. They whistle a warning to all and sundry at the approach of a predator.

Each woodchuck has a separate burrow, arranged along a low bank with a doorstep of packed dirt that they can stand on to get a better view of local goings-on. Unless there's an abundance of food around, there'll generally be only one old male, two or three breeding-age females, and a collection of juveniles that are old enough to leave mom but not truly off and gone as of yet. The females are righteously independent, but pretty much everybody takes their lead from the dominant male. Whenever something interesting is going down, they'll crouch in their doorways and watch him to see what's what. If he don't like it, they know pretty quick and make theirselves scarce.

That whistling is one good way to locate their burrow. Once you know where it is, you can apologize for disturbing them by augmenting their diet with something delectable like lettuce— which they truly love—out in plain sight on a little grassy picnic spot at first, until they learn to trust you some, then conveniently located in the back corner of a trap.

Rockchuck is the western cousin of the woodchuck. His other name is yellow-bellied marmot. He tends to live in a harsher climate than his cousin, so his hair is thicker, but in general he's about the same size and weight.

A couple of guys have told me that the best way to get yourself a marmot is to spy out his hole and then dig him out when he's taken leave of the afternoon sun. I've never done this myself. Not only is digging in the kind of country that these boys call home a seriously exhausting business, I don't get on with the idea of digging a guy's house up and tossing it around. I like to use my wits if I can, and if that fails, there's always the dependable chicken at the corner market.

Like woodchucks, rockchuck and hoary marmots will whistle to alert their brethren that a predator is about. If you like to hunt with a rifle from a distance, you can play the rockchuck against himself. Lay yourself down on the rocks with your head low so he can't see your silhouette and then whistle; one short burst will do. Pretty soon, some young male will stick up his head to see what the fuss is all about. His head's not much bigger than a large apple, but if you're a good shot, you can do it.

I always use the kind of traps that catch the animal alive. That allows me to release females and young unharmed and spares both me and the woodchucks the nightmare of traps with jaws that as often as not maim and cripple the animals.

If that's not enough to convince you, then try to remember that any animal who dies a prolonged and agonizing death has plenty of time to flood the meat with musk, not to mention that traps with jaws inflict deep wounds that bleed the animal to death. The meat will be dry and have a rank and sour taste and, to my mind, is not suitable for the table.

Field Dressing and Preparation

Field dress a woodchuck as you would a rabbit (see page 140). When cleaning a woodchuck, don't forget to remove the musk sacs in the small of the back and under each forearm. After skinning, scrape the fat away from the body. Woodchucks in the wild seldom live longer than four or five years. More often than not, two is gonna be the average age of all the adults you encounter. They get from 5 to 15 pounds, and an old male will taste just as good as a youngun.

Creative Cookery Goes over the Edge

Hunting woodchuck is fraught with more hazards than meet the eye. The animal's habitat—the northeast quadrant of the U.S.—lies within the domain of the cult personality, Punsxutawney Phil. For those of you who follow Phil's psychic predictions (whether from true religious fervor or because an appearance by that charismatic creature is always good for the turning of a few dollars here and there), I apologize if the presence of gourmets in your fertile woods causes distress.

In Texas, cattle are considered sacred, but eating them is not only permitted, it's practically mandatory. Speaking of Texas, I've a friend living there in Austin, by the name of Jim, who wields a free hand in the kitchen, and I want to take a minute here to warn against letting yourself go all around the field like that boy does. I've been telling you all along that you should feel free to make substitutions here and there, but I'm telling you about Jim now, so you'll understand that if you start cooking up the kitchen sink thinking my sauce and a few potatoes will make it toothsome, then you shouldn't oughta blame me if it doesn't serve up quite like you were expecting it to.

While I was about writing this book, I sent one or two recipes off to a friend here and there, just to get a feel for what they thought of them. I'm forever making guinea pigs of casual strangers, but I find that I'm cautious of setting it in print without I first test it out on a stomach I'm acquainted with. I sent this one to Jim and what that boy did with it can't be described in any words but his own, besides which, I'm struck dumb with amazement when I try to repeat it so that naught comes out of my mouth but a breath of air, like a seashell at the ocean. To this end, I am quoting the letter he sent me:

> *Tried this recipe last night, but unfortunately, and I say this with love, it wasn't one of your better ones. Of course, we did make a few changes, but they were minor. For example, we didn't have a wood-chuck, so we used leftover fish from Long John Silver's. And we were out of cardamom, so we used grated peanuts instead. The last onion in the basket had gone over, so in place of that, we substituted iceberg lettuce and a red pepper. But nothing really major, you see, was changed. Perhaps you should rethink this one and get back to me.*

Soon as I got that letter, I called and talked to a few friends thereabouts who knew Jim pretty well, and they told me that his health was fine and he had not, to their knowledge, been hit over the head with a pole-ax or some such similar object any time recently, so they could vouchsafe the fact that his person was intact. I can only conclude that Jim was born for adventures and to that end, he took my recipe for a hard ride and put it back in the barn sweaty.

Woodchuck with Quince

Serves 3

Woodchuck meat is tender and succulent. To my taste, it's much better than rabbit and easier to hunt. It has a satisfyingly firm texture that holds its own during the cooking process, but a bite of it in your mouth is easy to chew. Woodchuck can't be bought in stores, so if you haven't scared one up lately, then you can substitute lamb, rabbit, or almost any poultry.

> *½ cup fresh cranberries*
> *¼ cup ground coriander*
> *3 quince, cored*
> *2 tablespoons fresh lemon juice*
> *2 pounds woodchuck meat, boned and cut into manageable pieces*
> *2 tablespoons olive oil*
> *1 teaspoon ground cinnamon*
> *½ teaspoon ground nutmeg*

In a small saucepan, heat the cranberries in a couple of inches of water over medium heat until the skins begin to split. Add the ground coriander to it and remove from the heat instantly. Drain and set aside to cool. If you did this right, you might not have to drain it, as most of the water will have steamed away and what is left is mostly cranberry juice.

Cut the quinces into fifths and sprinkle them with the lemon juice.

In a large skillet over medium-high heat, brown the meat in the olive oil, searing the surface but not cooking through, 4 to 5 minutes per side.

Preheat the oven to 400°F.

Place the meat in a nonstick casserole. Start with the larger pieces—thighs and haunches—and reserve the smaller pieces to line the edges. Layer the cranberries over the pieces of woodchuck and place the quinces in a decorative pattern. I like to use a long dish and arrange them into three stars. It's not actually tricky to cut the quinces into five slices each and it looks pretty. Sprinkle the cinnamon and nutmeg over the top.

Bake, covered, for about 20 minutes, then lower the oven temperature to 350°F and continue to bake until a test stick inserted into the meat comes out clear. The best way to test this is to insert a very sharp knife and slip the stick in beside it.

Serve immediately.

 **Protestant Woodchuck Ethics**

I'd love to sit here and relate a humorous anecdote painting woodchucks in a favorable light, but I can't. Truth is, woodchucks are not funny people. The only funny thing that ever took place between me and a woodchuck was more on the order of peculiar—the kind of funny that makes your spine itch.

Woodchucks are too damned serious to be funny—they are absolutely devoid of a sense of humor and less apt to laugh than a chunk of two-by-four is to get up and dance. They got that outraged set to their face like a religious fundamentalist booked into a hotel what's hosting the annual drinkers' and gamblers' convention.

I never saw a woodchuck play, not even the younguns. They have an extremist creed—no dancing, no drinking, nor any undue carrying on, and even breaking into a smile borders on mortal sin.

Many's the time, when I'd spent a little of it with these creatures, that I'd got down on my knees and thanked the Lord that I was not born a woodchuck. If I hadda been, I'd long since have been locked up in woodchuck prison. I can't not have a good time and if I'm not, I'm surely out looking for one. Laughing and playing are life itself to me, and a woodchuck just purely can't stand the sight of somebody gettin' down on a good time.

Once, many years ago now, I tried to strike up a conversation with a woodchuck. I was hoping to chat about the problem and shed a little light on woodchuck ethics, as it were. I'm not saying I didn't learn something useful, but I don't think I got to the heart of the matter, either.

My folks always taught me that understanding people was the key to learning to love them, so I give it my best shot.

I had been putting out lettuce and, naturally, the old boy I was dealing with would no way act like he knew it was there until I'd made myself scarce. I figured we could pass the time getting to know one another. I told him a bit about myself and munched on an apple whilst I was about it so he would know that my canine teeth didn't rule my life. Throughout, he had such a sour face pasted on that I up and asked him, all of a sudden-like, if he had indeed ever laughed once in his life.

Friends, I had no sooner got the words out of my mouth than he commenced to grind his jaws, pulling his mouth down hard, and working the fat of his cheeks around a low threat that seemed to be stuck to his tongue. He'd skinnied his eyes down to slits, gleaming black and angry at me, so I figured that I'd committed some grave infraction by talking about laughing.

I suspect that it's like talking about sex to a Baptist—it's one of those things we all know about, but it's considered in terrible bad taste to bring it up in polite company.

Well, that was that for any little friendship me and that one old boy might ever have struck up. From the way he narrowed his little eyes ever time he saw me, I got the feeling that he had sized me up as one of those fallen creatures that keeps God up nights with a headache.

I expect he's right, but I saw no reason why a personal matter like my private doings should come between us; after all, I never proposed to actually laugh out loud in his presence, nor had I ever brought along a bottle while I was sitting at our chat nor even offered to teach him how to play cards.

I honestly felt bad about disturbing his peace, so I made amends by bringing him a variety of tasty greens to soothe his troubles. I figure if the only pleasure a fella will agree to take out of life is the simple taking of repast, then I could surely do my bit to make that one spark in his life a brighter light.

For a couple of days, while the man in charge and his family learned to expect lunch from the hands of an unreformed sinner, I brought them a selection of lettuces from iceberg to Boston red tip and kept my opinions to myself while they ate it. I went so far as to cover my mouth with my hand when I felt a smile coming on.

Naturally, when I changed the program and offered them the lettuces from the back of a cage, the old man was the first to venture in there to get himself a bit of it.

I came by that same family near a year later and by that time, they had chosen another head man, a younger fella from the look of him, but the spittin' image of his predecessor, right down the dour, no-nonsense expression carved on his face. I offered him a friendly good morning, but he only set his heels and barked at me. His little black eyes squinted in the dim light filtering through the trees.

You'da thought I'd asked him to dance with me.

Such a load of disdain for me and mine poured out of those eyes that I couldn't do naught but burst out laughing. Hoarse wheezing commenced to whistle out of my nose before I could get hold of myself, and by that time, my audience had taken himself underground and kicked dirt out of the hole to let me on as to his opinion of the whole affair. He couldn't have called me a washout any plainer.

Seems as if I'd been born a woodchuck, I wouldn't have kinfolk one who didn't think me a disgrace to the clan. On that score, it wouldn't be so different from what it is now.

Woodchuck Paprikash

Serves 2 or 3

If you don't have woodchuck and you end up substituting either lamb or beef, then you have to tenderize the slices with one of those attitude-adjustment mallets that they sell in kitchen stores. Pound it good until you've taken the fight out of it. If you use either chicken or goose, then the tenderizing step is not necessary.

All-purpose flour
Salt and freshly ground black pepper
2 pounds woodchuck, boned, cut into thin slices
¼ cup olive oil
1½ cups chicken stock
2 pounds fresh mushrooms, halved
1 large onion, very thinly sliced
1½ teaspoons sweet paprika
⅔ cup sour cream

Season the flour with salt and pepper and dredge the meat.

Heat the oil in a skillet over medium-high heat and brown the meat in it, cooking lightly on both sides. As they are browned, transfer the slices into an ovenproof casserole dish with a scant ¼ cup of the chicken stock in it. Cover and cook over low heat while you prepare the mushrooms and onion.

Sauté the mushrooms in the oil remaining in the skillet until brown. Remove with a slotted spoon and set aside.

Sauté the onion in the oil until golden yellow. Add the paprika and the remaining 1¼ cups chicken stock. Simmer for a few minutes, then pour it over the slices of browned meat.

Add the cooked mushrooms to the casserole dish.

In a small bowl, stir 1 tablespoon of flour into the sour cream. Dilute with 2 or 3 tablespoons of the broth from the casserole. Blend completely and then stir it into the casserole. Cook the whole works for 7 to 8 minutes without allowing it to boil (this will separate the cream and ruin the taste).

Remove from heat and serve immediately.

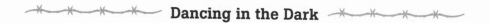

Dancing in the Dark

I was spying out rockchuck holes one day when the sun broke through the clouds and commenced to try to burn the back of my head. Naturally, I'd gone off and left my hat to home, so after I spotted the chuck sign I was looking for, I stuck a few sticks in the ground, wove some tall grass in amongst them, and laid myself out to take a little nap under the bit of shade I'd made for myself. I figured that the critters I was after were probably holed up waiting for the clouds to come back and no use cooking the back of my neck watching for them.

Did I mention how much I purely like to sleep?

Well, when I woke up, it was pretty near dusk. The sun was about to rest his haunches on the mountains and lengthy shadows were stretching along the ground. Rubbing sleep out of my eyes, I crept up to the ridge I was using for cover and peered over towards the holes I had been watching. From where I sat, I could see three chucks. One was lounging on his doorsill, scanning the sky, and the other two were standing in front of their holes with their hands crossed over their bellies.

I reached back and found my rifle with the tips of my fingers and pulled it up beside me, but I never got a shot off. I took my eyes off the chucks for a couple of seconds to load the chamber and when I looked back the scene had changed.

One of the chucks was standing out in the open grass with her back to the burrows. The other one was approaching slowly, swinging his head from side to side. I'm using him and her in this story 'cause that's the only way it makes any sense.

You can laugh all you want. . . . I do. Every time I tell this.

The one chuck walked up to the other, stood up on his hind legs, and tapped the shoulder of the chuck that was standing there looking at the grass. She turned around, looked him up and down, and then put up her hands, palms out. Friends, those two chucks struck a pose like that and then commenced to dance, back and forth and round and round, right there in the grass in front of me for upwards of three or four minutes.

I kept rubbing my eyes, but it kept happening, just like I'm telling it.

I have since heard other marmot hunters tell similar tales, and only a couple of them were apt to take a drink now and then, and none of them, like myself, will touch the stuff when handling guns is the order of the day.

The truth is rockchucks enjoy a slow waltz now and again. Ya gotta love that in a marmot.

Rockchuck in Coconut Curry

Serves 4 or 5

Rockchuck is not quite so tender as its eastern cousin, the woodchuck. Harsh climates have their little drawbacks. Nevertheless, the meat is dark, rich, and satisfying to the taste. I have a real passion for curries myself, and I came up with a recipe a number of years ago when it seems that all the lamb I could come by in the stores musta been raised up in a pen where they didn't get any exercise, 'cause they were all as fat as little pigs. The extra grease in my diet made me feel slow, so I took to experimenting with other meats to satisfy my urge for a good curry now and again. I found out that woodchuck, rockchuck, and rabbit did it up the best, though I still cook it up with lamb, or sometimes chicken, if the mood strikes.

¼ cup peanut oil

2 rockchucks (marmots), boned and cut into chunks about 5 inches long, about 4 pounds

1 teaspoon mustard seeds

1 onion, finely chopped

3 cloves garlic, minced

1- to 2-inch piece fresh ginger, peeled and minced

3 fresh green chiles, seeded and finely chopped

1 tablespoon ground coriander

1 teaspoon ground cumin

1 teaspoon ground turmeric

1½ cups coconut milk (canned or powdered)

½ teaspoon cayenne pepper

¼ cup shredded unsweetened coconut, toasted

Heat the oil in a large skillet over medium-high heat. Brown the marmot, about 10 minutes, turning and stirring constantly to avoid burning. Remove from the pan and set aside.

Pour all but a couple of tablespoons of the oil into a measuring cup for use later.

Throw the mustard seeds into the oil remaining in the skillet and cook for about 1 minute. Add the onion and sauté over medium heat for about 5 minutes. Then stir in the garlic, ginger, chiles, coriander, cumin, and turmeric. Cook for 1 to 2 minutes longer. Add the browned marmot pieces to the pan and stir to coat them in the spices.

Add the coconut milk and bring the whole thing to a low boil. Do not allow it to come to a full rolling boil. Cover and decrease the heat to low. Cook for 35 to 40 minutes.

Remove from heat and transfer the whole works to a handsome serving bowl. Add the cayenne and coconut and serve.

Porcupine

Porcupines are just as addicted to salt as any man ever was to his morning coffee. To hunt porcupine, you simply put out a few blocks of salt and wait. If you have an old pair of work boots that stink pretty bad and the soles have gone too far to be repaired, they'll work just as well. To a porcupine, those boots reek of the salt you've sweated into them over the years. If you live in porcupine country, you already know this, especially if you've ever left your boots on the porch or your gloves hanging on the fence to air. If they can't get it anywhere else, porcupines will chew up the handles of tools that you've dripped your sweat on.

Thanks to the interstate highway system and the popularity of cars and trucks in America, the porcupine population suffers great loses through accidental encounters with motor vehicles. Their formidable defense system works against them in this case. Porcupines rarely run from anybody. Why should they? Nobody much is stupid enough to take them on. Even the most determined predator generally gets just close enough for the porcupine's quills to adjust his attitude permanently. It's a painful lesson that no one has to learn twice.

Trouble is, porcupines rely so heavily on their reputation that they expect cars to back down as well. They move fairly slowly and resent having an intruder try to hurry them, with the result that a sizable number of them end up as roadkill.

Personally, I've never shot a female or an immature youngster either. Salt blocks are cheap, and waiting until a middle-aged male happens along is not too much to ask for the preservation of the animal's future.

While I'm on the subject, I should mention that I've rarely had to spend bullets on porcupine at all. Enough young males cross the road each year to make guns virtually unnecessary in the hunting of these animals. So long as there's ample snow on the ground and the body hasn't been lying there long enough to cool, it's safely edible. To check, cut open the chest and feel the heart—if its cold, he's been dead for two hours or more, and all you can do is move him off the road for decency's sake. Best not to make a meal, even in winter, of any animal that's been dead for more than one hour.

Field Dressing and Preparation

To dress porcupine, you will need a good pair of leather work gloves and a couple of blocks of soft Styrofoam. You can get the quills out safely with the Styrofoam just by touching the flat surface to the tips. The quills are confined to the back—from the shoulders to the haunches—and to the tail.

When the spines have been removed, field dress as you would for rabbit (see page 140).

Most folks think of porcupines as small, but they're not. They can grow to be up to 30 inches in length (excluding the tail, which is generally 9 or 10 inches long) and weigh up to 30 pounds.

✳──✳──✳──✳ Sweating the Small Stuff ✳──✳──✳──✳

Remember what I said about porcupines and their love of salt? Well, I'm here to tell you that no matter how careful you are, if you live in porcupine country, those babies and their habits are gonna get you sooner or later. I've lost many a hoe and shovel handle to the salt craze. I guess on that score, I've been lucky, or relatively so, since I've heard horror stories of porcupines that got into folks' barns and chewed up the saddles and tack. At least all the stuff I've lost to this salt madness of theirs has been replaceable, mostly.

One year, I put in a sizable garden, much bigger than I would have for just me and my son alone. I had the space for growing things, and a good number of friends who didn't have none planted stuff in that plot of ground and helped out with the water bills, if not always with the watering. Consequently, on weekends when everybody gathered to weed their plots, I had quite a throng of sweaty folks taking a break on the corner of my porch. A lot of guys took a bit of relief for their sweaty backs, flopped over on those cool boards of a hot afternoon.

I had never painted the porch because it was under a substantial eave and I liked the way the wood looked. In the winter, I'd haul out the storm windows and block in the porch so that it never suffered from snow buildup.

The porcupines got to it in the fall, scarcely a week before I was planning to put the windows up. Seems all those sweaty boards drew them out of the woods of an autumn night because when I came out the door the next day, that hapless porch had been gnawed and clawed at something terrible.

I can't say I blame the poor creatures. I knew they'd be looking for their salt presently, but I hadn't bought any that year. Likely, they were accustomed to me putting it out, so they came by my place to look for it. I expect that I got somewhat of what I deserved for pandering to their habits like that and then slipping up on the supply.

Porcupine in Pomegranate Sauce

Serves 2 or 3

Porcupine meat has a surprisingly sweet flavor to it so it lends itself really well to recipes with fruit sauces. The meat is light and juicy but tends to dry out if left to bake uncovered or unadorned by a sauce of some sort. Wood-chuck, prairie dog, or lamb also works well with this recipe. Most birds, with the exception of roadrunner and turkey, will do as well.

This dish goes well if served with rice or couscous.

> ¾ cup dried apricots
> 1 large Vidalia onion, diced
> ¼ cup peanut oil
> 2 pounds boneless porcupine meat, cut into large stewing cubes
> 1½ cups water
> ⅛ teaspoon ground cardamom
> Pinch of lemon pepper
> 2½ cups pomegranate juice

Soak the apricots in hot water to cover for 1 hour. Drain well.

In a large skillet over medium-high heat, brown the onion in the oil just until it turns a handsome amber. Add the porcupine meat as soon as the onion turns yellow, but before it reaches the amber stage. Sauté the meat, stirring constantly to prevent sticking, for 5 to 7 minutes.

Add the water, cardamom, and lemon pepper. Bring to a boil and cook, covered, over medium heat for about 10 minutes. Add the apricots and continue to cook over low heat for 40 minutes. Add the pomegranate juice and cook for 10 minutes to allow the flavors to resolve.

Transfer to a serving dish and serve hot.

⟶✳⟶✳⟶✳ Seeing Red—But in a Good Way ✳⟶✳⟶✳

Porcupines love the color red. Their love for the color red is even greater than their love of salt. You want to make friends with a porcupine, then leave out a red flannel work shirt that's acquired too many faults to be repaired any longer. What with red and the odor of salt in the same item, they'll happily take the offering.

Spring is a good time to leave them presents, since they dearly love to use bits of old flannel to line a nest to receive their kitten. Porcupines have only one kitten a year, and they put considerable affection into their young. The little ones are hardy and can climb trees and forage for themselves within a few days of birth. Their quills are soft at first—just like any other hair—but by the time they are able to get around, the quills have hardened and they can go out in the world with their defenses armed and ready.

I've put out many a scrap of red flannel myself, and I know a host of other folks who do the same. If there are any nearby, porcupines will collect red flowers to brighten up the nest for the kitten.

I had a guy tell me once that he lost an entire set of long johns (colored red, naturally) that his wife had washed and hung on the line out back of their place. I would dearly love to have seen that while it was happening. I can't imagine how it was accomplished, but I suspect if you want something bad enough, you'll manage. Somewhere out near Talpa, New Mexico, there's a family of porcupines with an impressive family heirloom in their possession.

Flattened and dyed, porcupine quills make excellent embroidery material. There are books out there that will tell you more about the techniques for doing this work.

You can collect porcupine quills for quill embroidery by using an old piece of wool blanket that's secured to a post. A quill is just specialized hair, and, like your own hair when you brush it in the morning, a porcupine's quills are regularly falling out and being replaced. If you tie the bit of red blanket firmly to the post, but leave it so as it has a narrow tail at one end, the porcupine will deem it a good thing if he just chews off the bit of tail, but while he's at it, his backside spends some time rubbing at the blanket and he'll leave a number of quills in it.

My son figured a faster way to get more quills using a blanket. You notice I did not say better, just faster.

He determined that you could coax a porcupine into donating a few hundred quills if you followed him about with a blanket—watching him careful-like to see when he was about to get fed up with your uppity ways—and then pitch the blanket over his back just about the time he was prepared to teach your sorry ass a lesson. Just before a porcupine slaps you with his tail, the muscles along either side of his spine bunch and shiver a bit. If they're already into the shivering stage by the time you fling your blanket, then your covering action might be a tad late. You need to cover yourself by covering him exactly when he starts to bunch.

Like I said, faster, but not better. Maybe it's just 'cause I'm starting to get older, but some things are just way to exciting for my taste.

By the way, porcupines do not throw their quills at you. That's a myth. They move pretty slowly unless they're mad, so at first, it may not seem like they're capable of moving so quickly that you can't see them doing it. Temper equals lightning speed in a porcupine. He bunches his muscles for the event, then he jumps up, slaps, and turns in a partial circle so quick that you need a high-speed camera to catch it. Mind you, I'm not recommending that you follow him around annoying him with a camera unless you just like trouble.

Porcupine Stuffed with Walnuts and Spinach

Serves 6

The small amounts of meat on the front legs and the lower part of the rear legs of the porcupine are very difficult to apply to this recipe, but I sure wouldn't want you to think that they have to go to waste. They work very well ground and used in the recipe for chipmunk patties on page 204.

If the technique for getting yourself a porcupine is eluding you, then try this recipe with chicken, turkey, pork, or woodchuck.

1 porcupine, about 4 pounds
2 tablespoons ground cardamom
1 teaspoon ground cinnamon
⅔ cup plain yogurt
4 cups fresh spinach, tough stems and veins removed
¾ cup walnuts, halved
½ cup matzo meal
1 teaspoon onion powder

Bone the porcupine thigh meat, taking care to remove the bone without cutting through the meat entirely—you want to have a small pocket, resembling a pita, when you have removed the bone. With the rib and shoulder meat, fillet very close to the bone.

Stir 1 tablespoon of the cardamom and ½ teaspoon of the cinnamon into the yogurt and allow it to sit for about 30 minutes. Add the spinach and the walnuts.

Put the matzo meal into a shallow dish and stir in the onion powder and the remaining 1 tablespoon cardamom and ½ teaspoon cinnamon.

Stuff the walnut-and-spinach mixture into the cavities you created in the porcupine thighs. With the fillets, you can choose to either layer them like sandwiches or use a bit of heavy thread and stitch the edges until you have made a small pocket out of two together. If you use the thread method, be sure to use white or natural thread so you can see it and so you don't add dye chemicals to your repast. Don't forget to pull out the thread before you serve the porcupine at the table.

Preheat oven to 350°F. Lightly grease a large baking dish.

Lay the pieces of stuffed porcupine in the matzo meal, turning them gently until they are coated on both sides. This is where the thread method makes handling the meat much easier.

Place the pieces in the prepared baking dish. Cover. Bake for about 30 minutes, until a sharpened stick inserted into the thick part of the meat comes out clean. If any blood is present or if the stick is stained pink, bake for another 10 minutes.

Remove from the oven, transfer to a serving dish, and serve immediately.

Raccoon

The reputation that raccoons have for carrying rabies is well earned. They didn't get it by accident. If you aren't familiar with the species, then don't go out hunting one without a companion who knows their little ways. While we're on the subject—don't ever follow a raccoon into the water—they'll climb on top of your head and try to drown you. Dogs get drowned by raccoons this way all the time. If he goes up a tree, trust your gun to bring him down. Climbing up after him is the best way I know to get your face rearranged short of taking a paring knife to it. The results are pretty much the same. If you make this little mistake, you can save yourself a lot of embarrassment by telling your friends that you had a little too much to drink and fell out of the hayloft into the harvester.

Field Dressing and Preparation

If you bring down a sow, then the field dressing is pretty straightforward. So long as you don't rupture the spleen or the bladder, the meat will taste sweet. A boar has to be handled a bit differently. Make a light cut down the belly—just deep enough to split the skin and allow you to peel it back from the flesh. Now go really careful, just like you were trying to peel a tomato without getting juice all over your wife's new tablecloth. Start high up on the chest, but don't let the breastbone fool you into bearing down too hard with your knife. Cut the skin and slip your hands inside the carcass to force the opening wider. Cut a mighty big circle around the testicles and the anus, being very careful not to nick them anywhere. With your hand in the carcass, pull downward, scooping the guts into your palm, and carry the whole works out and away and lay them on the grass. If you nicked anything you will know it when you dress the meat for cooking, because it will stink to high heaven of raccoon musk.

Remove the glands from under the skin in each foreleg and one on each side of the spine in the small of the back. Scrape away all visible fat.

Preferably, the raccoon should be less than two years old to reduce toughness. Raccoons grow to be nearly 4 feet in length, with about 10 to 12 inches of that accounted for by the tail. A big boar will weigh in at around 35 pounds; that's not the one you want to eat. Pick yourself a youngster about one year old and under 20 pounds, or not even champagne will tenderize the meat. Even the strongest teeth will feel the strain of trying to chew a mature boar. You don't believe me? Next time a hound dog of your acquaintance kills a raccoon, ask him if he ate it. If it was an old boar and he says yes, then he's either a liar or he hadn't had nothing to eat for better than a week. Desperation and starvation, unfortunately, still account for a big part of a dog's taste in edibles.

Interiors by Idle Hands, Inc.

Raccoons have clever little hands and can perform such charming stunts as opening jars and such. They also open cage doors pretty well and are bright enough to figure out just about any cage mechanism. Folks that keep raccoons for pets generally keep the cage door shut with a sturdy combination lock or padlock.

For myself, I can't figure out why they keep them in the house in the first place, since they don't make especially good pets. You can't go off and leave them alone in the room, unless you want it to look like a tornado's been through there, and they resent being locked up so much that they generally spend the time incarcerated planning what outrage they're going to commit.

I had a friend once who had a son with a pet raccoon. Seems that one day the kid forgot to lock up his pet before he left for school, and nobody else in the house knew the animal was afoot (hiding under the bed like as not, and since the boy's mom wasn't doing the laundry or nothing, nobody had looked under there).

As soon as the house fell silent, the raccoon came out and started getting those clever little hands of his into everything he could reach. Trouble is, he could climb pretty good, too, so there wasn't much he couldn't reach. By the time the family returned home, he'd done up the place so as to win an interior decorator's gold star—that is if the decorator in question happened to be a raccoon.

For starters, he musta thought he'd kick back and listen to a couple tapes and have a snack because a whole tribe of CDs and cassette tapes crouched in the middle of the carpet with cookie crumbs scattered in amongst them.

Cookies must not have been doing the trick for him, though. From the evidence, he wanted something in a bowl and just couldn't find one he liked that was big enough to suit him. Most of the cereal bowls and a couple of serving dishes had been discarded on the kitchen floor none too gently. In the end, he settled for the sink as a likely repository for his repast, and he dumped a box of grits in there and poured maple syrup over them.

I coulda told him that grits aren't much good until they are cooked, but naturally he didn't ask. He messed it around a bit, but he didn't eat much of it. He ate a bunch of fruit, but the only place he could wash it in was the toilet. He did pretty well for awhile, then he managed to get a grapefruit stuck in the pipes.

There was water in his cage, only he didn't want to get in there for it—somebody might come home and close the door on him.

He found plenty of water in the refrigerator and succeeded in washing slices of cheese in it for awhile until he got greedy and tried to dunk a handful of marmalade. Yes, raccoons feel compelled to wash everything before they put it in their mouth, even if most of it dissolves in the process.

Sometime during the day, he found he'd eaten so much that nature was calling him so he found himself a nice soft spot in the back of an overstuffed recliner to relieve himself, then he covered it up with a handy afghan.

The family, even the kid, was none to happy with this behavior. Seems the tapes had belonged to the boy, and the chair had been the old man's favorite before the raccoon requisitioned it for a toilet.

They offered him to me as a sacrifice to the barbecue pit, but I didn't take them up on it.

I make it a policy never to eat a friend or a friend of a friend, even if the aforementioned friends are not on speaking terms any longer.

Raccoon with Garlic and Scallions

Serve 4 to 6

If you don't want to risk being seen buying cheap champagne, then get into the habit of scavenging half bottles of flat stuff laying around the house after a sizable New Year's party. It's okay to pour together the remainders out of drinks that your guests have left laying around on the furniture since the whole thing is going to be cooked anyway. Raccoon meat is a little greasy, and I don't recommend eating it at all without marinating it first. A good alcohol-based marinade will help draw out some of the fats and improve the flavor of the meat considerably. You will need a barbecue or smoker grill big enough to allow for ample space to cook the raccoon without crowding. Use charcoal—not wood—so the fire is even and stays hot long enough to cook the meat clear through.

I once cooked up a pit-smoked raccoon that had been marinated in brandy overnight. I cut the carcass into manageable bits and smoked it over mesquite, basting it with a mild citrus-based sauce instead of the traditional tomato. It turned out to be very toothsome indeed, though more than one guest present informed me that it was something of an acquired taste. I don't know about that—I acquired it the minute I set lip to the stuff.

Beef, lamb, chicken, pork, and rabbit all make adequate substitutes for raccoon. This recipe is great served with roasted corn and salad.

> *1 raccoon*
> *1 (750-ml) bottle cheap champagne*
> *½ cup honey*
> *3 to 4 cloves garlic, peeled*
> *A bunch of scallions, white parts only (save the greens*
>   *for the salad)*

Clean the raccoon thoroughly, rinsing the body cavity with a dollop of champagne. Don't be cheap; you can spare it and it really does make a difference in the final result.

Quarter the carcass by slicing along the spine first, then divide the breast into halves and separate from the hind quarters. Dilute the honey with ½ cup champagne and rub the mixture all over the meat, especially inside the gut. Put the whole works down in a deep glass bowl and pour the rest of the champagne over it. Let it rest in the back of the refrigerator for 6 to 8 hours. If you can spare the time, leave it overnight.

Remove the meat from the champagne bath and lay the pieces out on a cutting board. Using a good sharp knife, make a host of little slices in the flesh and push the garlic and scallion heads into the cuts. Use it all. You can't get too much onion and garlic with a raccoon.

Prepare a hot charcoal fire in a grill.

Roast the meat over charcoal for about 30 minutes a pound, or until you can easily pull the meat away from the bone with a fork. If you're using a thermometer, it should read 170°F.

The meat reheats well so you can either prepare it ahead of time or serve it hot off the grill.

Beaver

I got into the habit of eating beaver that were caught by other folks. Beaver are not in any danger in the wild, since they breed easily, and they have no qualms about setting up housekeeping near human habitation, if that is where their path leads them. They've been known to flood small creeks running through posh subdivisions, so it's not like the beaver is a shy retiring fellow that needs to be coaxed into looking after number one first. If a likely source of water beckons, he'll lay a trap for it and build his lodge, regardless of whether or not your Mercedes floats away in the process.

Beaver fur is highly prized by those who know about such things, though for myself, I prefer wool. Wool fluffs up nicely, snuggling down next to your skin and making itself to home. I've never trapped a beaver myself. Since I have no interest in their skin, and I won't kill anything if the skin is all that I am after, I never had the opportunity to taste the beaver until somebody offered me one. It's very good, but I must confess, I can give you no hints as to how you would go about acquiring one.

I'll say it one more time: If I'm going to kill something, then I'm going to use all of it that I can or else find a home for it with a friend who wants it; otherwise, me and that animal are never going to cross paths at all. It's respect, as much as anything else. I don't believe in waste, and killing something for the sport or the skin is plain and simply a waste. If you know somebody who traps beaver now and then for the skin, offer to take the meat and learn to cook it.

Field Dressing and Preparation

Field dress as you would for rabbit (see page 140). Remove the glands in the armpits and in the small of the back and along the inside of the thighs. Locate the castor gland directly in front of the genital area—in the extreme lower belly—of both males and females. Remove the castor gland, being especially careful not to cut it. Soak the meat overnight in water to which 2 tablespoons of vinegar and $1/4$ cup salt per gallon have been added.

An adult beaver can weigh between 50 and 75 pounds, and, oddly enough, an old beaver actually tastes better than a yearling.

Beaver Moussaka

Serves 5 to 6

If more folks took the time to scrape the fat away and cook the beaver instead of just collecting the skin and leaving the carcass, then beaver might well be on the list of animals that are raised for meat and hide like cows and sheep are. There's usually quite a layer of disagreeable-looking fat just under the pelt, so I suspect that's why folks don't give it a fair shake. Well, that and the fact that humans have this prejudice against anything that looks vaguely like a rodent. Go figure.

Lamb, beef, and woodchuck all make adequate substitutes for the beaver in this recipe.

> *2 pound boneless rabbit*
> *2 pounds beaver (stick with the hindlegs, loin,*
>   *and saddle for best results)*
> *3 large eggplants, peeled*
> *¾ cup plus 5 tablespoons butter*
> *¾ cup all-purpose flour, plus more for dredging*
> *6 cups milk*
> *Salt and freshly ground black pepper*
> *1 teaspoon ground nutmeg*
> *1 cup olive oil*
> *2 medium onions, finely chopped*
> *2 cloves garlic, minced*
> *2 cups red wine*
> *2 cups tomato paste*
> *1½ cups chicken stock*
> *¼ teaspoon dried oregano*
> *½ teaspoon ground cinnamon*
> *1 pound fresh mushrooms, halved*
> *1 cup freshly grated Romano cheese*

Put the rabbit through a meat grinder and set aside in the refrigerator. (This is where you can use all those little bits of leftovers that are too small to use anywhere else—shoulders, front limbs, etc.) Slice the meat and cut into 1-inch cubes. Set aside with the rabbit.

Slice the eggplant into thin slices and cover with 2 quarts water and ½ cup salt. Allow it to sit for about 30 minutes, then drain and rinse. Drain thoroughly and pat dry with paper towels.

To make the béchamel sauce, melt ¾ cup of the butter in a saucepan over medium-low heat so as to prevent scorching. Add ¾ cup of the flour, slowly, stirring it into the butter with a whisk. Cook, stirring constantly so that the mixture does not scorch. If it starts to turn brown, ditch it and start over. You screwed up. In a separate pan, heat the milk until almost boiling. Add it hot to the butter-and-flour mixture. Now you really have to stir and I mean vigorously. Cook, stirring all the while, until the mixture thickens, then allow it to simmer for another 5 minutes. Don't give up on that stirring. You don't have to do it at such a furious pace, but check it now and again to be sure it isn't sticking. When you think you've had enough and you're ready to allow it to cool, season with salt, pepper, and the nutmeg.

Heat some oil in a large skillet over medium-high heat. Dredge the eggplant in flour and brown on both sides, working in batches to prevent crowding the pan. Drain. Clean the pan. You're fixing to use it again.

Melt 3 tablespoons of the butter in the pan and add the onions and garlic. Sauté until the onions are golden.

Add the beaver to the pan and brown for about 5 minutes before adding the rabbit. Cook for another 10 minutes.

Add the wine, tomato paste, chicken stock, oregano, cinnamon, and some pepper. Cook until very little of the liquid remains in the pan, 10 to 12 minutes.

In a separate pan over medium-high heat, sauté the mushrooms in the remaining 2 tablespoons butter, until the mushrooms give up their juices, about 8 minutes.

Preheat the oven to 400°F.

Oil the biggest roasting pan you have. It should be 3 to 4 inches deep, and it could stand to be at least 12 by 18 inches or some such equivalent size. Arrange half of the eggplant slices in the bottom. Next, layer the meat over the eggplant. Layer the mushrooms over the meat and, finally, cover with the remaining slices of eggplant.

Pour the béchamel sauce over the top and sprinkle the Romano cheese over the top.

Bake for 1 hour. Let stand for 10 minutes before serving.

Rattlesnake

Is there anybody out there who doesn't know that (1) rattlesnakes bite and (2) they're poisonous? Right, now that I have your complete attention let me just add for the benefit of those of you who like to live dangerously that you shouldn't go poking around in the bush for one of these babies unless you've done it before—successfully—and/or you go along with somebody who's good at it.

If you're not sure if your friend is stringing you along or not, then check his hands, knees, and ankles for bite wounds. These are the most common places to be bit and survive the experience. You get a bite high on the stomach, the meat side of your armpit, or anywhere above the shoulders, then the last thing you're going to be worrying about is dinner.

If you go out hunting snakes, take the time to learn the difference between a male and a female, and restrict your attentions to the former. A female rattlesnake only produces three to four clutches of young in her lifetime. Killing even one puts a serious crimp in the population. Since the animals are dedicated to a family territory and survivors will seldom leave it to mate again, you should never clean out a den and bag every snake you find. Leave the females and at least one beau for the next generation.

Snakes bite, but don't kid yourself, nobody packs a rougher bite that does more damage or lasts longer than man does. When you're out there digging around, have some respect, for yourself and the snakes.

Field Dressing and Preparation

Skin the snake and split him down the belly with a sharp knife. Pull out all the organs and rinse with water. Some folks scrape with a spoon to clean. You're welcome to do that if it suits you.

Hopefully, you cut off his head and tail in the field. Keeping the tail is fun—it dries easily, but keeping the head is not only foolhardy, it's dangerous. A rattlesnake can be dead a long time and still bite you. That sac of poison will stay there in his head for weeks waiting for a bit of soft flesh to brush against the teeth. Basically, until the entire head is dried out and desiccated, you can count on that poison still being in there waiting for somebody to come along and claim it. Don't you do it. When you kill a snake, cut off the head, dig a hole, and bury it a foot deep, and thank you, friend, for taking the time to do it right.

It's always necessary to steam a snake a bit first if you want to cook it without the bones. A snake's muscles hook right onto the vertebrae, overlaying each other in a long line. There isn't any such thing as boning a snake without steaming it first—if you try it, you'll end up with a pile of scraggly bits. That's why you hear so much about snake stew. Stewing a snake is the easiest way to deal with claiming the meat from the skeleton.

Boning a snake is hard work and takes lots of practice, but if at first it eludes you, not to worry. Make rattlesnake pot pie out of the bits and try again later. You'll get it right with time and experience.

⚊✳⚊ An Apple That Day Kept the Rattlesnake Away ✳⚊

Most folks think that all you have to do to find a rattlesnake is walk out in the fields and kick around a bit—not true. Contrary to popular opinion, snakes are not prowling around looking for somebody to bite. Most of the time, they hear you coming and slip away someplace quiet. They'd just as soon you leave them alone and be about your business elsewhere.

In fact, walking around a field with boots on is one of the best ways to clear out the snakes so the kids can play football. Carry a stick to swish the grass with, stomp about and yell back and forth to your buddies if you want to put a snake on the highway out of town. They hate uproar and they'll run before they'll fight.

That's partly why hunting them is an occupation that is best approached with no small degree of caution. In order to hunt a snake, you have to be deadly quiet and poke him out of his hiding place without his knowing that you're looking for him. If you don't think this is likely to piss him off, then try imaging how you'd feel if a snake crept up on you and caught you taking a nap.

To hunt rattlesnakes you need at least two people; three is even a better idea (in case somebody gets bit and you have to carry him back to the truck). Wearing boots is a must. A good leather boot will turn a bite to the toe into a bad scare instead of a trip to the hospital. Generally, a .22 rifle will do the job; and unless you're a good shot, it's easier to handle than a pistol.

Blowing away something as small as a snake's head with a pistol is something that generally happens most often in the movies.

Carry a rifle and take advantage of the fact that a small but accurate sight helps a lot when drawing a bead on a snake. Also, everyone should carry a sharp hunting knife and a small folding shovel for burying the heads. A canvas bag will help you get your booty back to the truck without having to sling it over your shoulder.

You can do it that way, but don't count on wearing that shirt to a party later.

A forked stick about four to five feet long will help you keep your snake pinned while you cut off his head. Herpetologists deplore the use of the forked stick because it hurts the snake. When pinned in this fashion, the snake will naturally try to pull his head out, causing injury to the spine. If all you want to do is look at your snake, it's kinda cruel to leave him with a neck cramp without the benefit of a chiropractor, but if you're gonna cut his head off anyway, I don't see the harm.

Rattlesnakes like to hang out under rocks and around the base of prickly pear cactus. Creeping along turning over rocks with the tip of your shovel is one good way to find a few snakes, but your chances of finding a really big one that way are slim. A rock big enough to satisfy a good-sized snake is going to be too big to turn over easily. If you get your shoulders into the business, then you're much too likely to have the soft part of your belly or your face in the line of fire when your intended quarry figures out just what's going on and makes up his mind to put a stop to it. Not good.

Prickly pear taste pretty good in their own right, so one good way to find a snake is to head for an impressive growth of prickly cactus and start taking it down with a long-handled shovel. Don't be so foolish as to put your foot on that shovel to push. Use your shoulders and cup the end of the shovel handle with your palms and push that way. It's a good idea to have your friend stand nearby with his rifle in case you make somebody really mad when you start taking down his home.

If you're lucky, the snake will take off running out the other side. Another good reason to bring along three people is to give you an extra to cover this option. Once out in the grass running for his life, the snake is vulnerable.

Generally, he will strike to let you know he's had enough of your fooling around, and your best bet to get your stick on his neck is in the first second after he recoils. With his head pinned to the ground, you can cut it off with your knife, but just you secure your position with a boot to back up your stick before you try it. You can slip pretty easy bending over, and you want more on your side than just a little stick that doesn't have a thing to lose by slacking off for a few seconds. A few seconds is all a snake needs.

With his head cut off and buried, he's not only harmless, he's lunch. On to the next stand of cactus and good luck.

A friend and me scored a couple of sizable rattlesnakes with a pick-up truck once. The pick-up had a big hole in the floorboard, namely, the entire passenger side floor. We were driving through a field, sort of a shortcut to his house, though I don't think his wife thought much of it, since the corner of her cornfield got in the way during our little sojourn.

Halfway across the field, we ran over a snake, and the wheels threw it up into the seat with us. It was pretty rowdy in the cab for a while, but since the snake was still recovering from a close encounter with a steel-belted radial, I got the upper hand and cut his head off with a knife.

It might have turned out differently if I hadn't been quartering an apple about the time he joined us, but then, the fortunes of war often turn in our favor on the simplest of details.

I was ready for it when the second one flew into my lap and made quick work of the business. I must admit, my friend invented a truly original way to hunt snakes, but I don't recommend this method to amateurs. Not only is it way too exciting for most people, it can contribute to a heart condition.

I didn't think to check my friend for bite marks until after. He had too many suspicious scars on his hands and shins to my way of thinking.

Rattlesnake Stuffed with Ground Chicken and Pecans

Serves 6 to 8

You'll need a big rattlesnake because you can't stuff anything smaller than 4 feet in length. That said, I have to add that diamondbacks and timber rattlers are your best choice.

> *1 big rattlesnake, skinned and gutted*
> *2 cups ground chicken (available in the grocery store)*
> *1 tablespoon peanut or safflower oil*
> *1 cup chopped pecans*
> *1 teaspoon dried tarragon*
> *½ teaspoon onion powder*
> *1 cup mushroom gravy*

Put the snake in a steamer pot well above several inches of boiling water and coax the meat away from the bone gently.

While the snake is taking his steam bath, brown the ground chicken in the oil over medium-high heat until it's about half pink still. Let cool.

When the half-cooked chicken is cool, mix in the pecans, tarragon, and onion powder.

Remove the snake from the steamer and allow to cool before you mess with it. The meat should come off the bones easily with only a little pulling. Don't use a knife unless you want to lose half your filling out of the hole you're gonna make. You should be able to slip your fingers into the cut you made and pull the bone away with your other hand.

Preheat the oven to 325°F.

Lay the snake meat out on a cutting board and begin scooping the chicken filling into it, bearing in mind that you can't sew it shut if you mound it up too high.

Using a simple gathering stitch, take up both sides of the cut. Leave the thread completely visible so you can pull it out again before you serve the snake at table.

Bake in an unglazed clay pot with a lid for about 45 minutes. Pull out the thread and cut into 4-inch lengths.

Serve with mushroom gravy for a special treat.

──✳──✳──✳─ The Summer of My Discomfort ─✳──✳──✳──

Remember I recommended you take a buddy with you rattlesnake hunting? I don't always follow my own advice so good and, on one memorable occasion, insolence and greed got me as close as I ever want to get to big-time trouble. Course, I was a kid when me and this particular snake of memory ran across each other's path, so there's a lot of room there for me to let myself off the hook, but considering that the tragic outcome turned out to be the best thing that coulda happened, I'm grateful for it and I try to recall it in vivid detail before I set out for snake alone again.

Okay, I'm getting ahead of myself. Here it is. Picture it: High summer in the Texas hill country. Mesquite, scrub cedar. The grass is a good knee deep and waving its yellow stalks in the breeze. Grasshoppers, horned toads, and rattlesnakes are the only folks about that aren't sitting on the porch with a glass of ice tea, fanning themselves. Even the windmill is turning slowly, doing its work without building up a sweat.

I could hear my mother in the kitchen, and a little voice in the back of my head told me that if I didn't clear off, I was about to be elected to walk into town for butter, or sugar, or some such stuff I didn't have any interest in. Naturally, I picked up a stick and headed through the corn instead of over the fields where I could be easily spotted from the house.

I had recalled a nice stand of break rocks on the hill over the tank and how it had sprouted a thick head of prickly pear that summer. I checked to make sure that my knife was in my jeans and all was well with the world in that regard.

Turns out, I didn't have to go all the way to the hill above the stock tank to find snakes. The biggest snake I ever saw before or since found me.

I was coming along the row, along the main thoroughfare as it were, and this big boy just brazened out in front of me. I guess right-of-way doesn't mean much if your front bumper is equipped with an impressive set of fangs because I clearly had it, and he clearly had no intention of giving an inch.

Well, the truth is, there wasn't much traffic, just me, and I wasn't making much noise to let him know that I was coming. The dirt in the row was soft, and I was moving slow so the sun would slide over me and not draw a bead. That snake didn't even look at me.

I'm thinking later that he must have smelled a mouse or something and couldn't take the time to worry about something so insignificant as a kid with a stick. We both would have come off better for it if he hadn't been so dead set on answering his stomach or either I had walked into town for that butter.

As fate would have it, we met in that corn row, and I even had a reliable stick in my hand. I didn't think about the fact that his body was twice bigger around than my arm, until I had his head pinned and was occupied with reaching for my knife. I never got to that part.

Friends, he knew he was bigger than me, and he wasn't having any nonsense. As soon as I bent down to hold his head, he wrapped his body around my arm and gave me a little warning squeeze. Too late. By that time, I was already picturing the look on everybody's face when I broke from the corn with a snake who was longer than my Uncle Henry was tall.

It's hard to think clearly with a swelled head. Mine was so big at that point that I wonder that my neck muscles could hold it up.

When his first overture didn't get results, he got serious and I quit fumbling for my knife to get a good grip on him. I'm guessing that pissed him off because no sooner did I get both hands on his neck than he doubled his efforts to squeeze me. He wrapped around my arm all the way to the shoulder and threw himself over to the other side, but he wasn't hugging me for any friendly feelings.

I don't know where that little voice was that warned me of my mother's intentions to send me on an errand. It certainly had nothing to say about snakes and right then, I coulda used a little inside advantage.

I knew I needed help cutting off his head, so I started back up the row, carrying my prize out before me. He most definitely didn't want to be carried away from whatever it was he was tracking for lunch, plus, he'd decided himself to teach me a lesson for grabbing him up like that.

He took a good hold of my arm, bunching his muscles and drawing back on his head. Each time he did that, he made maybe a hair's breadth in his efforts to pull his head out of my grip, but it wasn't long before I could see that in time, he would pull his head out altogether. No matter how hard I squeezed on his neck, there was nothing I could do to stop him. When he got his head loose, he'd be wrapped around me with his business end free to take whatever revenge he deemed due.

I was sweating pretty heavy by this time, and I truly don't think the summer sun had a thing to do with it.

I started hollering for my dad even before I cleared the corn and that's when the curse hit me hard. . . . He had walked into town to get my mom some butter.

At that point, I was never happier in my life than to see my brother up on the roof of the house, hunting for lizards. The tip of that snake's nose was just then disappearing under the shadow of my fingers.

Between us, we got a good grip on the menace and unwound him, pitching him into the empty oil drum my dad used for a trash barrel rather than put him down on the ground where he could come at us.

My mom came out the backdoor just in time to catch sight of us and jump straight out of her shoes. She recovered quick enough though and got a better grip on my shoulder than that snake ever had. She dragged me into the house and stripped me down to search for bites. My brother came along quietly—he was always the good kid in the family.

I was just getting dressed again when I smelled the smoke. Out in the yard, my dad had returned and pitched a bunch of brush he had cleared away that morning into the trash barrel. We burned stuff like that every other day or so and the flames from this batch were licking the heat out of the sky when I tore out of the backdoor—too late—to rescue my snake.

He was burned up in the bottom of the trash barrel. All I ever saw of him again were a few blackened bones. I'm grateful that I didn't get bit though.

They say stupidity is its own reward, but I missed mine that day.

Lucky is too mild a word for it.

Rattlesnake Pot Pie with Prickly Pear Apples

Serves 4

I usually end up making this out of leftovers or the temperamental small-fry that come after me when I'm harvesting prickly pear apples, thus the combination in this recipe.

1 small rattlesnake, skinned and cut into pieces
¼ cup peanut oil
12 to 14 pearl onions
6 medium prickly pear apples, whole or quartered, as you prefer
⅓ cup cold butter
1¾ cups all-purpose flour
¼ cup cold water plus ¼ cup room-temperature water
1 cup cooked fava beans
Pinch of freshly ground black pepper

Steam the snake for about 10 minutes, or just until you can coax the meat away from the bones with a fork.

In a large skillet over medium-high heat, brown the snake meat in the oil. Toss in the onions and prickly pear apples a scant minute before the snake is ready to be removed from the heat. Set aside.

Cut the cold butter into 1½ cups of the flour with a pastry blender or two knives. When it is crumbly in appearance, toss in the ¼ cup cold water, and mix until a smooth dough forms. Don't overwork it. You'll make it tough.

Divide the dough into two balls, one slightly larger than the other. On a lightly floured surface, roll out the larger ball of dough with a rolling pin until it is ⅛ inch thick and use it to line a greased pie pan. Prick with a fork.

Place the prickly pear apples in the pie pan in a rough star shape, saving one for the center. Arrange the snake and the onions around them and fill with the fava beans.

Reheat the oil remaining in the pan over medium heat. Make a thin gravy by stirring in the remaining ¼ cup flour and a little pepper into it for taste. Keep it smooth by stirring with a fork and add the ¼ cup room-temperature water before it can scorch. Keep the heat low to avoid scorching. Pour the gravy over the pie.

Preheat the oven to 350°F.

Roll out the remaining pie dough and seal the pie by laying it on top and crimping the edges shut. Prick the top with a fork.

Bake for about 40 minutes, until the pie is golden brown.

Serve hot.

Radical Cure

When my cousin Carlton and I used a snake to cure his mother of rheumatism, she paid us back by soundly thumping the two of us with a piece of firewood. True, we didn't know at the time that our contribution to her otherwise wearisome afternoon was the long-sought-after cure, but I thought that she would have expressed her gratitude in a more positive fashion. When we brought her the snake, we were only trying to cheer her up.

To my way of thinking, her violent reaction to our proffered pleasantries goes a long way to prove that it is most definitely *not* the thought that counts.

Carlton's mother, Aunt Connie, was a tiny little woman with small hands and delicate features. She was nearly forty when Carl, her only child, was born. The whole thing took her a bit by surprise, but she stood up to it bravely. She didn't do as well with the events that followed that gala affair.

Aunt Connie didn't camp quite so happily with Carl on the rampage in her little domain.

By the time he was eighteen, Carlton's mother had aged into a perpetually fatigued semi-hunchback. Her tired eyes sought out soft, comfortable furniture and quiet corners. She looked much older than her fifty-six years. To explain this, she divided her life into two eras: B.C. (before Carlton) and A.D. (after the delivery). She claimed to anyone who would listen that since A.D. 1 she had aged three years to every one of Carlton's, making her de facto age seventy-four on Carl's eighteenth birthday.

He was an active child.

On the day in question, Aunt Connie had been complaining about her bones aching for several years. You couldn't rouse her to a brisk walk if the house was on fire. Even Carl couldn't blast her out of her customary nest, surrounded by pillows on the end of the sofa. We left the house on our mission, never suspecting how much our lives would change that afternoon.

Maybe if Carl hadn't had his pistol with him, then the thing would have stayed just another story in our repertoire instead of landing the particulars of that afternoon squarely in the realm of living history.

The day was bright and sunny, throwing long, deep shadows where the sunlight was cut into shafts by the trees. Oak leaves littered the ground, and the smell of pine sap, released by the heat, was thick and sweet in the air. We were about three-quarters of a mile from the house when we came to a fallen oak lying across our path. Carl stepped over it and strode on ahead. I was straddling the thing when I happened to look down and noticed the ground slithering by on its way to a thicket of twisted grass and branches that hugged the path.

The ground that day had a curious pattern to it—patches of brown and gray diamonds.

When I say slithering, I'm exaggerating. That damned snake was a good six feet in length and too big to slither very quickly. He was dragging himself along the side of that oak, keeping his heavy body in as much cover as he could find.

I hesitated for a second, pondering whether it might be a good idea to shout for Carl and alert him as to my situation. Shouting invariably alerts everybody, not just the one for which the alert is intended, and there was one party in particular that I didn't care to alert.

Lucky for me, Carl turned around to see what the holdup was. I had an anxious moment after that. Carl had never learned how to be discreet. He plodded up the path making a racket that would alert a deaf-and-dumb rock as to his intentions. The snake froze in place at his approach, and I thought more than once about the chairs on Aunt Connie's front porch and how pleasant it would be to be sitting in one of them with a glass of cold tea in my hand. I swear, I couldn't think of a thing about the creek that inspired me to want to walk down there and see it.

Carl's head swung back and forth while he sized up the problem, then he prodded the thicket with his boot for a couple of seconds, searching for the head that went with the monumental body strung out along the trunk of the fallen oak. When he found it, he blew a couple of holes in it, and I began to breathe again, testing the air in great gulps.

Besides the pistol, Carl was sporting a knife big enough to skin the moon. He made quick work of that rattlesnake's head, cutting it off clean just behind the jaws and wrapping the stump with his handkerchief. By that time I had swallowed enough air to revive my interest, and I busied myself rooting around in the leaves uncovering the rest of the snake. He turned out to be an impressive specimen. Even without his head, he was longer than Carl was tall.

"Six feet if he's an inch," Carl grinned, holding the snake up for me to admire, though he was having trouble keeping his prize in a straight line.

Thing is, that snake didn't know he was dead yet. Snakes are like that. For up to an hour after you sever his head, a snake will twist and turn and wrap around stuff, just like he's surprised that he can't see where he's going.

Naturally, there was nothing for it but we had to show that big boy to Aunt Connie.

"Hell, she's been down these last couple a months," Carl confided in me, pulling his lips into a line of irrefutable concern. "Worse than usual. She won't hardly even talk to anybody."

By unanimous vote we came to the felicitous conclusion that telling Aunt Connie the story of the snake wouldn't be nearly so much fun as showing it to her in the flesh. Carl and I decided, I mean. The snake didn't say no so we took that to mean agreement.

Later, when the debris had settled, we asked Aunt Connie about it, but of course by then, her opinion of the entire afternoon was pretty well documented.

Carl borrowed my handkerchief and we pressed a handful of grass against the bleeding stump and tied the cloth over the top.

"She won't be none too happy if we get blood on her floors," Carl reasoned.

It sounded reasonable to me.

We took turns carrying the snake, but by the time we got to the house, Carl had been elected designated bearer by unanimous vote—the snake's. He had himself wrapped pretty convincingly around Carl's arm and chest, and it seemed somehow counterproductive to waste energy on a switch off when our companion had expressed such satisfaction with the transport he already had.

When we walked into the living room to show this herpetological marvel to Aunt Connie, he was winding and unwinding himself from his perch with breathtaking vigor. Carl had a determined grip on the bundle of rags and grass to keep from dripping blood in the house, but Aunt Connie was too transfixed to notice such an insignificant detail like the absence of a head. What she saw was a really big snake, and that's pretty much all that she saw.

She screamed with enough power to rattle the windows bone naked, and then she leaped up onto the sofa in a single bound, scattering cushions and books with her frenzied thrashing.

If we'd been a little quicker on the uptake and made our getaway right then and there, perhaps we wouldn't share such a wealth of stigmata as visible proof of our adventures.

Before we could beat a hasty retreat, Aunt Connie spotted the woodpile and our world came crashing down.

Graceful as a deer, she sprinted from the sofa to the handy sticks of wood and started beating us with the first piece that came into her hand.

Just like Aunt Connie to pick out the real villains in a crowd of likely suspects. She didn't spare a single blow for that damned snake.

We might've joined him in never-never land that day if it hadn't been for Uncle Clifford. He sized up the situation with admirable calm and slapped Carlton across the head two or three times. He took a couple of swings at me, but I'm shorter than my cousin and I ducked better.

Since I was unencumbered by such weighty problems as wriggling serpents or even flying firewood, I was able to exploit the gift of agility and make for the exit with all due speed. From out on the porch, it sounded pretty lively in that house.

Less than five minutes passed when Uncle Clifford came tearing out of the door bearing the snake in his arms. Carlton followed hard on his heels pursued by Aunt Connie, though mercifully she had been disarmed, probably by Uncle Clifford.

He never fails to catch the little details and take care of them.

The rest of the afternoon exhibited a remarkable tendency to combustibility, but after the initial explosion, things started to settle a bit. Uncle Clifford was so mad that he took a swipe at Carl every few minutes just for good measure. My guess is he wanted to make sure Carl wasn't thinking about committing another outrage anytime soon.

A couple of weeks later, when he noticed that Aunt Connie was moving around with renewed agility and taking part in family activities again, he apologized.

Stir-Fried Rattlesnake with Mushrooms and Whole Baby Brussels Sprouts

Serves 3

Practically any meat will work with this recipe. I fix some version of stir-fry a couple of times a week because it's quick and nutritious and versatile. If rattlesnake is handy, that's my first choice of meat.

Serve hot with rice.

> *1½ pounds rattlesnake*
> *¼ cup peanut oil*
> *2-inch piece fresh ginger, peeled and minced*
> *2 cloves garlic, minced*
> *2 tablespoons ground turmeric*
> *1 pound mushrooms, stemmed*
> *10 ounces whole baby Brussels sprouts, trimmed*
> *¼ cup sake or dry white wine*
> *¼ cup soy sauce*

Prepare the rattlesnake by steaming away from the bone, taking care not to overcook. It should take 15 to 20 minutes, depending on the size of the snake you brought home. A five-footer will take longer than a three-footer, obviously. Let cool enough to handle and remove the bone.

Heat the oil in a wok over high heat. Toss in the ginger and garlic and sauté until fragrant, about 1 scant minute. Add the rattlesnake meat to the oil and stir-fry until it begins to brown, 8 to 10 minutes.

Sprinkle with turmeric and add the mushrooms and Brussels sprouts to the pan. Cook for about 2 minutes, or until the mushrooms begin to absorb the turmeric and turn golden. Pour the sake over all and stir in. Add the soy sauce and cook for 2 more minutes.

Serve hot. If you wait more than a half hour, the cooling damages the fragile flavor marriage between the sake and the soy.

SMALLER GAME

Squirrel

Squirrel is the easiest wild meat to come by since it's only wild in
the technical sense. You can even get squirrel in New York City—
big, fat, sweet-tasting squirrels.

   To bag a mess of squirrel, you will need: a wrist rocket, a plastic
jar with just a little taste of crunchy peanut butter in the bottom, a
sack of bread crumbs that you've soaked in peanut oil for a couple
of minutes, a canvas bag with a square bottom so it'll stand up by
itself, a small hammer, and one good sturdy glove for your off
hand. Put all your stuff in the bag and head to the park.

   Pick yourself a likely bench that's not too conspicuous, and set
yourself down on one end with your canvas bag just beside your
knees. Don your wrist rocket and wedge your ammunition
between your legs for easy access. I like ball bearings, but marbles
work really well, too. When you're all arranged, set the bait.

   Take the lid off the peanut butter jar and set it in the grass
right by your foot. Sprinkle a few of the breadcrumbs in a wide
circle and wait for volunteers.

When a squirrel comes, he'll start by eating the peanut-flavored breadcrumbs and slowly make his way into the jar. Remember, he lives in the park so he expects handouts. The only thing he might be suspicious of is that he might not get all of the food before you get up and leave.

Your volunteer naturally will try to get the peanut butter in the bottom of the jar. This means that they have to stick their head in. When they do that, they get some on their ears. Squirrels will always stop and clean this off before venturing in the jar for another taste of the good stuff. This puts him—and his empty little head—just by your ankle.

Draw back your rocket and pop him one on the skull. As soon as he falls, take out your hammer and give him another whack for good measure. You have to pick him up quick, so that you don't risk getting any blood on the grass, otherwise you have to move the whole thing to another bench.

Using your gloved hand, pick up your squirrel and dump him in the bag. A glove may seem redundant at this point, but you're wearing it just in case the little bugger isn't quite dead when you pick him up. A squirrel bite, especially one that is arguably justified, hurts worse than one from a rat, though thankfully it's not so dirty. Squirrels do bite people, but mostly because the person had something, namely food, that the squirrel expected to get.

They get mighty pissed off when they feel they've been cheated.

Field Dressing and Preparation

Squirrel yearlings can be fried just like chicken, but older specimens need to be either included in a stew or ground like hamburger. Remember that both the fox and the gray squirrel varieties are quite tasty, but their cousin, the rocky mountain squirrel, has a musky flavor and should be avoided.

If it's hot outside (70°F or higher), then get your kill home and dressed within 2 hours. Cooler temperatures give you more time (3 hours at 60°F, 4 hours at 50°F). To dress squirrel, remove the front legs at the elbow. Make a cut in the skin on the lower stomach, just at the base of the tail. Hold the squirrel by the back legs and pull the skin away from the stomach and breast until you have pulled it as far as the head, then stand on this free flap of skin and reverse the process, pulling the remaining skin over the back legs. Remove the feet and the head. Gut carefully, making sure to remove the two glands in the small of the back and under each front limb. Rinse the cavity with water to which a few drops of lemon juice have been added.

Squirrel Roasted in Brandy Sauce

Serves 3

This one came to me in a dream. Well, not really, but close. It had been a tough year for art sales, and park squirrels were becoming a staple in our kitchen, plus I had a cold that I couldn't shake off. I was nursing my discomforts and a glass of brandy with lemon and honey, trying to get a little ease out of an old easy chair whose sprung springs had given up on the concept of human comfort. I was about to nod off when everything happened at once. My son came in with a mess of squirrels. He took one look at me and suggested that I'd be better off with a big glass of orange juice; and all of a sudden, I had a vision of a new and better way to prepare the same ol' same ol' we had not been enjoying much lately. Here it is, and I hope you like it as much as me and mine do.

You can also use duck, goose, chicken, woodchuck, or beaver.

5 to 6 plump squirrels, about 1½ pounds each
1 cup plus 2 tablespoons orange juice
½ cup plus 2 tablespoons brandy
¼ cup all-purpose flour

Cut the squirrels into manageable-sized pieces. Put the pieces in a deep bowl and pour 1 cup of the orange juice and h cup of brandy over them. Stir it around so that all the pieces get their fair share. Let it sit in the refrigerator for at least 4 hours.

Preheat the oven to 350°F.

Drain and roast the squirrels in the broiler or over an open fire for best results. Slip a pan under it to catch the drippings. In the broiler, roast for 8 to 10 minutes on each side, then transfer to an open pan and bake in the oven for an additional 10 minutes.

Tie the front legs forward and the back legs back, and roast over an open fire, turning every 5 minutes, for no longer than 25 minutes. The meat inside of the thigh joint should be tan all the way to the bone when the squirrel is done.

Brown the flour in 3 tablespoons of the drippings. Then add the rest of the drippings plus the remaining 2 tablespoons each of orange juice and brandy. Simmer for about 10 minutes.

Serve hot off the grill, passing the gravy on the side.

The Boys Upstairs

Squirrels in the park are much easier to deal with than the ones who presume to move into your house with you. It doesn't matter how long you have lived there, once a squirrel takes up residence, in his mind, you're a squatter. Go figure.

When my son was about six years old, we were living in an old house where the upstairs bedrooms had slanted ceilings about halfway up that flattened out to accommodate the floor of a narrow attic that ran down the middle of the house. Lots of big, old trees grew up close to the house and, with the gable windows open, it was cool and breezy upstairs in the summer. All and all, not a bad spot.

The second year we were there, a family of squirrels took up residence in the attic by gnawing through a corner of the vent. By and large, the squirrels weren't much of a bother—in the beginning. They had a bunch of younguns in the spring, and the patter of little feet over my head gave me cause to wonder if I shouldn't clean them out of there and repair the vent, but in the end, the summer turned hot that year, and I spent more time on the porch thinking about getting out the ladder than I did in making a move towards the shed. Besides which, there was a sizable family of daddy longlegs living in the shed that my son liked to play with, and I didn't have the heart to break up his friendships.

He'd go in there and stand in the dusky shadows with his hand up against the rough wood wall, and before you know it, his new buddies would take up the invite and climb off onto him, bouncing on their skinny legs and crowding one against the other for the best spot. They purely loved the feel of his skin under their feet, and it tickled him to have them climb around on him.

I spent that summer drinking tea and easing my lazy carcass over to take advantage of the shade, and my son played with his friends and grew at least an inch and a half. While we were about that business, the squirrels wrote long heartfelt letters to their relations and invited one and all to come and live at their place. Friends and neighbors, in the fall, the party began.

Sometime in October, I noticed that the number and timbre of the little feet over my head had surely grown. They were having a family reunion and partied all day and well into the early evening. That night, while my son and I were asleep in our beds, the neighbors upstairs decided it was time to clean up after the gathering and take out the trash.

I remember hearing a distant gnawing sound, but I didn't put it down as meaningful information until my son jumped up out of bed flinging bits of pecan shells and leaves about the room. I turned on the light to see what was what, but what I saw didn't set my mind at ease, not one bit.

Just above my son's bed was a hole—a brand new hole—in the ceiling. Out of the hole popped a squirrel head. No sooner did the squirrel spot me looking at him than he took offense. Apparently, according to the squirrel— if I read that string of profanity and arm waving correctly—I had no business living in his trash dump, and he expected me to apologize and leave the premises right then and there.

He didn't think very highly of it when I took a poke at his head with a broomstick; in fact, he stayed up half the night fuming over it, returning to the hole now and then to deliver a fresh set of insults.

About three in the morning I thought of yet another use for duct tape and covered the hole sufficiently to discourage the dumping of any more garbage.

Over the next few weeks, we conducted a daily war wherein the squirrel and his kinfolk chewed a hole in the ceiling, and my son and I pounded the hole with the broomstick and taped it over with duct tape. In my off hours, I cussed the landlord for the cheap pasteboard he tacked up on the ceiling, and I cussed the squirrels for being squirrels.

Seemed appropriate at the time.

The ceiling looked like the backside of a minefield. In some places, the squirrels had chewed through the existing duct tape so that strings of detritus hung down with gnawed pecan shells sticking to it.

Along about August, a fella moved in down the street from us who had a lively terrier for a pet, and the idea of digging holes in the ceiling began to appeal to me. Me and my son sawed us a hole big enough to put that dog through. In next to no time, the squirrel clan made up their minds that our attic was not the happy home they thought it was. Friends, they were packed and out of there so fast, they didn't have time to leave us a forwarding address.

The duct tape repairs were so ugly that we put up a couple of sheets of plywood and painted it white, but we left the hole open at one end to put the dog through, just in case some of those boys decided to come back and pay us a visit.

Squirrel Parmigiana

Serves 3

The truth is, not all of the squirrels in our attic made a clean getaway. That terrier was having a fine time grabbin' them up by the neck and throwin' over his back. All in all, he killed near a dozen of them before the rest had gathered their belongings and cleared out. The man who owned the dog was Italian (still is, far as I know), and once he discovered that it was our sincere intention to make a meal of the deceased miscreants, he took over the kitchen and produced the unforgettable recipe below. Tony, I'm in your debt.

Naturally, veal and chicken are great substitutes for squirrel in this recipe.

> *Freshly ground black pepper*
> *3 to 4 pounds boneless squirrel meat, cut into strips*
> *¼ cup olive oil*
> *1 cup sliced mushrooms*
> *1 green bell pepper, seeded and finely chopped*
> *½ cup finely chopped Vidalia onion*
> *1 clove garlic, minced*
> *4 large tomatoes, peeled and chopped*
> *½ cup dry white wine*
> *½ cup black olives, sliced*
> *¼ cup freshly grated Parmesan cheese*

Preheat the oven to 325°F.

Shake pepper over the squirrel. Brown the meat in the oil in a large oven-proof skillet or Dutch oven over medium-high heat, about 4 minutes per side.

Add the mushrooms and sauté for about 5 minutes. Add the green pepper, onion, garlic, tomatoes, and wine. Cover and bake for about 30 minutes. Add the olives and bake for an additional 10 minutes.

Remove from the oven and sprinkle with the Parmesan cheese. Serve before it has time to cool unduly. It's much better hot and fresh.

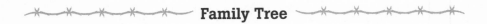

Family Tree

Some years ago, when my brother was a young man in his early twenties, he expressed a scientific interest in improving the intelligence of the squirrels in his yard. To this end, he designed a rash of experiments to help him see the thing through.

Truth is, he had more than enough material to work with. I don't believe that I have ever seen a place with more squirrels then he had around that house. Those squirrels there were making younguns faster than his dog and both cats could deal with. The neighbor's cat gave up absolutely and started hanging out in the house all day just to get some peace from the chattering.

Just to listen to them, the way they cuss and scold, you'd think that squirrels wouldn't be able to say enough kind words to one another to ever strike up the kind of relationship that leads to kids, but I guess they manage somehow. I expect they have the sort of love affairs where man and wife chase each other about the premises wielding frying pans and other handy objects of affection until they're too tuckered out to squabble anymore, and the kids come along as a result of the making up.

It sounds like a tiresome way to keep the family turning to my way of thinking. If it's true, then all I can say is, "Thank God and Grandma that I was not born a squirrel," because if I was doomed to getting a little love with a string of threats first, then I'd just as soon not have it.

My brother's first experiment (I'm going to keep using that word; though I can personally think of half a dozen others that fit the bill better, he is my brother and if I'm inclined to finagle the truth on his behalf, you'll just have to indulge me) involved a counterbalanced stick with a cluster of juicy walnuts on one end and a lead weight, roughly two-thirds the weight of the average squirrel, on the other. He picked open the walnut shells first and ate the meats, then glued the shells back together and glued the empty shells to the end of the stick, providing a tempting, if hollow, reward for the unsuspecting squirrels.

When the glue dried, he positioned the stick over a branch, carefully balancing it so that the stick slanted upwards towards the nuts, but wouldn't slide off onto the ground. The squirrels quickly discovered that walking the length of the stick in pursuit of the toothsome treat caused the fragile balance to swing wildly out of control. One particularly stout male rode the stick all the way to the ground and spent the better part of an hour cussing the dog and tugging frantically at the stubborn walnuts before he finally succeeded in cracking one.

If madder than hell equals smart, then that had to be the smartest squirrel in three states.

A couple a days later, my brother decided that the squirrels had not developed any new talents thanks to his experiments, so he moved on to phase two.

Phase two introduced a ten-foot pole with a platform bolted to the top. Naturally, a pile of delectable nuts crowded the platform in full sight of God and the squirrels. The pole was wood better than halfway up (easy climbing), then a metal pipe with the platform bolted to the top slipped down over the wood. The metal would have been a challenge unto itself, but Mike had taken the time to give it a thick coating of lard, just to keep things interesting.

The squirrels, not to be outdone by cheap tricks, made a manly run at it and fell sprawling to the ground every time, their bellies slick with lard.

About this time, I happened to notice that the squirrels he had to deal with may or may not have been showing signs of increased brainpower, but their numbers were definitely increasing. Seems putting out stacks of walnuts, empty or not, tends to attract a crowd, if the crowd you were intending to attract is into that sort of thing. I figured that my handy wrist rocket was just gonna make matters worse, seeing as how the bodies of the fallen were likely to set off a riot, and I didn't know if we had enough help in the person of cats and dogs to deal with a riot of squirrels.

Since my brother was dead set on experiments, I suggested that we see if squirrels could figure out a trap. The losers would forfeit and help with dinner—if you get my meaning.

In less than a week, we'd cleared the squirrel population down to about half their numbers, and the surviving citizenry proved to be smart enough to avoid me and my brother and any device we were seen fooling with.

That trend held to the next generation, so somebody learned something— just what, I can't tell you.

After much thought, I still can't actually say whether or not my brother made those creatures smarter by the stuff he did or just meaner. Squirrels are pretty foul tempered and ornery anyway, so it's hard to tell. I know for a certain fact that they learned to hate me and my brother pretty good, especially after we started catching and skinning their kinfolk.

Nobody can teach a squirrel a new cuss word. They know them all and then some, but my brother's experiments encouraged them to use all they knew in breathtakingly long and creative sentences.

If even one of those curses had actually hit home, my brother would be in a bad way for sure.

Squirrel with Crab Apples and Quince Wrapped in Grape Leaves

Serves 4

I used to make this all the time with either lamb or chicken, but during the prolonged art drought when my son and I were becoming accustomed to squirrel on the table and lots of it, I borrowed a couple of crab apples and some quince from a tree in our neighborhood and tried it out with what we had to hand. Squirrel is not as tender as chicken, nor as oily as lamb tends to be, and the flavor is a bit like rabbit only darker.

> *2 quinces, peeled, seeded, and quartered*
> *2 crab apples, peeled, cored, and thinly sliced*
> *¼ cup golden raisins*
> *¼ teaspoon ground cinnamon*
> *⅛ teaspoon ground nutmeg*
> *⅛ teaspoon ground cloves*
> *1 tablespoon honey*
> *1 teaspoon fresh lemon juice*

3 pounds boned squirrel meat, minced
¼ cup olive or sesame oil
2 tablespoons red wine
8 large grape leaves, preferably the bottled kind
¼ cup pomegranate juice

In a glass dish, combine the quinces, crab apples, and raisins. Sprinkle the cinnamon, nutmeg, and cloves over and stir together. Stir in the honey and lemon juice. (Hint: It's much easier to stir honey into something if you let it sit in the windowsill for about an hour and heat up. Cold honey is an obstinate ingredient, but it becomes more agreeable by measured increments as it warms up. In the winter, you can set the honey jar in a pan of warm water for a bit.)

Brown the meat in 2 tablespoons oil in a skillet over medium-high heat, turning it quickly to avoid sticking. When the meat is brown all over, pour the wine over it and remove from the heat.

Arrange the grape leaves on a cutting board and fill each (slightly off-center) with a couple of spoonfuls of browned squirrel meat. Top each off with the mixture of the sweetened fruit.

Brush with oil and fold into a tightly contained little package. This is accomplished by first folding down the ends, brushing them with oil and then rolling the remainder of the leaf into a tube.

Preheat the oven to 350°F.

Brush the outside of the wrapped grape leaves with oil and place in a casserole dish. Pour the pomegranate juice over them. Cover.

Bake for 20 to 25 minutes. If the tops of the grape leaves begin to darken too quickly, decrease the heat. If the weather is very dry, it may only take 20 minutes for the fruit to suck up the pomegranate juice, so keep an eye on them and be prepared to remove it from the oven and chow down 5 minutes early.

When all the pomegranate juice has been absorbed, remove from the oven and serve.

Chipmunk

Chipmunks are so small that only the thighs are edible. An adult chipmunk is no more than 8 inches long and rarely weighs more than 4 or 5 ounces.

You can catch them the same way as squirrels, but you don't need the wrist rocket. In fact, chipmunks are not as trusting as squirrels (also a lot smarter) and their heads are so much smaller that if you manage to hit one with a ball bearing, I want to get a letter from you, complete with photographs.

Generally, you can't get close enough to a suitably cautious chipmunk to bring out your weapon, and unlike squirrels, who are not only accustomed to handouts, they expect them, chipmunks have a healthy grasp on the true relationship between man and every other living thing on the planet. In other words, a chipmunk is not likely to trust you as far as he can throw your pick-up truck, brother.

On to plan B.

Here's where traps come into play again. You will need: a trap, one that catches the victim alive, and by the way, you will need one big enough to catch a small dog; a big canvas bag; a plastic jar at least 8 to 10 inches in diameter; and ½ cup of crunchy peanut butter.

Drill a couple of holes in the plastic jar and run a wire through it so you can secure it to the back of the trap. If you get lucky, you'll have a dozen or more chipmunks after your bait and they are quite capable of wrestling the prize out of harm's way. Consider yourself the harm and use your head here.

With the jar secured, scoop the peanut butter and push it all the way to the back of the jar. You want to make them work for it but at the same time providing enough of an incentive to get them working together for the common good—namely stuffing themselves with enough high-fat vegetarian treat to keep them warm all winter. Set your baited trap between a couple of rocks and take a seat about 30 feet away and read a book. Don't whittle. Chipmunks know

good and well what a knife is and they're not likely to turn their backs on you long enough to concentrate on the peanut butter.

Wait for it. A big trap takes a bit of tussling to set it off and bring down the door, so wait for it.

The chipmunks will have eaten at least half of the peanut butter and as a group, they will be thoroughly involved in trying to get that jar out of the cage and off to someplace private when they spring the door on themselves.

Put the cage into the bag and drive away with it. Getting them out of the cage is something you want to do in the privacy of your garage.

When all the doors are firmly shut, set the cage on its end so that the door is up, facing the ceiling. Open it and quickly slip another bag over the top. Chipmunks can jump quite a distance and by now they've been practicing for their great escape.

Should I mention that they bite? Wouldn't you under the circumstances? They'll also chew through your bag soon enough, so move quickly. Wear a pair of heavy leather gloves and pinch off the neck of the bag, letting the chipmunks out one at a time into a smaller cage.

It helps to have a confederate to knock them in the head, unless you are truly dexterous and can hold the bag in one hand and take aim with a hammer while the prey squeaks and threatens behind you.

If they chew through your bag before you're done, they'll scatter. Eventually, they'll take up residence in your yard. You might as well give up ever trying to catch them again. Chipmunks, unlike most people, learn from their mistakes.

Good luck.

Field Dressing and Preparation

Clean and dress as you would a rabbit . . . only much, much smaller (see page 140).

Chipmunk Patties with Sesame Seed and Ginger

Serves 3

If you don't have a meat grinder or a food processor, then get yourself a really sharp knife, like the kind you see in fancy Japanese restaurants and practice with it until you can do the job (see Note, page 72).

In the absence of chipmunk meat, you can always substitute pork, chicken, or turkey. To some extent you can use lamb, though you need to substitute cardamom for the ginger and 1 tablespoon of pomegranate molasses (page 63) for the soy sauce.

¼ cup white sesame seeds

2 pounds chipmunk meat, ground

3 tablespoons very finely chopped onion

1 teaspoon minced garlic

2 teaspoons fresh ginger juice

1 tablespoon soy sauce

1 tablespoon sugar

2 small eggs, lightly beaten

¼ cup peanut oil

Sweet-and-sour sauce or hot mustard

Toast the sesame seeds in a small skillet over low heat until the seeds turn a light brown, about 2 minutes. They'll start to pop slightly, like popcorn. Set aside.

Mix together the chipmunk, onion, garlic, ginger juice, soy sauce, sugar, and eggs in a bowl. Form into patties by slapping back and forth in your palms until they are approximately ½ inch thick.

Heat the peanut oil in a skillet over medium heat. Toss in the patties and cook for about 5 minutes, or until golden brown on the bottom. Turn the patties over and sprinkle with the sesame seeds. Cook for 3 to 4 minutes longer.

Serve with either sweet-and-sour sauce or hot mustard.

 **Dorothy Is in the House**

Remember I said that you need to keep a handle on how many chipmunks slip out into your yard, or they'd take up residence there? Well, I bet you thought that chipmunks in your yard would be a harmless enough event, didn't you? Cute even. Well, maybe now and again. They're probably real cute when they're asleep.

I don't know what came over me. I'd done that transfer act with chipmunks some half-dozen times, when one day I just went brain dead in the middle of the grand event, and half of the little devils got past me and clean out of my grasp.

They were a little bummed by the landscape of my locale at first. After all, I'd kidnapped them from a place where they'd never had opportunity to see a house and damned few of either cars or dogs, and now they had a selection of each on a daily basis. I suspect they were going through a chipmunk version of "We're not in Kansas anymore."

The place I was living at the time wasn't exactly Oz—they had everything they needed to set up housekeeping and prosper, and no wicked witch was after their precious slippers, so they adjusted quick enough.

I expect I would have qualified for the ogre in a fairy tale. I didn't have one eye in the middle of my forehead, but by chipmunk standards, my canine teeth are a formidable threat, and I did eat their kinfolk. On the other hand, Ogre Jr., in the body of my son, was busy passing out peanuts, peanut butter, bread crumbs, and croutons, as well as every other comestible treat that a chipmunk's little heart could desire.

In no time at all, that boy had an army of admirers who praised him from morning till night and even told him that he was good looking. They had a minor falling out when he offered his new buddies a bit of garlic toast. My boy found out right quick that vampires are not the only creatures that squeak and hop out of the path when you shove garlic in their face.

By the following spring, they had taken up residence in the eaves adjoining my son's second story window. A little high and drafty for chipmunk tastes, but it had the advantage of being close to the kitchen help, as it were.

I resented the way they had renovated the property without permission from the existing residents—namely me and mine—but since I didn't get too fired up the year before when the wrens had busted into the attic by way of the vents, I guessed that it would be out of character to start practicing outrage now, so I let it be.

I offered to give them a ride back home, but the grin on my face gave me away, and they wouldn't go into my cage. Besides, by this time, they had little ones who were born in my yard, and they didn't want to transfer to new schools in the middle of the year. Over the winter, the spirit of colonialism had hit them, and they were busy setting out flags and marking off territories.

Oh, well, I had to try.

The trouble started when the pecan trees in my yard decided to produce a bumper crop of nuts. No way could I crack and eat them fast enough. No worries, the chipmunks could and would work in shifts.

They discovered the first day that the eaves had a lot of spare room and that they could pack a great many nuts into the space behind their huts.

For a couple of weeks there, there was a mad dash for property. The squirrels, in a fit of pique, started burying as many as they could gather to keep the chipmunks from carrying them off to their storerooms. My garden and the flowerpots on the porch offered the softest, quickest place to dig. In no time at all, those particular places were graced with more pecans than dirt. To my mind, the squirrels spent way yonder too much time picketing for their rights. While they were cussing and chattering in the trees and generally going about the political end of things, the chipmunks made short work of the nuts and won the war.

Soon, the chipmunks were seen standing on the gutter above my front porch, munching peacefully on pecans while the squirrels scolded them from the trees.

The upshot of this little fracas was that I learned to wear shoes. I have always resented shoes and only wear them if I absolutely have to. Thanks to the chipmunks I ended up having to wear shoes just to go out and get the paper. Now I can and have gone out for the morning paper, skipping barefoot through a foot of snow, but splintered pecan shells is another kettle of goods altogether.

It got so's you didn't dare leave my house without shoes on unless you had a mind to pick shells out of your feet for near half an hour. I raked shells near everyday and used them in the smoker to add flavor to fish and poultry, but I couldn't rake fast enough to keep ahead of those chipmunks; besides, they had a knack for dropping them broken side up.

I tried it myself and it always came up fifty-fifty—half the time up, half down.

The luck of striped rodents never fails to amaze me. They had found a way to confound me and all they had to do to accomplish it was munch on one of their favorite treats.

In the end, the squirrels suffered yet another setback because of the chipmunks. I took to practicing with my wrist rocket and found that I could easily waste eight or nine shots and risk the windows of the house tryin' to take down a single chipmunk, but the squirrels that came down to cheer over the body of the fallen made excellent targets. They had bigger heads and I tended to get one on every second or third shot.

Chipmunk with Sweet Pot Cheese and Spinach

Serves 4 to 5

I had a really hard time deciding whether I should put this recipe under chipmunk or under rattlesnake 'cause the truth is, it gets fixed either way. Rattlesnake does this recipe up proud, but if you don't have either a good, fat snake or a mess of chipmunks, you should try it anyway with something like chicken, squirrel, or woodchuck. It works with lamb, but it's a bit oily done that way, and you need to add a bit of cardamom to the spices.

> *2 to 3 pounds boneless chipmunk meat, ground*
> *2 tablespoons peanut oil*
> *2 cloves garlic, crushed*
> *1 tablespoon sweet paprika*
> *½ cup very finely chopped red onion*
> *3 pounds fresh spinach, tough stems removed*
> *½ cup plain yogurt*
> *½ cup sweet pot cheese or farmer's cheese*
> *Pita bread or any flat bread*

In a large skillet, brown the chipmunk meat over medium-high heat in a scant tablespoon of the oil. Sprinkle the meat with garlic and paprika while it is cooking. When it begins to brown, throw in the onion and stir to keep it from sticking. Remove from skillet and set aside in a bowl.

Heat the remaining 1 tablespoon oil in the skillet over medium-high heat. Throw in the spinach and stir until wilted, less than 2 minutes. In a medium bowl, mix the wilted spinach with the yogurt.

Preheat the oven to 325°F. Butter a large casserole.

Place half of the spinach-yogurt mixture in the casserole. Layer the browned meat over the spinach. Spoon the sweet pot cheese over the meat and, finally, finish off the casserole with the remaining spinach and yogurt. Cover and bake for about 20 minutes.

Serve hot with pita bread.

Prairie Dog

Prairie dogs set sentries that warn of the approach of anybody and everybody that isn't a member of their family. Sneaking up on them is not an option.

Ditto on the bait idea. Prairie dogs don't want anything from you but your absence.

To hunt prairie dog, you will need: five or six good-sized traps, five or six large-diameter clothes-dryer exhaust hoses cut into three-foot lengths, a box of matches, and a couple of wads of green grass strung together with a few slivers of tree bark. A little chicken wire comes in real handy, but you can survive without it if you have several guys helping and you're quick about it.

Once you've located a suitable prairie dog town—they're called that because there are typically hundreds of occupants and all of their burrows are strung together by a system of tunnels not unlike city streets—scout around until you've found their boltholes.

A prairie dog town has numerous bolt-holes—sometimes called a plunge hole because it dives straight down between 8 and 12 feet before it begins to branch out. The dogs also dig themselves a number of escape holes. The boltholes are arranged at a higher ground level than the escape holes to allow for ventilation within the town. When the wind blows over the boltholes, it pulls fresh air up through the escape holes and throughout the system.

Arrange your traps at the escape holes by shoving the dryer hose into it and feeding the open end into your trap. You may have to use burlap bags to make up the difference in size and shape. This is where the chicken wire comes in handy, if you decided to go that route. Duct tape helps too.

Once you have your traps in position, pick an escape hole that you haven't blocked and set a match to your plug of grass and bark. It'll be hard to light, but when you get it going, it will put out quite a bit of smoke, which will, naturally, be pulled into the town by the wind rushing over the plunge holes.

With smoke wafting through their burrows, the prairie dogs will rush out to see what's up. At least some of them will find themselves in your traps. Set the traps on end quickly, pull out the dryer hose, and shut the doors to the traps.

Inspect your catch and turn loose any juveniles and pregnant females.

If you find yourself with a really big, formidable male in one of your traps who's telling you in no uncertain terms that you and your family are in grave danger if you don't apologize immediately, then you should do the prairie dog town a favor and turn that big boy loose. Those towns are run by a patriarch, and chances are that's the one who's cussing you out. They'll need him to help reorganize after their fright.

Oh, and be sure to stomp out your little fire and bury it in the dirt somewhere so the youngsters don't find it and scorch their feet.

The burrow system is efficient, and the smoke will clear in only a few minutes.

More than one case of black plague has been associated with prairie dogs. Apparently, they harbor the fleas that carry the disease, so take all due precautions when hunting them. Prairie dogs also fall victim to the plague. If, when you have your quarry in the traps, you notice more than one dog looks a little faint—more so than can be accounted for by smoke inhalation—then turn them all loose immediately and get yourself to a doctor. Hey! Nobody ever said the path to gourmet dinning was either safe or easy.

Seriously, there's no way to tell if a prairie dog has the plague without testing, so educate yourself on these matters before you go after a batch of tasty dogs and remember to take every possible precaution.

Field Dressing and Preparation

Clean and dress as you would a rabbit (see page 140). Remove the small, hard glands in the armpits and the groin.

Prairie Dog with White Kidney Beans in Tomato Sauce

Serves 4

This recipe came from a friend who keeps horses out in South Central Wyoming. Naturally, he's out there with a rifle picking off prairie dogs pretty often in an attempt to spare his horses the inevitable broken leg when they step into a prairie dog bolt hole. I stopped by his place one weekend that I was planning to spend fishing and found my friend apologizing for having such a slim larder from which to offer me dinner. "That I don't get," I explained to him. "You've got dinner all around you, and you're shooting some of it everyday." He took the hint and the next time I was by his way, he offered me prairie dog with kidney beans. I've changed the recipe a little bit, but not much.

Chicken, turkey, and pork also make up real well. It's also real good cold with a firm-crust bread to sop it up.

> 3 prairie dogs, meat cut into rather large chunks
> ¼ cup olive oil
> 1 onion, finely diced
> 2 cloves garlic, minced
> 3 to 4 carrots, sliced
> 1 pound dried white kidney (cannellini) beans
> 4 tomatoes, peeled and chopped (I like to use canned Italian
>   tomatoes for the herbs)
> ½ teaspoon dried thyme
> ½ teaspoon dried marjoram

> *2 small leaves purple basil or green basil*
> *Freshly ground black pepper*
> *Water*

In a large skillet, brown the meat in the olive oil over medium-high heat for about 5 minutes. Add the onion, garlic, and carrots. Cook for about 5 more minutes.

Transfer everything to a large pot and add the beans, tomatoes, thyme, marjoram, and basil. Sprinkle with a spare pinch of pepper. Cover with cold water. Bring to a boil. Cover and allow to simmer for about 3 hours, stirring occasionally to check the water level. When it's done, the beans should have absorbed most of the water, but sometimes you need to add a spare cup here and there to prevent them from allowing the rest of the ingredients to dry out.

You can serve this hot, or save it for later.

Who's the Fairest?

If all you want is one or two prairie dogs, and you don't want to have to buy your buddies a six-pack to get their help, then you can strike off on your own and take down a couple of dogs with a hand mirror, a wire-hook bird-feeder stand, and a pistol.

Once you've located a suitable town, scout around for an escape hole and place your bit of mirror at the entrance. You should set the mirror so that it catches the light of the sun and sends those bright rays as far down the hole as possible. To this end, you likely will be setting it up about a foot from the opening, wedged into a mound of dirt that you have scraped up just for that purpose.

Make yourself scarce somewhere nearby where you can peer through a bunch of grass and watch the hole and the mirror.

Pretty soon, at least one prairie dog will follow that bright light to its source. By the time he gets to ground level, he will have been staring right at the light from the mirror for several minutes and will naturally be dazed and at least temporarily blinded. While he stands there blinking at the mirror, you have plenty of time to aim and shoot.

Retrieve your dog with the wire-hook bird-feeder stand and wait for the next dog to try his luck with the mirror.

Watching the prairie dogs play with the mirror is more fun than watching your cat lick peanut butter off the roof of his mouth. If left unmolested, the prairie dogs will pose, lie down and roll, talk to their reflections, and even chase other dogs away from it. They get these peculiar looks on their faces like they was approaching a state of rapture or somewhat.

I was using a small, pocket-sized mirror one day when a particularly vain and pretentious dog ran off all the other contenders who presumed to approach the new toy. In the end, he managed to get a good grip on it and carry it down in the hole with him.

I've gone back to that town several times since to see if some weird religious cult has sprung up, but if it has, then they haven't put up no signs or banners to go with it, so I guess I'll never know. I expect if some social or religious change took place in that town, then it's an underground religion anyways and best left undisturbed.

Sometimes when you're out stomping around looking for a prairie-dog town, you find one where the inhabitants have long since moved on. In that case, come back in the fall on a cool day and bring a shovel with you. Abandoned prairie-dog towns are prime locations for scaring up snakes in the winter months. Once a snake has gone to ground in the winter, they're generally less feisty and you can dig them up without undue risk to life and limb. They need the sun to put spark in their resistance. That doesn't mean that they're helpless, just a tad easier to deal with. A snake's temper is heat driven. Without it, he's more likely to leave you a few openings where you can grab his tail and hoist him into a sack. Hint: don't ever try to dig a snake out on a hot summer day. They can hear you coming a mile off and they'll lay off on a side burrow and take a bite out of your knee when you're off balance leaning into your shovel.

Tandoori Prairie Dog

Serves 4

Tandoori prairie dog is another one of those recipes that sprang from the combination of my intermittent poverty and my unquenchable love for Indian food. Besides which, prairie dog is tastier than chicken, just as tender, and virtually free. Chickens invariably have owners that expect remuneration, whilst prairie dogs are free agents. Along the same road of experimentation, I found that woodchuck and beaver make excellent tandoori as well.

Serve with basmati rice and onion kulcha or other flatbread, naturally.

¼ cup ground cinnamon or 2 (3-inch) sticks

3 tablespoons cardamom

1 tablespoon cumin seeds

1 tablespoon coriander seeds

1 tablespoon ground cayenne pepper

1 tablespoon whole cloves

1 tablespoon black peppercorns

1 teaspoon ground nutmeg

1½ cups plain or vanilla yogurt

2 tablespoons fresh lime juice

2-inch piece fresh ginger, peeled and chopped

2 to 3 prairie dogs, cut into large chunks (3½ to 4 pounds meat)

Combine the cinnamon, cardamom, cumin, coriander, cayenne, cloves, peppercorns, and nutmeg in a spice grinder and grind them into a fine powder.

Combine the yogurt, lime juice, ginger, and ground spices in a blender and reduce the whole thing to a smooth paste.

Place the prairie dog meat in a deep glass dish and pour the contents of the blender over it. Cover with plastic wrap and allow to refrigerate for 6 hours. You can actually leave this for longer without hurting anything, but after 2 days, I'd definitely make plans to cook it soon.

Preheat the oven to 400°F.

Remove the meat from the spicy yogurt paste and place it in a roasting pan. Roast for 30 minutes, or until golden brown.

Serve immediately, before it has time to cool off. It tastes much better hot.

Field Mouse

Don't go turning your nose up on me here. I'm not talking about rats. Field mice are vegetarians and their meat is tender and sweet. If they were easier to clean and dress, more people would take advantage of this tasty treat.

Let me be the first to admit that cleaning them is a royal pain. Forget getting any meat off of them anywhere but their chunky little thighs, which are a perfect bite size.

Generally, field mice can be caught pretty easily with the kind of trap that lures them in without killing them. They spoil pretty fast, so unless you want to sit nearby and clean each one as it's killed, the traditional rat trap method is a bummer. Once you've bagged the desired number, you're in for the grunt work.

Field mouse is a tasty meat, plentiful, and relatively easy to acquire, but in view of the advances made on humanity by the hantavirus, a few words of caution should be said here. Hantavirus usually is transferred to humans by contact with mouse droppings, but enough fatal cases of the stuff have been contracted of late that all due caution should be exercised when you hunt the mouse. Always use gloves—the disposable kind—when handling mice and wear one of those masks that filters out sawdust and paint fumes in the shop. Better yet, get a mask that meets NIOSH Standard N100. You can get these masks from laboratory supply companies. If you have long hair, tie it back and make sure that it doesn't brush the ground when you are skinning and cleaning. At first, hantavirus seemed to be contained generally in the Southwest, but recently reports have come in from locations in the North and East as well. It's been more than twenty-five years since an incident with a trap led me to discover the subtle taste of this meat.

At that time, hantavirus was so rare that even folks who lived in the Desert Southwest were unaware of the danger. Lots of folks died before the cause was discovered. By taking the proper precautions, you can avoid contracting the virus, but do take the proper steps to protect yourself. You wouldn't hunt rattlesnakes in sandals, would you?

Field Dressing and Preparation

Cut away the thighs and skin by splitting carefully down the inside lengthwise and peeling back the skin with the tip of your knife. Make a pile of the bodies and don't feel bad about leaving them in the field. The coyotes will love you for it. They dote on this particular delicacy, and they never bother to bone it. To a coyote, a mouse is just as good tasting as a squab is to a society dame and eaten in much the same way, crunching up the bones with the meat.

✳——✳ And the Whole World Flocked to Our Door ✳——✳

I would never have thought of eating field mice without considerable help.

A man in Texas who I know does a turn of business as a taxidermist and got a chance a few years back to work his skills by putting together a wildlife diorama for a museum. The contract didn't pay much, so not too many folks took up the offer, but my friend thought well of seeing his name on that little brass plaque, so he fought for the contract and set about the business intending to make a grand show of it.

Mostly, the museum provided him with the specimens: deer, bobcat, javelina, and the like. For the smaller animals, they expected him to provide his own as well as do the mounting.

We got a raccoon and an opossum easy enough. He didn't have much experience with ringtail, and he ended up donating a good denim jacket, about a square foot of previously unscathed skin, and an unknown quantity of blood on that venture.

It seems the ringtail took umbrage to my friend's unwelcome familiarity when he tried to pick up his quarry by the neck—an action that warrants a well-placed warning: namely, always make sure whatever you just shot is truly dead by poking it with a stick before you volunteer any part of your body to justifiably angry teeth and claws.

When he showed me his stitches and told his story, I was truly glad that I'd had the flu and didn't go along on his little venture that time. The wounded ringtail got away (probably with less long-term damage than my friend), and my friend ended up having to trade a deer haunch to another guy in order to get one. Even then, it turned out not to be worth the price, since it had a sizable hole right between the eyes that had to be patched with a scrap of raccoon, which didn't exactly match.

Bagging a few mice for the display seemed like a cinch job, so we set out with our trap (we couldn't get one the right size and, in hindsight, it's pretty obvious that the one we took for the job was way too big) to camp out for the night and return the next morning with a few live mice in a box.

Even though our mousetrap was decidedly sub-par, we got lots of takers.

The trap was designed to catch the mice alive. With an animal so small, it's pretty hard to mount them realistically if they have any visible wounds. So much for great plans destroyed by too much thinking.

We set our trap and cooked ourselves a hearty dinner of sausage, baked potatoes, and roasting ears and stretched out under the stars in our sleeping bags, content with all the world. Sometime during the night, our trap had a change of heart, or developed a mean streak, or some such cockeyed madness. Anyway, when we checked it at just about dawn, over a hundred dead mice crowded one end, like the victims of a disaster film piled up at the morgue, only they weren't gonna get up and go home when the film stopped rolling.

Contrary to the leaflet that came with that contrary trap, those creatures were all sincerely dead. Friends, it was truly an awful sight.

Standing there looking at them, we scratched our heads and tried to retrace our steps. Somehow we did everything just right, and it all came out wrong just to spite us.

Well, we were not to be outdone by a worthless contraption. If those mice were dead, then we would just have to find a use for them. There was still some ice in our cooler, so we picked out the best-looking half dozen for the diorama and set about cleaning and dressing the rest.

The coyotes must keep our names and my friend's license number in their address books under "parties thrown by total strangers." There were enough little mouse bodies to satisfy a pack of coyotes that night.

The succulent meat we took home with us fed lots of human beings as well, fewer when some of them found out just what they were eating, but some people were born stuck up and at least we found that out before we trusted those folks to watch the kids or feed the dog for us.

Hot Hunan Stir-Fried Field Mouse
Serves 4

One of the best things about this recipe is the subtle flavor of the meat. Field mouse tastes nothing at all like chicken, but rather a bit like rabbit only darker, more tender, and with a slightly sweet overcast that's elusive but nonetheless distinctive. Also, the pieces are uniform, bite-sized chunks without any special cutting. Since a field mouse weighs about 4 ounces and you're only eating the thighs, six to eight mice per person works out about right for this recipe.

Stir-fries are always good with beef or chicken, but you might want to try this one with duck, woodchuck, beaver, prairie dog, or rattlesnake. All are just wonderful.

Serve with rice.

> *20 to 30 field mice, dressed*
> *¼ cup peanut oil*
> *3 to 4 cloves garlic, finely minced*
> *½-inch piece of fresh ginger, peeled and sliced paper thin*
> *¼ cup Hunan sauce (available where Asian foods are sold)*
> *1 onion, diced*
> *4 to 5 carrots, cut into 2-inch matchsticks*
> *1 cup trimmed green beans*
> *½ cup whole almonds or cashews*
> *1 (4-ounce) can baby corn*
> *1 (3-ounce) can water chestnuts*
> *¼ cup soy sauce*

Steam the mouse thighs for about 3 minutes to facilitate removing the bone. Cut straight down the inside of the meat and find a little bone about twice as thick as a toothpick and two thirds as long. Remove the bone. With the bone removed, the meat forms a dense little oval that fits in the palm of your hand. You can leave them in one piece or cut them in half if you have children or older guests.

Heat the peanut oil in a wok over high heat. Throw in the garlic and fresh ginger. Toss in the mouse thighs and quickly stir in the Hunan sauce.

When the mouse is better than half cooked, 3 to 5 minutes, add the onion, carrots, and green beans. Stir vigorously another few minutes, adding the nuts, baby corn, water chestnuts, and soy sauce a scant minute before you intend to serve.

Serve in individual bowls at the table.

Note: If you keep fresh ginger in the freezer, you can slice it as thin as a sheet of onion skin writing paper and never lose a drop of the precious juice into your cutting board.

 **Store-Bought Goodness**

One of the folks that I served mouse up to took such a liking to it, that he determined to have it once a month on the first Sunday. Trouble is, he was born and bred to city living, and he hadn't a notion of how to go about hunting anything more elusive than theater tickets.

He was possessed of a wickedly creative turn of mind, though, and soon enough, he solved the puzzle for himself.

Along one wall of his place, he had put up a sizable stand with several aquariums on it. Seems he had quite a liking to tropical fish and took great delight in admiring their lovely colors through the glass. Well, things took a turn for him when the pet store he frequented added boa constrictors to their stock.

Pet stores being what they are, they never sell anything what they don't supply the customer with the means to feed and house it as well. With boa constrictors, this means white mice.

Now, this is something that I never knew before, but all things considered, it makes sense—namely, that white mice for sale as snake food are graded from small to jumbo, like eggs in a supermarket.

Okay. At first, the pet store wasn't sure how to handle the situation when my friend informed them that he wanted to skip the one at a time bit and buy jumbo white mice by the dozen. He made the mistake of telling them that he didn't actually own a snake and that the mice were for him. Thereafter, he had to buy his mice from another store.

Like I said earlier, some people are way yonder stuck up and have some funny ideas because of it. It seems that they were all for it when they thought he wanted a dozen mice for pets, and it was still cool if he owned a tribe of hungry snakes and planned to dangle live mice at them one at a time, but Katie bar the door and call the police when he told them that he planned to dip them in tempura sauce.

Eventually, he found a pet store that would special order a dozen jumbo white mice for him once a month and not ask pushy questions, the answer to which was rightly none of their business. Thereafter, he enjoyed mouse tempura on the first Sunday of every month without interruption. He kindly invited me to join him once or twice, though I couldn't help but notice that he was more than grateful to have me arrive early and help with the cleaning and dressing.

Domestically raised white mice from the pet store stock have a kind of bland taste to my way of thinking, though I don't see why it wouldn't be possible to keep the little buggers penned for a few weeks and feed them sugar water and sunflower seeds. My friend seemed to prefer the domestic variety to the deer mice that I brought him now and then, but I can't tell you whether that is due to the difference in taste or the origin of the meat in question.

I did say he was born and bred to the city. Perhaps he had his suspicions of meat that didn't hale from a store, any store.

Field Mouse Tempura

Serves 6 to 7

Usually, tempura is served with a dipping sauce that is made from ginger and soy. That's good, but field mouse has a tender flavor all its own and works better with something slightly sweeter than salty. Crossing cultural barriers in search of a unique taste is not a crime. You want to serve chile rellenos with a pasta dish, go right ahead. With field mouse tempura, I like to put out a dipping sauce made from tamarind paste. Some Asian markets sell tamarind concentrate in a liquid form, making the whole process much easier, but in any event, if all you can find is the blocks of paste, then take the time to mix it with a little water, boil it, and strain out the seeds. It is sweet and sultry and complements the mouse very well. Enjoy.

You might also try this one with chicken, duck, beef, woodchuck, or prairie dog.

> *20 to 30 field mice, dressed*
> *4 to 5 cups peanut oil*
> *3 egg yolks*
> *2 cups very cold water*
> *½ teaspoon lemon pepper*
> *3 cups flour (garbanzo flour lends a nice flavor to the batter)*
> *2 garnet yams (sweet potatoes), sliced ¼ inch thick*
> *2 sweet yellow onions, sliced ¼ inch thick*

Steam the mouse thighs for 3 minutes to facilitate removing the bone. Cut straight down the inside of the meat and find a little bone about twice as thick as a toothpick and two-thirds as long. Remove the bone and slice the thighs lengthwise into halves.

Preheat the oven to 200°F.

Heat the oil in the wok to 365°F.

While the oil is heating, mix the batter. Beat the egg yolks with a fork and add the cold water, mixing lightly. Stir in the lemon pepper. Add 2 cups of the flour all at once and mix just enough to combine. Don't fret, it's supposed to be lumpy. Set the remaining flour nearby for use in dredging.

Dredge the slices of sweet potato one at a time in the flour, then dip into the batter. Shake off excess batter and slip into the hot oil. Fry until crisp, 3 to 4 minutes. Remove from the oil and drain well. (Hint: If you don't want the tempura to get soggy, it's a good idea to drain them on a very fine wire screen. You can use paper towels if you want, but change them frequently.) After cooking, keep the individual servings warm in the oven for a few minutes so they're edible when you offer them to your buddies. Repeat the entire process with the onion.

Repeat all that again with the field mouse thighs, but cook them for 4 to 6 minutes to ensure doneness. Drain well.

Serve on a decorative platter and arrange in overlapping rows for a handsome presentation. Tempura should be served hot or it gets gummy textured.

Armadillo

Besides man, armadillos are the only animal known to carry leprosy. Bummer, huh? I've never heard of a case of anybody catching the disease from hunting the animals, but you never know. It wouldn't hurt to take a few precautions.

Field Dressing and Preparation

Wear disposable gloves and don't take anything home with you but the dressed meat. While we're on that subject, dressing armadillo is not so hard as it might look at first glance. The armored banding that protects them from predators is open at the bottom, like a skirt. You can separate him from the shell by scraping your knife through the heavy skin that binds him to it, but keep your blade firmly against the inside of the shell—you don't want to slash the flesh. It's also a good idea to carry an aluminum pot and some water since the best way to remove the hair from his underside is to dip the carcass in boiling water for a minute or two. After dipping in boiling water, you can scrape the hair off as easily as if you were scaling a fish. Clean and gut as you would for rabbit (see page 140), only you don't need to bother skinning him. Once the shell is off, you've done your duty.

Armadillo Sincerity

The biggest difficulty in hunting armadillos is trying not to laugh. Armadillos are really noisy as they plow their way through the undergrowth and at no other time do they make more racket than when they are feeling amorous.

To this end, the surest way to hunt them is to get yourself a good solid wooden baseball bat. Make your way out to the scrub country where they prefer to live and take a seat on a suitable rock.

The armadillo mating dance consists of a riotous ballet where the female—playing the coy debutante—runs away (but not in a direct line—that would defeat the purpose), angling her escape in a series of wide circles like the coils of a spring.

The male designs his circle dance to intersect hers but not follow directly in her path. In this fashion, they pretend to be going about their separate business, all the while making enough noise to keep the other aware of their presence, and allowing for the occasional exciting interception where they invariably whistle and turn flips.

Well, the male turns flips. After all, he wants his ladylove to see how excited he is to run into her, doesn't he? Trouble is, he's not exactly designed for flip turning.

The armadillo's body curls up beautifully into a clever little ball when he feels threatened, but the very design that permits him to do this puts a serious crimp on the business of flip turning. Not to be deterred by anything so insignificant as genetics, he nevertheless turns a flip to impress his lady.

That is, he starts off to turn a flip. What he does, in fact, is launch himself into the air with his nose pointed to the sky, wriggling his feet madly in a vain attempt to throw his weight into an arc. Partway into this amazing performance, he realizes that it can't be done, so he pulls his head in just in time to land on it with a thump, whereupon he leaps up and rushes off to try it again.

Believe it or not, the female is duly impressed by this display of male bravado, which goes to show you that women love nothing so much as sincerity.

It is possible to thump them in the head with your bat at any time during the mating dance, though personally, I think that's beyond the bounds of fair.

Despite the constraints of their armored bodies, armadillos are pretty active. If you wait until after they have mated, the female will trundle off in search of a few bugs for her postcoital snack and you can walk right up to the exhausted male and end his life with one quick blow. Great chili and the fellow in the pot died happy. Who could ask for more?

Armadillo Chili

Serves 6 to 8

Armadillo makes the best chili in the world, but don't say this out loud in front of somebody who raises cattle. They feel threatened enough without you reminding them that there are alternatives to beef.

Now that I've said that, I can almost feel somebody taking aim at me with a lawsuit—the same way you can feel it when somebody's pointing a gun at you.

Let me just say that I don't have a thing against beef. I've probably consumed something close to a small herd in my lifetime. I have a particular fondness for blue shirts too, but I do occasionally wear another color, if for no other reason than that I like blue all the better the next day. Lighten up.

When you make this chili, don't do anything so low as to stoop to putting in beans. Folks add beans to stuff when they're too cheap to fill out the volume with meat. Beans are a side dish. You like beans, fine, then make them available at the table, but don't dilute the beauty of a great chili with beans.

Great chili can also be made with beef, goat, sheep, or buffalo.

6 strips of bacon, cut into 1-inch pieces
1 cup chopped onion
3 cloves garlic, minced
4 pounds boneless armadillo meat, cut into cubes
2 cups canned tomatoes (I prefer the Italian varieties
*   for their flavor)*
¼ cup chili powder
2 teaspoons ground cumin
½ cup picante sauce

In a large pot, brown the bacon over medium heat until the fat is rendered but the bacon is still soft, about 4 minutes. Throw in the onion and the garlic and sauté until the onion is clear.

Add the armadillo meat to the pot and brown on all sides, stirring regularly to prevent sticking.

Add the tomatoes, chili powder, cumin, and picante sauce. Cover and simmer for about 4 hours.

This stuff is best made the day before and heated up when you're ready to treat your guests. For some reason, the flavors like to spend a little time together in the fridge and work out their differences. Of course, it's right good if served up the same day it's made.

Grasshopper

You can chase grasshoppers with a butterfly net, or you can get lazy about it and string up seines in corn fields. If you've been reading this book and paying attention then you know that I'm about to let you in on the laziest path to success that I can think of.

Get yourself a raggedy old seine and tie it up between a couple of poles. If you're really lazy, then you're way ahead of me and figured out that using the clothesline poles is the easiest way to go. Be sure that your seine has a very fine gap, not more than ½ inch; if it's much less than that, then you will lose the larger, tastier grasshoppers simply because they won't any more get hung in it than you would catch your foot in a post hole no bigger than the heel of your shoe. It takes a little fiddling, but when you get it right you'll know it. The right-sized gap will catch all the larger grasshoppers and a few of the medium size, but it will allow the smaller ones to skip through.

Now, the next thing that you need to do is sit down nearby with a bucket of fair-sized stones to chuck when the crows happen to see what you are up to and drop by to rob your catch. Makes sense, sure . . . why chase a bunch of hoppers yourself when some enterprising human has set out a buffet?

They're not just ready and willing to steal a bunch of hoppers from you; if some buddy of theirs developed thumbs overnight and set up a similar device they'd steal his hoppers, too. Crows are nothing if not egalitarian.

Those stuffed scarecrow things work best when the wind is blowing up a storm, and that's no good 'cause you're likely to catch fewer grasshoppers if that is the case.

Grasshoppers like it hot and still. A lot of hunting is sitting and waiting and knowing when to keep your peace and when to shift your carcass quick-like. I suggest you keep a goodly amount of stones handy because if you have to go and pick up another load, then while your back is turned, half of your hoppers will disappear and at least one crow will have managed to get either a foot or a wing hung in your seine. This usually means that you have to scrap it and make another net.

When my son was little, I used to pay out in chocolates for him to play some noisy game near where I had my nets strung. The grasshoppers could care less what he was up to, but the crows found him annoying and stayed pretty well off. I did, too, but since I had to cope with that sort of thing on a daily basis anyhow, I figured I may as well get a few hoppers out of the deal.

Field Dressing and Preparation

Clean and prepare the grasshoppers by removing the wings, the antennae, the forelegs, and the lower portion of the back legs. You should be left with the body and the thick upper portion of the back legs intact.

Grasshoppers Roasted with Piñon Nuts

Serves 3

While grasshoppers are a snap to acquire, piñon nuts are another matter altogether. The piñon is native to the southwestern United States, and gathering the nuts takes quite a bit of dedication. They are horribly sticky, and the cones they are hiding in have nasty little ridges that will grab at your hands in the tenderest places. It's work, but the taste is found nowhere else. If it all sounds too much for you, you can get close to it with pine nuts, which nowadays are available in most retail stores that sell gourmet foods and quite a few just plain food stores.

You can roast grasshoppers and piñon nuts in a metal bowl, if you've a mind to, but you have to have a pair of really big mitts, and they need to be double thick at that 'cause it gets some hot. Believe it or not, the Pima Indians used to do this trick in a basket. Naturally, this was a trick performed by the women, since it requires enormous skill and dexterity to cook the piñon nuts and not burn a hole in your basket. They cooked piñon nuts in this fashion, but I don't know if they ate grasshoppers or not. That taste treat was added by me.

By the way, you can pan roast grasshoppers in oil all you want, but piñon nuts, no matter which method you use to do it, have to be dry roasted.

> *2 or 3 dozen fresh grasshoppers, wings, antennae, and legs removed*
> *½ pound of piñon nuts*

Layer the bottom of a large, sturdy wooden bowl with grasshoppers and cover them with piñon nuts. Cover the piñon nuts with a layer of hot coals and commence to shake the whole thing, rolling the contents of the bowl against one another and keeping the whole works in constant motion. By this method, you should spare the bowl most of the stress of the heat and cook the grasshoppers and the piñon nuts to a tasty turn.

Dump the contents of the bowl onto a tight wire screen when you think you are done. Allow to cool and pick out the coals with tongs. After a while, you can do this with your hands.

Food Group Smart Trail Mix

Serves 10 to 12

This trail mix provides a fine blend of all the vitamins and minerals you need to keep in good form. There's actually plenty of sugars in the grasshoppers, but the taste of a little chocolate gives the mix that extra bite it needs.

For those of you who haven't tried them, Jerusalem artichokes are the roots of sunflowers. Sliced thin and pan-fried, they have a pleasant al dente crunch that complements a bag of mixed nuts and fruits very well.

1½ cups fresh grasshoppers, wings, antennae, and legs removed
Butter or peanut oil
1 cup Jerusalem artichokes, cleaned, trimmed, and thinly sliced
1 cup dried crab apple slices
1 cup dried cranberries
¾ cup currants
¾ cup golden raisins
1 cup pine nuts
¾ cup cashews
¾ cup almonds
½ cup betel nuts, shelled
¾ cup roasted sunflower seeds
1 cup M&M's

Place the grasshoppers in a large, sturdy wooden bowl and cover with a layer of hot coals. Shake, rolling the contents of the bowl to keep them in constant motion, until well roasted. Dump the bowl onto a tight wire screen. Allow to cool and pick out the coals with tongs.

Heat a little butter or peanut oil in a skillet. Toss the Jerusalem artichoke slices until they begin to turn a handsome gold and start to brown around the edges. They have a nice, even grain and don't do much curling unless sliced too thin. Drain on paper towels and let cool.

Toss the roasted hoppers, Jerusalem artichoke chips, and remaining ingredients into a paper bag and roll down the top. Shake it around until it's well mixed. Distribute into plastic bags with good seal on them and take off for your walk.

Ant

Red ants are those half-inch monstrosities that crowd the western plains with mounds the size of a prairie dog town. Red ants have such a strong flavor of pepper about them that they make an exceptionally good substitute for it.

To collect them, you will need: an old glass milk bottle, two lumps of sugar, a smear of oil, and two or three mason jars.

As it goes without saying, though I'll repeat it here anyway: Remember to harvest your ants in a place where you are absolutely sure that nobody has been spraying for them. Ants are hardy and may well survive several attempts to poison them, though we can't be sure that you would be so lucky or so tough as an ant.

Locate a suitable bed of red ants and stake out your territory. Drop the lumps of sugar in the bottom of the milk bottle. Smear a bit of oil inside of the bottle just past the mouth; you want the oil on the downward slope on the inside of the bottle and not around the inside of the mouth.

Dig a divot in the ground about three inches deep and set the heavy end of the bottle in it at an angle. Use the extra dirt to build a ramp to the mouth of the bottle and to support it. When you're done, the bottle should be elevated slightly but not radically and the ramp of dirt should be a gradual climb. The whole business shouldn't be further than three or four feet from the mouth of the anthill.

Get a good book and wait—not too close to the bottle, but close enough that you can easily get a good look at it and monitor the situation.

If you did this right, the ants can get into the bottle, which of course they really want to do, but they can't get out again. That sugar is too good a prize to pass up. The benefits to the anthill would be tremendous if they could get it out of that bottle and back home again. To this end, more and more workers will join their friends inside in an effort to rescue the prize.

When the bottle looks to be getting a tad crowded, relieve the pressure by dumping the contents into a mason jar and resetting the bait. If you let the bottle get too full of ants before you harvest, those crafty little devils will do something that humans rarely try—

namely, they'll cooperate with one another. Given enough numbers, they'll build a chain and hoist the sugar and all of the ants they can reach out of the trap.

After two or three such harvests, you should have enough ants to cook up a fine batch of ants and pistachios.

Red Ants Roasted with Pistachios

Serves 4

Some people like to put a touch of sugar in with their ants, but I think it kills the natural peppery flavor. Sadly, red ants lose a lot of their flamboyant color when cooked, but they will keep cooked for at least a week without benefit of refrigeration.

If you like curried cauliflower, try trimming the cauliflower very fine and cutting half your curry powder with red ants. It makes for quite an exciting variation.

> *2 tablespoons peanut or safflower oil*
> *2 cups red ants*
> *½ cup pistachios, finely chopped*
> *Pinch of nutmeg*

Heat a little oil in a wok and pour the ants into it all at once. Stir at your own risk. It's best to wait a minute before you stick a spoon in there. Add the pistachios and nutmeg as quick as you can and then begin to stir. The whole business shouldn't take more than 3 minutes tops. Allow to cool and serve.

FISH AND SEAFOOD

Catfish

Catfish like to hide under a ledge and watch the parade go by, picking and choosing a meal from the line of offerings. This makes them a little chancy to catch, since if you drop a worm or other offering, they'll simply take it and dive back into their hole, and you're left with the serious business of reeling him in while your line rasps against rock. Good way to have to refit your reel. Believe it or not, catfish are attracted to Ivory Soap and will follow a cube of it if you drag and tease them. Cut a small cube and bait your hook with it. Set yourself up in a place that does not allow for a bank that's cut back so that you can be well assured that the catfish you are after is not under your feet. Then drag your soap through the water a couple of times. When they bite it, they'll be out from under snags and you can bring them in pretty easily. Soap has the extra advantage of being repugnant to turtles, so you don't have to bother deciding whether to throw back an endless stream of turtles who are stealing your bait or have turtle soup that afternoon and be done with it.

You can catch a lot of fish by hunting with tobacco. Spit on a small chunk a couple of times and work it with your fingers for a minute, then toss it into the water. Tobacco paralyzes fish and you can scoop them up with a net. I've heard of guys fishing with dynamite; but for one thing, it kills too many, and for another, it's loud and that tends to attract the game warden, who takes a dim view of such methods.

I have to say that I more than agree with them. Not only is it overly greedy to kill more fish than you can eat, dynamite does a lot of damage to the area and afterwards the fish populations, from small-fry to game fish, take a long time to recover.

Now and then a dynamite fisherman blows up his boat or donates a couple of fingers to the cause of greed and stupidity, but since that charity is already overflowing, I think we can safely dispense with adding to it.

While tobacco is not inherently dangerous to the fisherman (unless he happens to be smoking it or chewing it while he's fishing), the big trouble with dropping a wad of tobacco in the water is that it is indiscriminate, namely, it doesn't care whether the fish it kills are legal size or not. You might not either, but if you take too many of the young ones before they're old enough to reproduce, then you will begin to care a lot when the fish population dwindles so low that there are none left to catch. On the plus side, the tobacco method is free of game warden intervention and subsequent fines, if you're reasonably careful with it. If he happens by and sees you chewing, he'll just think you're stupid and will go about his business, though he might check back on you when you think you're alone, so its best to actually keep your line in the water and listen for surreptitious footsteps.

For myself, I always find that a fish tastes better if I play the game according to the rules.

Fish, bless their lovely little hearts, come in all imaginable sizes. Rainbow trout average from 2 to 5 pounds but have been recorded at over 30 pounds. Brook trout usually weigh 2 to 3 pounds but can weigh several times that amount. Lake trout tend to weigh about 6 to 8 pounds and rarely much more. A healthy largemouth bass ranges from 8 to 10 pounds and his cousin, the smallmouth bass, averages about 6 pounds. The spotted bass covers both ranges but tends to average between 6 and 8 pounds.

My favorite, the catfish, is the most amazing of all. The stonecat and the bullhead are small and rarely exceed 3 pounds, but the channel cat can easily weigh up to 20 pounds, the flathead can grow up to 5 feet in length and weigh up to 50 pounds, and the blue cat can exceed 150 pounds. Ya gotta love that in a fish. Apparently, the catfish will grow to fill the limits of his environment and some members of the species live in places with lots of elbowroom.

Catching fish is an art that is way yonder too involved for me to go into here. If you don't know somebody who can teach you, then nothing I can say will help. Once you've caught it, I can guide you through cleaning, but catching it is up to you entirely.

Field Dressing and Preparation

Begin to clean your fish by scraping with a knife blade in the same direction as the scales. You'll find that your knife is accumulating a layer of slime; if you remove this before cutting into the flesh, your fish will taste much better when you eat it. Next, use your knife or an old fork and scale the fish by reversing your scraping action and working from the tail forwards to the head.

Wipe your knife clean and cut through the backbone just behind the head, making a short horizontal cut. That done, slit the skin on both sides of the dorsal fin from the upper edge of your cut behind the head all the way to the tail. Cut out the dorsal fin and then cut off the tail. Grip the head firmly in one hand and push down, passing the fingers of your other hand under the backbone and lifting up firmly. The fillets will come out free of the skin, head, and the entrails.

If you want boneless fillets, you can do this slightly differently. Slit the skin from head to tail along the back beside the dorsal fin. Next, slit the skin from just above the head to the front of the anal fin, then alongside the anal fin to the tail. Lift the skin back at the point of your initial cut (behind the head just along the spine). Grasp the skin at the point and pull it back to the tail. It helps to use your knife as a guide to give you a firm grip. Slice the fish from head to tail down the backbone and cut the fillet away from the head and the tail. Repeat this for the other side.

Catfish Piccata

Serves 2

I love a catfish, and a goodly number of my friends had been raised with folks who just stuck the thing on a grill or poked it in the oven without first showing the fish the respect it deserved. I made up my mind to show those folks just how good fish could be and here is the result.

> *2 to 3 catfish fillets*
> *2 tablespoons plus 1 teaspoon lemon juice*
> *½ cup plain yogurt*
> *½ cup all-purpose flour plus more for dredging*
> *¼ cup grated Parmesan cheese*
> *¼ cup grated Romano cheese*
> *1 cup milk*
> *¼ cup peanut oil*
> *2 plum tomatoes, cubed*
> *2 tablespoons butter*
> *½ cup white wine*
> *Freshly cracked black pepper*

Marinate the catfish in the 2 tablespoons lemon juice and yogurt for at least 3 hours.

Blend together the flour, Parmesan, Romano, and milk until you have a smooth paste.

Remove the catfish from the marinade, pat with a little extra flour, and roll it in the paste.

Preheat the oven to 375°F.

Heat the oil in a large skillet over medium-high heat. Add the fish and brown for about 3 minutes per side. Drain on paper towels.

Lay the fish on a rack in a baking pan and bake for 12 minutes.

While the fish is baking, sear the tomatoes in the butter over medium-high heat. Add the remaining 1 teaspoon lemon juice and wine. Reduce for 5 minutes (simmer until most of the liquid has boiled off and left the sauce thick and aggressive).

Pour the sauce over the fish and sprinkle with pepper. Serve hot.

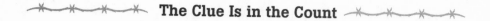 **The Clue Is in the Count**

Another reason I don't get on well with guys who fish with dynamite is that they sometimes take other folks along for the ride.

Pardon me for being so fussy, but I don't particularly like dodging flying debris. It makes me edgy, and I find myself entertaining an irresistible desire to give somebody a good whacking about the ears.

I don't even care for it when I'm the fool who set the world into motion, so naturally, I've got my whacking stick cleaned and oiled in defense of my right not to be belted across the side of the head with a dead fish when a certain party comes to my place uninvited.

By now you know that I'm thinking of a particular time, so I'll get on with the telling of it and not string you any further down the path than we need to go to get there.

One of the ways you can get yourself a nice catfish without fighting the rocks and logs he lives under is to put out cornmeal cakes for him. I've already said a few words about what a load of trouble catfish are to lure out from under the rocks, but there's more than one way to skin a fish and more than one way to hook him as well. This method ensures that your fish is well filled out and sweet tasting when you finally bring him in, but you have to visit the same site every day or so for upwards of a couple of weeks for it to work.

Catfish, like many another animal, man included, can't resist a sweet cornmeal cake. They'll take it right up and grow fat and happy on it. With this in mind, you can seed a favorite fishing hole with bits of leftovers and be assured that your fish will grow so accustomed to occupying the middle of the stream, laying in wait for today's cake, that when you drop one in with a hook attached, he'll snap right onto it and pop out of the water free and clear of the rock ledges along the bank where he's like to spend the rest of the day.

I had been feeding a beauty of a catfish for better'n a week and was just about ready to harvest when this old boy came along with his tomfool ideas on fishing and ruined the whole business for me.

I'd seen him many a time before. He was the uncle of a friend of mine. The man worked with heavy machinery for a living, and he was so good at it that he was missing three fingers—that ought to tell you something right there.

If I'd seen him coming, I woulda had for him before he got his matches out and that woulda been the end of it, but he snuck up on me whilst I was busy admiring my fish, and so the culprit was fully involved in assaulting nature and his fellow man before I even had a clue that he was there.

My own fault, that. I shoulda been listening for footsteps, but I had just fed my fish and was admiring his lovely skin as he skimmed the surface, playing up for more treats.

I'd about made up my mind that I'd as soon come back everyday just to feed him and look at him and forego laying him out on the table when Uncle Doofus stepped into the picture and took the decision clean out of my hands.

First thing I knew, there was a soft "whop," and a couple a bucket loads of creek water and a handful of small fish flew up into the air and doused me a good one. I shook myself off and tore out of the bushes I had been hiding behind, running along the bank to where the idiot with the dynamite was lighting up another.

Not content with dumping half the contents of the creek onto dry land, he was trying for the rest of it. I expect the look on my face musta said it all because he hesitated in his toss, dangling the lit stick from the ends of his fingers for a second before he remembered that it was there. Then he started up quick and dumped it towards the creek.

It hit in about three inches of water that was swashing back and forth over a gravel bed. A second later, the two of us and every bush in a thirty-foot radius was pelted with flying scree.

The bushes had a buncha leaves tore right off them, and I suffered a broken finger on my left hand along with a rash of bruises along my arm and shoulder that measured an inch or so across. My friend's uncle took a couple of big pebbles in the chest and one on the end of his chin that mighta cracked the bone. Anyway, it was bleeding pretty free and I didn't see any shards sticking out so I wasn't much worried about him.

My catfish buddy came off the worst for it. I could see him clear and it was a pitiful sight, too. He was floating belly up, in what of the creek water had survived the assault.

I stepped into the water up past my knees to get him and carried him out by his tail.

Friends, I was so rightly angered by what had transpired that day that I walked right up to that dynamite-totting fool and clouted him one across the back of the head with that dead fish. Knocked him flat with it and served him right. Then I gave him a ride into town to the doctor's office.

I was still holding my fish by the tail and nursing the little cuts I had all over me when the doctor came out with my friend's uncle in tow. The old boy had more than a few bandages on him. The doctor kept looking at the bruises on my hand and at the fish, and I suppose he wrote a different story than what had actually happened because he offered us his wisdom before we left him.

"I want you people to try to get along with one another," he told us, solemnly wagging his head as doctors are wont to do when they are absolutely sure that they got the right of it.

For a minute, I toyed with the idea that the doctor could use a bit of fish across the side of his fool head, but in the end, I just turned and walked out.

My mother always told me that the more credence you give to an idiot, the more presumptuous he'll become, and I didn't know what that the doctor kept a stick of dynamite or two in his truck. I did notice that he was missing the end of his little finger on the left hand, and I deemed it a goodness to get away from him before he started up talking about fishing with me. After all, my dinner already had one bruise on it.

Fillet of Catfish in Coriander Sauce with a Yogurt Marinade

Serves 4

This recipe is right good with any white-fleshed fish. Trout is especially tasty here, though I hesitate to say it, since trout caught fresh is best with nothing more than a quick pan-fry. Some things are so purely heavenly that anything other than itself alone is an adulteration of true and natural beauty.

> ½ cup plain yogurt
> 1 teaspoon lemon peel, dried and ground
> 1 teaspoon curry powder (see Note, page 239)
> 4 catfish fillets, weighing not more than ½ pound each
> 1 teaspoon white pepper
> 2 tablespoons olive oil
> 1 tablespoon ground coriander
> 2 tablespoons fresh lemon juice
> ½ cup slivered almonds

In a shallow glass dish, mix the yogurt, lemon peel, and about ½ teaspoon of the curry powder. Clean and rinse the fillets, pat them dry on a towel, and immerse them in the yogurt marinade, turning them over several times to be sure they are evenly coated. Let them sit for at least 4 hours in the refrigerator.

Preheat the oven to 400°F. Grease a baking sheet.

Remove the fillets from the marinade and lay them on the prepared baking sheet. Sprinkle them lightly with the white pepper and the remaining ½ teaspoon curry powder.

Bake for about 5 minutes.

While the fish is baking, heat the olive oil over medium heat in a small pan and toss in the coriander. Cook for about 2 minutes, stirring to prevent scorching. Add the lemon juice. Cook for another minute or two.

Arrange the baked fish fillets on a serving dish, cover with the coriander, and sprinkle the whole works with almonds. Serve immediately.

Note: If you prefer a paste to curry powder, you can try another method that I like. Spread a little biryani sauce on the baking sheet and lay the fish on it to bake. It makes for a very interesting taste since the sweet, hot biryani is concentrated on one side and the coriander and almonds on the other.

Salmon

Atlantic salmon are more closely related to trout than they are to Pacific salmon. The brown trout can actually fertilize Atlantic salmon eggs. The Chinook salmon, sometimes known as the king salmon, the largest of the Pacific breeds, has both a spring and a fall run to spawning grounds and can be found in great numbers in the Columbia and the Yukon Rivers and sometimes in the early winter as far south as the Sacramento River in California, though the greatest numbers are to be found in northern waters. Since they primarily feed on other fish, the Chinook will take baits readily, but only young weighing 15 to 20 pounds can be brought in with rod and tackle and then only by the most skilled of anglers.

Field Dressing and Preparation

Clean and dress as you would any fish (see page 233), though with a salmon of 10 pounds or greater, it can be gutted and cut into steaks easily.

 **Fishing the Fisherman**

If you take yourself to the Pacific Northwest in the fall, you can harvest quite a few salmon by watching the bears and retrieving what they leave by the wayside.

Late in the fall, when bears are trying to add as much fat as possible with a minimum of effort, they will strip the fat rich skin off of a salmon and throw the rest of the fish away. Dozens of skinless salmon flop on the shoals when the bears are hard at their fishing.

Sneaking along behind the bears and picking up these fish is a fast way to get quite a few, but not an easy one. Bears tend to take offense at strangers profiting from their work, and they will defend their right to fish in the privacy of their favorite family fishing hole with sudden outbursts of violence that would astound the most jaded woodsman. Add to that the fact that bears are pretty testy in the late fall and resent being disturbed at the serious business of preparing for winter.

Even at the best of times, bears are an uncertain element, certain only in the grim reality of their speed and strength. A group of them fishing, bent on consuming much-needed fats, is something that should only be approached by a seasoned veteran of bear behavior, and then only if he has put his affairs in order first.

I can't think of a better way to commit suicide than to irritate a bear, unless maybe you'd prefer to push over a row of motorcycles parked outside of a rough bar. Truth is though, a bunch of angry motorcycle jocks are a way yonder easier to reason with than a bear who thinks his space has been invaded.

I have collected fish from bears in this fashion, but I've also been told that there's something seriously wrong with me. Could be.

Salmon Steamed in Spinach with Hot Peanut Sauce

Serves 4

This is something of a difficult recipe in terms of getting the timing just right. Sticky rice is contrary, and it stiffens within 15 minutes after cooking, so you should plan this to be ready just when you need it. It also helps to get the rice out of the pan and lay it out on a bit of waxed paper. It can be real hard to get out of the pan if you let it harden in there.

¼ cup fresh lemon juice

¼ cup olive oil

2 teaspoons ground cumin

2 teaspoons cayenne pepper

4 salmon fillets

6 tablespoons crunchy peanut butter

½ cup Thai hot peanut sauce (available where Asian foods are sold)

1 cup cooked sticky rice

Fresh spinach leaves, to wrap salmon fillets

In a shallow bowl, mix together the lemon juice, oil, cumin, and cayenne. Roll the salmon fillets in the mixture until they are well coated. Lay out flat on a large cutting board.

Stir together the peanut butter and peanut sauce and set aside.

Spread ¹/₄ cup of cooked sticky rice over half of the surface of each salmon fillet, spooning ¹/₄ of the peanut sauce mix into the middle of the rice.

Roll up each salmon fillet, starting with the end you spread the rice and peanut sauce on. Secure temporarily with a toothpick. Wrap each fillet in spinach leaves and steam for 5 minutes.

Serve immediately, as they do not keep well.

Salmon Pan-Fried in Grubs

Serves 2

By now, at least one or two confused souls are reading this with a mixed sense of horror and wonderment, asking themselves if by "grubs," I might perchance mean those thick white things you dig up in your garden when you're turning it over in the spring. I surely do mean one and the same animal, and believe me, no richer source of sweet fat will you find if you wander to the ends of the earth. There is little to a grub other than fat and skin. The troublesome skin is a snap to get rid of, and I'm here to tell you how tasty the fat is. Grub fat has a sugary sweet flavor and cooks up pure and clear with a remarkably light taste on the tongue. For the fragile and often elusive heaven of fresh fish, grub fat is the one pan-fry ingredient you can use that won't overwhelm the flavors you spent all afternoon fishing for.

> *2 cups fresh grubs*
> *2 fresh salmon steaks*

Wash the grubs by dipping them in water in a net bag.

Prepare a fire and let it reduce to a few sprigs of flame and a healthy bed of coals. Shove a large cast-iron skillet into the coals so that the coals creep halfway up the sides and let it heat for a count of ten. Toss the grubs into the hot skillet. If the skillet was heated correctly, their skins will split open at once. With a metal spatula, separate the skins from the grub fat that is sizzling in the pan and toss them into the fire.

Before the fat can begin to brown, lay the salmon steaks in the pan and cook quickly—a scant few minutes per side is plenty. Enjoy.

Mesquite-Smoked Fish Sushi Rolls

Serves 3 to 4

The variety of fish you choose is not all that important since anything from speckled trout to salmon will do. Now that I've said that, I feel I have to put in a good word for bass. Even though bass is considered a panfish, it is awfully good in this recipe. Fish for bass in weedy ponds and slow-moving streams. They prefer cool water and are best caught just at nightfall when the air falls silent of daytime traffic. They feed along the shoreline and can be hauled in using noiseless lures. They like to lurk near logs that provide them a good hiding place, so some skill is involved in bringing in a sizable bass without snapping your line on a snag. But the taste of their flesh is well worth the effort it takes to learn their ways and outsmart the hidden threats to your fishing line that populate the bass's chosen home. If you go store-bought, chose pike or mackerel, the bass's cousins, for similar taste.

When it comes to sheets of nori, I am picky. I prefer Hon Asakusa Red, available from Nagai's. It comes in 8- by 7-inch sheets.

> 2 boneless fish fillets (any variety)
> 1½ cups water
> 1 cup sweet rice (also called sushi rice, glutinous rice, or short-grain rice)
> Nori sheets
> Scallions, trimmed and sliced lengthwise
> ½ cup pickled carrots, sliced very thinly
> ½ cup pickled ginger

Prepare the smoker with mesquite wood chips according to the manufacturer's directions. Lay the fillets on a flat pan in the smoker and do them up to your personal taste. Since this is a sushi dish, you can stick to the basics and smoke your fish for a scant 3 minutes or cook it clean through if that's how you like it.

To cook the sweet rice, pour the water into a small saucepan and bring to a boil. Decrease the heat immediately to maintain a gentle simmer and add the rice. Cover and simmer for 20 minutes. Turn off the heat and allow the rice to sit covered and undisturbed for about 5 minutes. This allows the condensation on the lid of the pot to resolve itself with the rice and join the party. Sweet rice becomes hard to work as it cools down so it is best to have all your other ingredients laid out on the board and ready to work with when the rice is done. If you leave the rice alone to its own devices, it will set up in the pan and become impossible to work in less than a half hour. It's best to transfer the whole works to a piece of waxed paper so it can be steamed for reheating if necessary. Don't forget to draw some water in the pan so you can clean it later without throwing out your elbow in the process.

Lay a sheet of nori on the sushi mat and spread a layer of sweet rice over about half its surface, working lengthwise, not side to side. Top the rice with a slice of smoked fish and then lay a couple of lengths of scallions, a few slices of pickled carrot, and the ginger on top of the fish.

Roll the whole thing up, starting from the side with the rice and fish layered on it and working towards the excess nori until you have a tube with at least a half sheet of nori covering itself. You can brush the nori with a dab of water (with a basting brush) so it will stick to itself without a struggle.

When you've used all your fish and you have a small pile of nori tubes on your cutting board where fish and veggies used to be, cut the tubes into handy rounds with an extra sharp knife.

Serve immediately. If you have any of that Japanese hot mustard sauce, set it down on the table near your favorite brother-in-law—the one who's always bragging that the world never made a pepper too hot for him. Keep a napkin handy unless you especially want him to see you laughing your fool head off.

Crab

Crabs are part of the ocean's clean-up crew. They generally feed on the bodies of the fallen and any other tidbit of detached flesh that they can grasp. Very large crabs will take small fish successfully as well as smaller crabs when they can catch one, but for the most part, count on the one you have in your net to have followed the general order of the day for crabs and to have been munching on carrion. Most of them do. To this end, it's a good idea to fish for crabs in water that is clean and free of stagnation or pollution.

Field Dressing and Preparation

No special cleaning needs to be done to cook a crab, though it's generally a good practice to rinse them off thoroughly with a hose before you put them in to boil. Tie up their claws with rubber bands before you put more than one crab in a bucket of water. If you don't, they'll fight each other and the winner will pull the loser's claws off.

Where's My Line?

Coaxing crabs out of the water is an art, but not one that is all that difficult to learn. Even rank beginners can do pretty well for themselves if they don't get in too big a hurry. Just remember that the only hook you have on the crab is his greed. He wants that free lunch, and he wants it bad, so encourage him to stick with it by pulling the string in slowly. Don't make it too much work, or your prize will turn back and look for easier pickings— namely, he'll dine on whatever he can find that seems inclined to stay put. If chasing down lunch gets to be too much work, he'll give up. If you do it too slowly, then he'll have most of his prize eaten by the time the beach hoves into sight, and he'll let go rather than risk exposing himself for so little reward. After a few tries, you'll get good at it. All it takes is a spot where there are plenty of volunteers, and a bait bucket with a goodly supply of chicken necks in it, although even this is not a problem. Once you get pretty good at it, you can re-use the same neck a dozen times before you encounter a wily old veteran who is clever enough to take it off you before you get him to the beach.

People who enjoy fishing for crabs end up with a favorite stretch of beach. I prefer the Gulf of Mexico myself. From the Florida Panhandle to Corpus Christi, Texas, there are dozens of great little coves with more crabs than the ecosystem can comfortably support. Every so often, I do my best to ease the population strain. The parts of the Texas shore that are protected by Padre Island have some especially profitable fishing spots. I taught my son how to crab along that stretch of beach. Since it's my favorite spot, you'll forgive me if I don't give away the exact location.

Here's where that warning about knowing your limitations and sticking with that comes in.

My boy was about six years old and inclined to think that he was big enough and ornery enough to handle just about any situation that came his way. Mostly that was the truth, but he wasn't used to being ganged up on, and that's what happened to him that day we went crabbing.

He learned how to tease that string right away and succeeded in pulling in a crab on his second try. Well, if that was fun, wouldn't taking on two strings be even better? Guess so. And two was plenty for a while. He got so good at it that he got bored. Up to that point, we hadn't had too many volunteers. One string at a time had a caller, and the kid had the knack of keeping a watchful eye on one line while slowly winding up the other. He was a natural. After a couple of hours, we counted up our catch, bound their claws, and dumped them into a big cooler full of saltwater so we could free up our buckets for more victims. Then we moved to another spot not more than half a mile away, where the locals hadn't warned their brethren about the hazards of following a meal out of the water.

My son settled under our lean-to out of the sun with a string on each thumb and another on each big toe. He was a fishing fool that day and he thought he had those crabs on the run. I suppose they'd had enough of his uppity ways after he pulled out a dozen of their friends and neighbors, and they decided to teach him a lesson.

I was binding claws when I detected the first sounds of genuine distress.

He had one on each thumb, coming up slowly, and another on his right toe. He was sitting in the sand with his foot a few inches off the ground, turning his ankle just enough to wind the string around his foot, determined to bring in his catch. He might of done it, too, if another crab hadn't seen through his game and decided to call his bet.

He had two at the edge of the water and another just visible where the string dove under when a truly impressive monster began making his way up the beach. That crab had the bait in one claw and a wad of string in the other. Seems like he had been thinking about winding in my boy one gentle tug at a time and had lost his patience.

Friends, he was coming after the prize, waving his monster's claws over his head. His eyes wove back and forth on their stalks and he clacked his jaws at the sight of all that tender meat just sitting there unguarded.

My ribs ached I laughed so hard, though I did stop and get the net in time to scoop up the crabs before they carried my boy back to their nest.

He still loves to eat crabmeat and grins with sheer delight with a succulent claw in his grasp, but he never ties himself down with more than one string nowadays.

I laughed a little too long and cut the margin of error too close for his liking. Not for the first time.

Crab Boiled in Chile Water and Ginger

Serves as many as the number of crabs your bag will allow

Serve with roasted corn and salad. Lemon juice is optional, but test the flavor of the crabmeat before you decide to dip in lemon.

Don't presume to cut the chile in this recipe. Leave it whole. The reason those little red peppers are deemed ornamental is that they are so hot that one is more than a dozen people can eat without burning their lips. Most of the damage comes from the seeds and the greenish yellow flesh inside the pepper. Cutting it allows the seeds to float and catch in the crabmeat. Bad idea. Trust me here. Plenty of chile flavoring will permeate the crabs if you just throw one whole chile in the water and let it be. If all this makes you a tad leery of ornamental chile peppers, then go buy one of those pleasant, sweet-tasting red chiles that most grocery stores carry, and play it safe. Two store-bought red chiles (4 to 5 inches long) are equal to one small ornamental ($1/2$ inch).

> *1 small ornamental chile*
>
> *1 piece of fresh ginger about half the size of your thumb,*
>   *cut into quarters*
>
> *2 to 3 crabs per person for however many guests you are expecting*

Put the biggest pot you have on the fire, filled better than halfway up with water. Add the chile and the ginger.

When the water is boiling hard enough to roll, throw in the crabs and boil until their shells are bright red. It's not a good idea to stand over the pot with your face in the steam because the peppers will make your eyes water pretty bad. Some folks turn redder than the boiled crabs.

Serve hot out of the water.

Crab, Line, and Stinker

My mother used to fix us grilled fish with okra and tomatoes. When I got a bit older, I figured that it was also right good with crabmeat. On one spectacular event, it got fixed with both fish and crab and that's how it got transmogrified into its present form. Providence called for that to happen, though I had to go and buy a few crabs to fill out the bill of fare.

The whole thing took place on a picturesque strip of beach on the Texas coast, near Corpus Christi. I was some young at the time. My son was still checking out the world from one of those papoose carriers. Up to that time, I had never proved to be the best fisherman to hand, so I can understand why my kinsman did what he did. What he did do is give me his old fishing rod as a birthday present. Since this left him without anything to fish with, he was obliged to get himself down to the tackle shop and buy a new one.

Well, even I could see the reasoning behind this. No way could he take me fishing if he didn't have a rod and reel, so we went together and picked out some gear that he'd been hankering over for some time and then made our way to the fishing spot he had picked out.

Right there's where he took one step too far and brought the scrutiny of the fishing gods down on himself—namely, he kept his favorite fishing spot a secret and took me to a place that he scarcely ever stopped by.

Either one of these two nefarious undertakings would be a piece of work that you could beg off on, but both and on a kinsman can't do nothing but bring retribution down on the head of the perpetrator.

We got to the stretch of beach, and he was telling me all kinds of tripe about how this was a right good spot, and he expected I would catch some fine specimens here. All the while he was running his trap, the fishing gods must've been taking notes.

I cast out a couple of times, with the result being that I got to practice reeling in my line. Long about the fourth cast, somewhat took ahold of my line and tried to tug it out to sea with him. Naturally I set up an argument on that account and the push and shove of fishing commenced.

He'd have his way for a bit, then I'd have him where I wanted him until he could see his way around me once more. He showed no interest at all in jumping, but wove from side to side, trying to slip the hook that way. Finally, he tired of that game and made a leap for it, splashing the water in a fit of pique.

Meanwhile, all this commotion had attracted a couple of seagulls, who naturally wanted to see if they could steal whatever it was that I was fooling with on the other end of that line.

About the third time my fish made a jump for it, one of the seagulls made a jump for him, only it didn't work out quite like he had planned it. He was trying to skim the water, grab the fish, and take off at an angle from me, I suspect to prevent me from chasing after him. Somewhere along the way, he got the line around one wing and in the fight to free himself, he got his toes hung up as well. The weight of the thing pulled the whole shebang into the water and bird, fish, and all thrashed in the surf, madder than hell.

The fish was a gafftopsail, one of the family of saltwater catfishes that live around coastal estuaries and harbors. He was too tired to argue by this time and let himself be dragged onto shore in company of a half-drowned seagull.

Along the way, the slack in the line between the captured seagull and the sea cat had snagged a good-sized crab, who joined the party waving his one free claw over his head threateningly, more a "Why, I'm gonna" than a "Why, I oughta."

The gafftopsail and the crab we put in separate buckets so they could cool down in privacy, but the seagull turned out to be another deal altogether. Just turning him loose was an ordeal.

We cut the line fore and aft, but then he proved determined to hobble off down the beach, bound and crippled, but no less rancorous. I stomped on the line to put a hitch in his plans, but that only hiked up his temper another notch.

In the end, my kinsman took off his shirt and threw it over the bird's head so we could keep track of where his beak was while we cut the line away from his wing. After a bit, we were satisfied that we'd done all we could to restore his dignity, so we yanked off the shirt and made a dash for the dunes pretty quick. Good thing, too, 'cause that bird skimmed the beach a couple of times just to be sure that we weren't up to any more insulting shenanigans.

He fixed me more than once with that cold yellow eye of his, so that I was glad when he moved on down the beach to fish.

We didn't catch another thing that day. After the fishing gods were through teaching my kinsman a lesson, they abandoned us altogether and naught else was forthcoming. We bought us a few more crabs to go with the one we had and shared dinner all around.

Crab Claws and Grilled Fish with Okra and Tomatoes

Serves 4

This dish is good with just about any kind of seafood, and so purely versatile that you can well play with it and make it all your own. It's real good with rice on the side.

> *Claws from 7 to 8 medium crabs*
> *1 tablespoon fresh lemon juice*
> *½ pound okra (choose small pods, no more than*
>   *1½ inches in length)*
> *1 egg*
> *¼ cup milk*
> *½ cup white cornmeal*
> *¼ cup yellow cornmeal*
> *2 tablespoons all-purpose flour*
> *Peanut oil*
> *Freshly cracked black pepper*
> *2 small fish fillets, any white-fleshed variety*
> *2 medium tomatoes, sliced into wedges*
> *2 to 3 scallions, trimmed and chopped into rings*

Boil the crab claws in water to cover until bright red. Allow to cool, then break open the shells and pull out the meat. Sprinkle lightly with lemon juice and set aside.

Wash the okra and trim the stem as close to the cap as you can cut it without cutting off the cap. Drop the trimmed okra into boiling water and boil for 2 minutes. Drain and allow to cool.

In a small shallow bowl, drop the egg into the milk and whip it up good.

In another shallow bowl, mix together the white cornmeal, yellow cornmeal, and flour.

Heat about 1½ inches of the oil in a large skillet to 365°F.

Dip the okra pods in the egg-and-milk mixture and sprinkle with pepper. Quickly roll them in the cornmeal mix. Fry in the hot oil in batches until the cornmeal coating turns a handsome golden brown, about 8 minutes. Drain on paper towels to absorb excess oil. Arrange them on a platter leaving a small space in the center and another around the rim.

Pan-fry the fish fillets in a bit of oil. Allow them to cool for a scant minute, then slice them down the middle.

Arrange the tomato wedges in the center of the platter and lay a row of them around the outside as well. Fill in the empty spaces with the okra. Lay the crabmeat and the pan-fried fish fillets over all and top it with the chopped scallions. Serve the whole thing hot.

Crayfish

You need the buddy system to hunt for crayfish. They prefer to take up residence in rocky shallows along the mossy sections of streams. The muddier the bank, the better.

You will need a couple of pairs of hip boots, a seine, a pair of heavy rubber gloves with ridged fingers, and a bucket with a lid.

Once you've located the crayfish, one of you takes the seine and stands downstream while the culprit with the gloves messes around amongst the small stones in the bed of the stream, scaring up the prey. When you get a net full, transfer them to the bucket, move downstream a couple of feet, and have at it again.

Sounds easy, doesn't it? Don't count on it. For an animal with a brain about half the size of a black-eyed pea, crayfish are pretty smart. Perhaps the prospect of being cooked and eaten has something to do with increased brain capacity. A dire threat like that could make a genius of the dullest cracked-rock stupid 300-pound lineman, even if he played for Philly.

All that said, I feel compelled to add that hunting for crayfish is an art best learned as a child from the apt hands of a skilled parent; otherwise, you're always fumbling in the dark for a truly successful technique, and the intended prey is getting such a good laugh off of you that the mud is fairly quivering around your ankles.

Even if you're good at it, it's a messy business at best. Crayfish thrive in areas where the mud is as green as it smells, and the mosquitoes are so thick they congregate in clouds. The last time I went crayfishing, I donated so much blood to those greedy little bugs that I had to have liver for dinner to get my strength back. Since crayfish taste best if caught and cooked in the same day, the whole episode defeated itself.

Call me lazy (or practical—sometimes it is truly the same thing), but I like to buy crayfish off someone who's good at it. They're not terribly expensive and a lot cheaper than a blood transfusion.

Field Dressing and Preparation

Since crayfish tend to browse in the rotten debris at the bottom of ponds and streams, you need to rinse them really well before you cook them; otherwise the proposed dinner starts to smell like boiling mud.

Crayfish is a poor cousin to the lobster, and you pretty much cook it up the same way you would a lobster. Namely, you drop it into boiling water and peel the shell away from the meat once it's cooked. It'll turn red when it's done. For a really tasty crayfish, boil it in a couple a gallons of water to which a teaspoon of lemon juice, a pod of garlic, and a small red chile have been added.

Crayfish Pudding

Serves 4

If you don't live in an area where crayfish are readily available, try this recipe with lobster or crab. Both are delicious, though the flavor lacks that satisfying bayou ambiance crayfish offers. Since crayfish weigh 2 to 5 ounces each, four or five per person is about right.

> *1 tablespoon butter*
> *A mess of crayfish, boiled for 5 minutes and picked*
> *½ medium onion, finely chopped*
> *1 green chile, seeded and chopped into 1-inch slivers*
> *6 eggs*
> *1 cup whipping cream*
> *½ cup chopped scallions*

In a large skillet, melt the butter over medium heat. Add the crayfish, onion, and chile and sauté. Stand there and stir it pretty often while it resolves the issue or you'll scorch the flavor out of it. This should take about 4 minutes.

Preheat the oven to 350°F. Lightly butter a large baking dish.

Whip together the eggs and cream, making sure that it is well blended without beating it frothy—good medium strokes and no frantic action is the key here. Fold in the sautéed crayfish mixture. Pour it into the baking dish. Set the baking dish in a roasting pan and fill the pan with water until the level is a scant inch below the lip of the baking dish.

Bake for 35 to 40 minutes, until a wood skewer inserted into the center comes out clean.

Allow to cool for a few minutes. Serve topped with the scallions.

Wrestling Alligators

The trouble with going crayfish hunting with somebody who grew up doing it is that they invariably have an agenda for the entire day, and these boys can get enough crayfish to satisfy you, your whole family, and every friend you ever knew and do it in half a day.

That leaves you sitting on the bank finishing off your sandwich at lunchtime while your crayfishing buddy slowly talks you into doing something that a fella with half the brains of that mud-sucking shellfish you just caught wouldn't do, even if you pointed a gun to his head. And you, you doofus, find yourself sitting there with a smile and saying something stupid like, "Yeah! Sounds good!"

You're kidding, right?

That's how I ended up napping in a small boat while the afternoon burned off to evening so I could be rested enough to wrestle alligators under the full moon.

The plan did not include actually wrestling with them, but with alligators, anything worth doing is worth wrestling about, so they tend to turn every encounter into a kind of wrestling match to some degree or another. They're truly handsome animals, and you would never believe how formidable their skin feels under your hand unless you touch one yourself, but for all that, bumping around with them in the water is just not something I enjoy doing.

Unfortunately, I found that out around about 1 A.M. while I was trapped in a small boat with a couple of fanatics who like doing nothing better.

I'm sorry, Don (I forgot your friend's name), but I lied when I told you I had a good time. All I can say is, if you believed me, then you must've lost every game of cards you ever played.

In the early part of the evening, the alligators we came across slapped the water and took the fish that my friend Don offered them from his hand, and all was mostly right with the world. None of the animals that we bumped around with was longer than our boat, and I felt reasonably assured that Don knew what he was about when he gutted a croppie and dipped it in the water for his toothy friends.

Then, long about one in the morning, a good-sized boy joined the party, sliding up under our boat like a big cat scratching his back on a fence railing. Don whooped and did a little dance of pure joy that must've pulled all that variety of emotion that was available in our environs to him, 'cause right away I didn't have any of it at all. I felt purely terrible all of a sudden, like I was about to be sick.

I kept thinking of all kinds of places that I'd like to be, but nary a time did a vision of that boat out on the bayou enter my plans.

Turns out, Don and this particular old boy were buddies of sorts and met out there on the bayou to wrestle now and again to renew old friendships. Don tickled his back with a stick and fed him a couple of fish. For his part, that big boy thwacked the side of the boat with his tail once or twice, then he left us be and went on his way, for which I shall always be grateful.

With the highlight of the party come and gone, Don and his friend picked out a suitable youngster to hook. Between them, they lured their choice up near the boat with a gutted croppie and slipped a noose over his nose while he was grabbing for the fish. That done, they dispensed with the formalities and pulled the thrashing beast up over the side and into our laps.

Things were real exciting for a few minutes while we got a canvas bag over the creature's eyes and a few nylon ropes about his limbs. According to Don and his buddy, most guys just shoot the alligator in the head first and drag him in dead, but, they claim, this ruins the flavor of the meat, which tastes considerably better if you kill it quick, just before it's cooked.

Well, you can't prove it by me. If it tastes worse than what I had, then I can't see why a wharf rat would want to eat it, much less a man and his friends. If somebody offered me a choice between alligator meat and a bit of pan-fried work boot, then I'd have to have a good look at the feet of the fella who wore those boots last, as well as a few of the places he took them for a walk, before I could make up my mind which of those two things, the alligator or the boot, I would be having for dinner.

Alligator meat is not tough, if it's cooked right, but nonetheless, it has an odd flavor that I can't make myself learn to put a tooth to without grimacing. It's like I'm afraid if I swallowed that stuff that something strange would happen to my poor unsuspecting stomach that neither God nor a passing good doctor could do aught to assuage.

Crayfish with Tomatoes and Green Chiles

Serves 2 to 3

Every time I think about doing up this recipe, I remember Don and his buddy, and I end up making it with either crab or lobster. Go figure. I got this recipe from Don, and I purely love to visit him and partake of the generous way he lays it out on the table, but I always check through it, too, just to make sure there's nothing strange in there, like one of his toothy friends.

> *1 leek, white part only, quartered and sliced*
> *Crayfish, at least a dozen*
> *¼ cup light olive oil*
> *5 firm plum tomatoes, cut into fourths*
> *2 green chiles, seeded and chopped*
> *1 cup cooked rice (either long-grain white or basmati)*

Boil the leek for about 3 minutes, until soft and chewy but not soggy. Drain and set aside.

Boil the crayfish for 5 to 8 minutes. Shell. Not as hard as it sounds, since all you want is the tail meat and it comes out of its shell a whole lot easier than its larger cousin, the lobster. Shelling crayfish can be accomplished with a small paring knife. Set the meat aside and resist the urge to cut it into smaller pieces.

In a large skillet, heat the oil over medium-high heat and quickly add the crayfish, tomatoes, and chiles. Decrease the heat to medium and brown, stirring constantly to prevent sticking and scorching. You can't hurt the chiles because the more you burn them, the hotter they get—they could care less—but have some respect for the tomatoes and the crayfish. After 3 to 4 minutes, add the rice and fold it in. Add the leeks last, when the rice has begun to take on some of the handsome red color of the tomatoes and has a light sheen of oil on it.

Serve immediately, as it loses some of its charm when it begins to cool down too much.

The Best-Tasting Raw Oysters

This one's not really a recipe or a story but just a tip for sweetening your oysters before you eat them. The only drawback to this technique is the noise befitting a grisly horror movie that will issue from your garage every few hours as your new friends enjoy their lunch. They're not shy about competing with their neighbors for a succulent morsel, and the sound of greedy sucking they make as they go about their business is sure to give the kids nightmares unless you clarify the situation for them.

You will need: a washtub full of oysters; two galvanized washtubs; two canvas bags, split up the back; 5 pounds coarsely ground yellow cornmeal; and $1/2$ pound sugar.

Lay the canvas bags in the bottom of two washtubs and array the oysters on top. Divide the oyster population in half so that there is plenty of room for them, half in each of the two tubs. Fill with just enough saltwater to cover the shells and cover them with the canvas bags again.

In a large bowl, mix the cornmeal and the sugar.

Four times a day, uncover your oysters and sprinkle them liberally with the mixture of cornmeal and sugar. The shells should be covered to at least $1/8$ inch in thickness. Cover again and let them alone with their dinner.

Once a day, drain the old water by removing the whole works, rinsing the canvas bags and setting up your oyster cafeteria again.

In four or five days, you will notice that your oysters are so fat that they are finding it difficult to keep their shells decently closed. Friends, those babies have been living in the land of plenty in your galvanized tubs and they've forgotten what it feels like to be hungry. They've also been purged of anything vile they might have eaten before they met up with you, and their flesh is the sweetest you will ever taste. Since they're so fat, they're also easy to open. *Bon appétit.*

Alligator Snapping Turtle

When you take it into your mind that you're going to hunt up an alligator snapper, don't count on a pair of gloves to save your fingers. These babies can take your fingers off with one snap, linesman's leathers and all.

Hunt them with a length of steel pipe wrapped in a strip of rubber and take a buddy with you who's especially good with an ax. When you taunt the turtle with your length of pipe, he'll grab onto it. He's not actually clever enough to know whether or not that piece of pipe is a piece of your hide or not, but he's surely hoping it is. He's used to biting quickly through whatever he grabs, so when he gets a good grip, he's too hardheaded to let go right away. While he's thus occupied, your buddy can take a good whack at his neck with the ax and step one to lunch is a fait accompli.

If neither of you is especially trustworthy with an ax, do not despair; you can do just as good a job with a really sharp set of hedge clippers. Use the big kind, not those little delicate things the hardware store puts out for women under five-foot-five. You can also use a long-handled limb pruner if you happen to have one.

Despite the press to the contrary, turtles are not at all shy about sticking their necks out. Good hunting, friend, and keep your fingers in your pockets and your toes out of reach. With any luck, your turtle is well fed enough already without you giving him a last meal.

Alligator snappers eat a lot of meat, most of which they find as carrion. If you have the room for it, it improves the taste to keep them penned for a week while you feed them stale doughnuts to clean out their systems. It also puts a little weight on them, as fats and sugars are wont to do. They don't normally subsist on such truck, but the sugars in doughnuts really appeal to them, so keep an ample stock handy. The sweet stuff won't improve their attitude much, so remember to keep your fingers out of their reach and keep a lid on the pen and the kids strictly away from it.

If you have boys, you might think that stale doughnuts are an item best found in mythology, since the doughnut is one item that is not likely to get enough free time in your household to grow old in. Not to worry. So long as doughnut franchises depend on untrained young people to do most of their work, there will always be managers who don't have a firm grasp on the concept of inventory management. It takes considerable experience to know your clientele well enough to make only so many doughnuts as will sell in one day. Most places sell day-old for a very fair price and now and again, you can locate a place with a fuzz-faced new manager who will spend the first week feeding leftover day-olds to the dumpster. Krispy Kreme franchises are so proud of their freshness that most will refuse to sell day-olds, but some will give them to you if you tell them what you are doing—and if you look sufficiently convincing enough.

Field Dressing and Preparation

To prepare a turtle for cooking, cut off the feet and the head and nail the turtle's tail to a piece of wood, with its back down and its belly plate facing you. Remove the belly plate by cutting away the skin around the lower edge of the back shell. Skin the neck, tail, and the limb quarters before removing them. If your turtle is a particularly large one, you can gut it to get to the tenderloins—the long strips of back muscle up against the back shell. Cut away all visible fat and rinse the tenderloins in water for 5 minutes to wash away bits of fat that might cling to them. Wash the skinned neck, tail, and limb quarters as well.

Alligator Snapping Turtle Cream Soup

Serves 2

Every time I've ever made this, I kept the turtle in question penned for about a week and force-fed him doughnuts. The soup was sweet and thick. Turtle is something of an acquired taste I'm told, but since I first tried it as a kid and liked it, I can't say much about that. I can say that the rumors that claim that turtles taste like fish is not at all true. It has a vaguely chickeny flavor, as if one of the chicken's parents was a sheep, or maybe a deer.

You can use any species of snapping turtle in this recipe. I use alligator snappers because they're bigger and therefore I only have to catch one for a big pot of soup.

> *Meat from 1 alligator snapping turtle*
> *2 cups heavy cream*
> *5 egg yolks, lightly beaten*
> *½ cup water*
> *½ teaspoon ground nutmeg*

Cut the turtle meat into cubes and steam for approximately 20 minutes.

In a large pan, blend the cream and the egg yolks together and dilute with the water. Cook over very low heat for about 15 minutes without allowing it to boil.

Add the turtle meat to the cream mixture and cook for about 10 minutes. Remove from the heat and sprinkle with nutmeg. Serve hot.

INDEX